Hegemony in the
Digital Age

Critical Media Studies

Series Editor
Andrew Calabrese, University of Colorado

This series covers a broad range of critical research and theory about media in the modern world. It includes work about the changing structures of the media, focusing particularly on work about the political and economic forces and social relations which shape and are shaped by media institutions, structural changes in policy formation and enforcement, technological transformations in the means of communication, and the relationships of all these to public and private cultures worldwide. Historical research about the media and intellectual histories pertaining to media research and theory are particularly welcome. Emphasizing the role of social and political theory for informing and shaping research about communications media, Critical Media Studies addresses the politics of media institutions at national, subnational, and transnational levels. The series is also interested in short, synthetic texts on key thinkers and concepts in critical media studies.

Titles in the series

Hegemony in the Digital Age

The Arab/Israeli Conflict Online

Stephen M. E. Marmura

LEXINGTON BOOKS
A division of
ROWMAN & LITTLEFIELD PUBLISHERS, INC.
Lanham • Boulder • New York • Toronto • Plymouth, UK

LEXINGTON BOOKS

A division of Rowman & Littlefield Publishers, Inc.
A wholly owned subsidiary of The Rowman & Littlefield Publishing Group, Inc.
4501 Forbes Boulevard, Suite 200
Lanham, MD 20706

Estover Road
Plymouth PL6 7PY
United Kingdom

British Library Cataloguing in Publication Information Available

Library of Congress Cataloging-in-Publication Data

Marmura, Stephen M. E., 1965–
  Hegemony in the digital age : the Arab–Israeli conflict online / Stephen M.E. Marmura.
      p. cm—(Critical media studies)
  Includes bibliographical references and index.
  ISBN-13: 978-0-7391-1772-9 (cloth : alk. paper)
  ISBN-10: 0-7391-1772-6 (cloth : alk. paper)
  1. Arab-Israeli conflict—Mass media and the conflict. 2. World Wide Web—Political
aspects. 3. Middle East—Foreign relations—United States. 4. United States—Foreign
relations—Middle East. I. Title.
  DS119.7.M3133 2008
  956.04—dc22   2007048938

Printed in the United States of America

⊗™ The paper used in this publication meets the minimum requirements of American
National Standard for Information Sciences—Permanence of Paper for Printed Library
Materials, ANSI/NISO Z39.48-1992.

For Michael Marmura

Contents

Acknowledgments

This book is largely based on a doctoral dissertation completed at Queen's University in the Department of Sociology. I was supported during the writing of both dissertation and book by numerous individuals, at various times and in various ways. First and foremost, my partner and best friend, Bridget Revell, actively supported my return to academic life after a considerable absence, well aware of the sacrifices that this would entail. This book would never have been completed without her ongoing patience and support. Vital also was the encouragement and academic advice that I received from my dissertation supervisory committee. I was fortunate to have a supervisor, Elia Zureik, with an accomplished background in the major overlapping subject areas dealt with in the book. It was Elia who convinced me that it was worth undertaking research which combined my long-standing interests in ethnic conflict, identity politics, and mass media, with attention to the internet. His guidance and support were greatly appreciated.

I was also fortunate to have on my dissertation committee two leading authorities in the areas of surveillance research and mass communication respectively, David Lyon and Robert Pike. As well as having undertaken extensive research in the area of electronic surveillance practices, David also has a keen interest and strong background in the sociology of religion. His combined interests in the areas of social ordering and control via digital technology on the one hand, and grassroots affirmations of identity and culture on the other, made him highly attuned to the overall direction and nature of my work. His advice was inevitably valuable. Robert Pike, who was a constant source of reassurance, also displayed great enthusiasm for my work while keeping me mindful of the politically charged and contentious nature of the subject matter with which I was dealing. His prompt and very close readings of my dissertation chapters were always appreciated, as was his sound advice.

I am grateful for support from other individuals as well. Important feedback was provided from Bart Simon, whose enthusiasm for my chosen area of research proved invaluable in getting things started. I would also like to express my thanks to Vincent Mosco, for his patient advice during the transition from dissertation to book. Further support came in the form of camaraderie from colleagues, friends, and family members struggling with their own projects in the capacity(s) of academics, activists, or advocates (or some combination of the above) or who were otherwise affected by the fallout. They include Jeffrey Brown, Heather Marmura, Elizabeth Marmura, Timothy Marmura, Martin Hand, Zoey Roy, Jason Pridmore, Jon Frauley, Jeffrey Rowell, Kyle Janzen, and Akrum Matuk. I will always feel indebted for the inspiration I received early in my academic career from my former mentors at the University of Guelph, Professors John McMurtry and Stanley Barrett. Finally, I would like to thank my daughter Hana and my son Alexander. Their positive and unlimited energy helped me stay grounded in the world off-line, directing much of my attention away from the always fascinating, but often depressing phenomenon of ideological struggle on the WWW.

Chapter One

Introduction

Identity and Authority in the Age of Networks

Ever since it became accessible to large segments of the American public, the World Wide Web (WWW) has held broad appeal as a media forum and social networking tool. Political parties, social movements, news bloggers, charities, religious organizations, and countless other citizen-based groups were quick to make use of this new information and communication medium. Not surprisingly, the Web's appeal has extended to marginalized individuals and "extremist" groups which have traditionally enjoyed little in the way of political influence or sympathetic coverage from the mainstream media. Examples are easy to produce, and include actors ranging from racist organizations, religious "cults," and militia groups, to those espousing such ideologies as deep ecology, radical feminism, and anarchism. As with more institutionally entrenched interests, the internet allows such identities to disseminate their messages and address a potentially vast audience with little fear of censure. In addition, the Net provides new potentials for political mobilization. It may readily be utilized to facilitate the communication, alliance building, and activist strategies of like-minded elements often physically separated by great distances and, increasingly, by international borders.

The enthusiasm with which internet technology has been embraced by citizen-based groups in the West—and increasingly beyond—reflects larger transformations associated with the arrival of the "information age." The most significant of these relate either directly or indirectly to the continued growth of the global economy, beginning in the 1970s. Of particular importance, the spread of global capitalism has been closely tied to the decline of the social-welfare state and its displacement by the security state, a transition which has in turn been linked to the undermining of organized labor, the dismantling of "inefficient" government social programs, and a growing state preoccupation with the management of risks and contingencies associated with transnational flows of consumer goods and persons (immigrants, laborers, refugees). Similarly, media convergence, both technological and organizational, has been marked by an accelerating global circulation of cultural/media products of primarily Western origin. And while the digital technology which underpins the global economy remains accessible to only a small portion of the earth's population, its proliferation and use by a growing variety of grassroots actors around the world continues to gain momentum. All of these developments have been implicated in a global resurgence of identity-based politics, the transformation of civil society in liberal democracies, and the establishment of new forms of social solidarity in which the state is no longer paramount.

Despite the tremendous scope and scale of such changes, it is often surprisingly difficult to ascertain what is truly new or novel in the world, particularly when considering the character and influence of corporate and governmental power, or the nature of ideological struggle among competing interests within or beyond the borders of states. Such is the case even when attention is restricted to the "impact" of the new information and communication technologies (ICTs) within societies like the United States, Britain, or Canada. Fortunately, the French social theorist Jacques Ellul has left us with an ideal point of departure for considering such matters. In *Propaganda, the Formation of Men's Attitudes*, Ellul (1965) directs attention to the widespread use of community-based (i.e. "alternative") media by minority groups within modern "technological societies," arguing that such use serves to reinforce the ideological boundaries which already separate them:

> Those who read the press of their group and listen to the radio of their group are constantly reinforced in their allegiance. They learn more and more that their group is right and that its actions are justified; thus their beliefs are strengthened. At the same time, such propaganda contains elements of criticism and refutation of other groups, which will never be read or heard by a member of another group. (Ellul 1965, 213)

Ellul also suggests that, paradoxically, this same tendency leaves individuals within each community vulnerable to the dominant "integration propaganda" emanating from within the power structure, and permeating the modern state society as a whole.

"One must not think, incidentally, that such partitioning is in conflict with the formation of public opinion. Although propaganda partitions society, it affects opinion and transcends the groups in which it operates" (Ellul 1965, 214). Such arguments invite us to question how the dynamics of ideological struggle, propaganda warfare, and communal solidarity might be altered were a diverse range of ethnic minorities, subcultures, and social movements to be regularly and directly exposed not only to the messages promoted by powerful state and corporate institutions, or produced from within their own ranks, but also to the ideologies and political projects of one another. It is the unique ability of the WWW to provide precisely this set of conditions which constitutes the central problematic with which this book is concerned.

Aims and Scope

Several closely interrelated questions guide the overall course of this book. First, are the ideological barriers which separate divergent social identities weakened or reinforced as a result of their "proximity" online? Second, when the WWW is employed to further the agenda of a particular individual, organization, or group, to what extent are the strategies these agents adopt a reflection of their ideological outlook and/or relative power in society? Third, which types of social actor appear to benefit most from their use of the internet *relative* to others in terms of larger struggles for political power and cultural influence? Finally, and in keeping with this book's overarching interest(s) in processes of hegemony, how does the Web transform those modes of communication, propaganda dissemination, and ideological rivalry formerly associated with "mass societies" and the widespread use of traditional print and broadcast media? These are ambitious lines of questioning which could never be fully addressed within a single investigation. However, I hope to show that a great deal may be revealed by limiting the scope of inquiry to a specific array of online actors and a clearly defined area of ideological contention.

Before proceeding further, readers should be aware that while I considered it necessary to refer to the Arab/Israeli conflict in the subtitle of this book, this reference is also potentially misleading. It will likely impart the impression that the book's main focus is upon the ways in which the internet has been exploited by Israeli and Arab actors vis-à-vis their long-standing enmity and/or ongoing warfare. In fact, this is not the case, or at least only indirectly so. Various dimensions of the Israeli/Palestinian and wider Arab/Israeli conflicts—along with related events, players, and U.S. government policies—are given attention. In fact, they are referred to on an ongoing basis throughout the book. However, while all of the organizations and social movements considered here have strong international ties, most are also based within the United States. The reason for this focus on American-based groups and interests will be returned to in a moment. In the meantime, it should be emphasized that continued reference to the Arab/Israeli conflict is made primarily for methodological purposes. When considered in terms of how it is interpreted by various competing identities, this conflict provides an extremely useful devise, or "boundary object," through which to assess their respective Web-based media and networking strategies.

As indicated above, all of the actors given attention in this book are considered primarily in relation to an American context. The reasons are fairly straightforward, relating both to the core agendas of relevant organizations, as well as to the parameters and key concerns of this investigation. Specifically, each identity has a direct interest or ideological stake in the role played by the United States as Israel's primary financial backer, arms supplier, and defender at the United Nations (UN). A desire to reinforce, fundamentally alter, or otherwise draw attention to American policies regarding Israel/Palestine has been a major motivating force and/or a favored propaganda tactic for all of the organizations considered here. Each recognizes that the future of the Arab/Israeli conflict—including such matters as Palestinian statehood, Israel's military power, and the contours of any future Israeli/Palestinian borders—will largely hinge upon American policies and interventions in the Middle East. Likewise, while relevant players are clearly interested in coordinating action and sharing information with affiliates around the globe, each identity is particularly concerned with influencing the beliefs and gaining the sympathies of the Western, and specifically the American, audiences, deemed most critical in influencing U.S. government policies.

The internet, and more specifically the WWW, does not represent a single medium, but rather a collection of modalities through which communication may transpire, or information may be stored or accessed. In fact, the Web's communicative and informational properties overlap considerably, may function in multiple ways simultaneously, and may facilitate vastly divergent ratios of individual, collective, or mass engagement; synchronically or asynchronously. In this light it should be noted that while the case studies considered in the forthcoming chapters draw attention to many of the ways in which the internet may be utilized for purposes of communication, identity construction, and mobilization, equal consideration is not given to all of the Net's continually evolving capacities and attributes. Instead, the dominant focus is upon the WWW's unique qualities as a *hypertext* medium. Hypertext is arguably the Web's most fundamental and unique feature; one that makes it both like and unlike earlier mass media. An emphasis on this "medium within a medium" is consistent with this work's overriding concern with the Web's potential to function as a mass medium while simultaneously facilitating intra *and* inter-identity communication, organizational strategies, and ideological warfare.

In the chapters that follow, attention will be devoted to the Web-based activism, communication and mobilization strategies, and propaganda warfare engaged in by three distinct sets of actors. Each corresponds to one of three forms of social identity construction conceptualized by Castells (2004) in *The Power of Identity*; project identity, legitimating identity, and resistance identity. The terms *project identity* and *resistance identity* are used to refer to distinct types of social movements and their representative social movement organizations (SMOs). More will be said about each type shortly. The specific cases considered in chapters 2–3 and 5–6 respectively, range from relatively mainstream human rights groups and political lobbies, to "extremist" fringe identities such as ultranationalist and racist organizations. By contrast, chapter 4 considers the well-known news corporation, *CNN.com*, in its role as a legitimating identity. Chapter 7 considers the collective significance of these case studies against the backdrop of globalization and the transformation of civil society, and in light of relevant theory.

Key Terms and Concepts

To begin, it should be recognized that all of the primary concerns dealt with in this book take on their significance within the broad rubric of hegemony theory. The concept of hegemony was most famously elaborated by the Marxist Italian dissident, Antonio Gramsci (1891–1937) in his *Prison Notebooks*. Gramsci's intent was to develop a theoretical framework which could better account for the workings of power in modern capitalist societies. Like other Marxists, Gramsci was perplexed by the fact that ruling elites were generally able to consolidate power without recourse to the use of force and with the implicit consent of the masses. The proletariat had not revolted against bourgeoisie rule—ostensibly pursuing their true class interests—as orthodox Marxism had predicted. To better cope theoretically with this reality, Gramsci developed an approach which viewed ideology as a relatively autonomous force in society. Most importantly, his approach worked from the premise that any group which hopes to gain and hold political/cultural leadership must demonstrate an ability to move beyond an explicit commitment to its own narrow program. Instead, it must appeal to the broader masses by co-opting the symbols, championing the values, and at least partially addressing the material and economic concerns of other groups, even as it attempts to gain state power primarily to further its own interests and/or impose its own particular vision of the good society (see Boggs 1976; Simon 1991).

Gramsci maintained that once in power, a dominant group or coalition of ruling elites cannot expect to take their dominant position for granted. They must continually strive to head off the challenges of other groups and interests, making their own values and programs appear commensurate with the values, cultural expressions, and needs of the masses and other significant interests in society. This is because new challenges continually arise "from below." Most contemporary accounts of hegemony assume that political struggle and ideological contestation among an indeterminate and shifting range of institutionalized and grassroots actors is ongoing within industrialized (or "post-industrial") societies. Many approaches also take into account the global dimensions of such struggles. In addition, it is widely understood that in countries such as Britain or the United States, struggles over meaning and culture take place primarily within the arena of the mass media; via the culture industries, advertising, and news production. It is here that dominant interpretations of reality and cultural values become stamped upon, or "anchored within" the media products sold to the public in the form of news, entertainment, and culture. Hence, by providing the basis of a shared symbolic universe, the mass media ultimately foster a common (if contested and unstable) culture as a lived system of meanings and values.

Relevant ideas consistent with the line of reasoning outlined above will be raised throughout the course of this book, and there is no reason to provide a more in-depth overview of hegemony theory here. However, it should be noted that for present purposes—and consistent with its application elsewhere—the term *hegemony* may be understood as embodying two closely related meanings which are in fact two sides of a coin (Fiske 1993). First, it may be used to refer to a process, "the struggle for hegemony," through which competing groups strive to outperform one another in their respective attempts to gain public favor and achieve cultural/political influence. In addition, this term is also commonly employed to refer to dominant or "hegemonic" interpretations of reality; those which have come to pervade political and media discourse. Significantly, such interpretations do not normally appear to most members of the public as interpretations at all, but rather as common sense representations of objective reality(s). This dual understanding of hegemony informs all of the case studies dealt with in the forthcoming chapters, which address the internet strategies of social actors falling into the three general categories referred to below.

Castells's (2004) typology of identity construction in the "global network society" is employed throughout this book as a useful means for distinguishing between the various social movements and commercial/political interests whose Web strategies receive scrutiny in the forthcoming chapters. The first to be considered are project identities, best understood here as networks of individuals, social movement organizations (SMOs), and political interest groups striving to promote universally recognized principles of social justice. The notion of project identity is similar to that put forward by Giddens (1990, 156) when referring to "life politics" or "emancipatory politics", which entail "radical engagements concerned with the liberation from inequality or servitude."

Ideological currents commonly referred to as "progressive" and associated with such causes as feminism, environmentalism, or the anti-globalization movement fit this profile. Much like the latter, the project identity SMOs examined in chapters 1 and 2 remain committed to affirming universalist values. As actors associated with the Arab/Israeli peace camp, their calls for social justice are grounded primarily through appeals to principles of international law, UN resolutions, and human rights conventions, ostensibly arrived at through deliberative political processes among nation-states.

Resistance identities refer to social actors who feel excluded, stigmatized, or otherwise oppressed by the logic of domination. They respond to persecution (whether real or imagined) through the construction of a defensive identity, one which "reverses the value judgment while reinforcing the boundary" which separates them from dominant institutions and ideologies (Castells 2004, 9). The stance adopted by these collective subjects is perhaps best summed up in the phrase "the exclusion of the excluders by the excluded" (Castells 2004). Examples of resistance identities discussed in this book include both the relatively influential Christian fundamentalist and Jewish ethnic nationalist organizations and lobbies given attention in chapters 2 and 3 (in conjunction with their project identity rivals), as well as the socially stigmatized white supremacist organizations and militant Islamist and Jewish fringe elements which provide the focus for chapters 5 and 6. In contrast to their project identity rivals, all of the latter draw moral authority from exclusivist interpretations of religious scripture, or base their claims to privileged status upon decidedly narrow conceptions of nationality or ethnicity.

Diani (2003, 301) describes the contemporary social movement as "a network of informal interactions between a plurality of individuals, groups and/or organizations, engaged in a political or cultural conflict on the basis of a shared collective identity." This formulation is very useful when referring to social movements of both the project identity and resistance identity type. An emphasis upon the network character of social movements is particularly important in light of the transnational ties which now characterize so many, and also when considering the wide assortment of organizational forms which may be included within a single network, or which may create overlap among disparate networks. There is presently wide agreement within the social movement literature concerning both the increasing importance of widely dispersed networks for contemporary political activists, and the key role played by internet technology in maintaining them (see van de Donk, et al. 2004). At the same time, it should be recognized that an overemphasis on structure may draw attention away from other equally important influences upon social movement growth, preferred activist strategies, and success rates in achieving stated goals. These include such factors as ideological outlook, relative political power, public image, and past experiences such as violent oppression by the state. Less obvious or direct inputs such as the adoption of ideas borrowed from other (often diffuse) sources, internal power struggles, or the idiosyncrasies of group leaders may also prove significant. Such influences will inevitably attenuate with others more attributable to social movement morphology, affecting preferred repertoires of action, and the manner in which networking technologies are utilized.

The third identity category employed in this book, legitimating identity, draws attention to the close interrelationships between state and corporate power, popular understandings of reality, and the perceived authority of messages circulating in the mass media. Following Gramsci, Castells (2004, 9) argues that it was the state's control over, or influence within, the institutions of civil society that traditionally allowed it to exercise ideological hegemony. The state's close involvement with institutions such as churches, charities, labor unions, education, and social work made it possible for governments to "legitimize" their authority by identifying with, influencing, and co-opting ideological and cultural currents generated at the grassroots level. However, with civil society either in decline or increasingly devoid of state involvement, it is now more difficult for governments to defend their institutions as the "natural" outgrowths of any collective, public will. In Castells's (2004) view, this situation is exacerbated by the state's recent loss of control over the mass media, arguably the most important means through which governments have traditionally been able to shape public opinion and promote ideological unity in a way favorable to their own long-term survival and success. This last point is particularly important since Castells's position on the mass media is rejected here. Rather—and in conformity with the considerable bulk of political economy research on the subject—I defend and build upon the premise that the mainstream news media continue to function as a legitimating institution in pluralist, democratic societies.

It should be emphasized that the terms resistance identity, project identity, and legitimating identity are employed here for heuristic purposes and should not be viewed as absolute or static categories. For example, Castells (2004) argues that project identities such as the gay rights or environmental movements often began as resistance identities. Alternatively, resistance identities may retain their exclusivist character while growing in numbers and confidence. Under such circumstances they may attempt, as other successful social movements often do, to achieve their goals through more direct participation in the established political order. Interestingly, Christian fundamentalist movements in the United States, such as those referred to in chapters 1 and 2, have historically wavered between a self-imposed isolation from mainstream society and vigorous attempts to reform what they perceive as a morally corrupt political system (Bruce 1998; Marsden 1980). To the extent that such identities are able to find common ground with established elites and/or effectively promote their values through the major institutions of society, they may attain some measure of cultural hegemony and hence (to varying degrees) adopt the role of legitimating identities.

A final concept holding importance throughout this investigation, "underdetermination," was developed by Poster (2001) as a means for identifying and isolating the unique "postmodern" qualities of the internet and digital technology; namely those which distinguish them from older analog technologies and media. Poster grounds his approach through reference to Althusser's ideas concerning the "overdetermined" nature of social institutions and cultural forms (historic or social objects). For Althusser, the influences serving to shape the character of social/cultural objects include both existing material conditions, such as those obtaining to the physical environment and the dominant mode of production in a given society, and autonomous ideological structures reproduced through the workings of state apparatuses such as the legal system, educational institutions, mass media, and so on (Gruneau 1988). Crucially, social objects and cultural forms are not to be understood as simply representing the products of creative individuals, or conversely, as merely the ideological by-products of the prevailing economic system. Instead, they represent the contingent "nodal points" of crosshatching (historic) ideological, political, and economic forces.

For present purposes, the concept of underdetermination holds significance in relation to what Poster (2001) terms digital or "virtual objects." This is because the contingent, indeterminate traits which characterize all social/cultural objects are *extended* in the case of virtual objects such as hypertexts. As is the case with other cultural forms, virtual objects reflect, embody, and "participate" in the complexities and contradictions of the social practices, institutional frames, and political and ideological discourses which coalesce in their formation. At the same time, virtual objects are "overdetermined in such a way that their level of complexity or indeterminateness goes one step further" (Poster 2001, 202). They remain open to practice in a manner and to a degree which distinguish them from other expressions of culture. Rather than directing subjects in clear paths, they "solicit social construction and creation" (Poster 2001). Hence, their inherent malleability makes them available for continual (re)appropriation and modification by individual and collective human actors pursing widely divergent agendas.

When directing attention specifically to hypertexts, Poster (2001) argues that their underdetermined qualities make them qualitatively distinct from traditional print media such as newspapers and books. Significantly, the characteristics which differentiate digital from traditional (analog) texts are argued to affect the subject position of both author and reader. In the case of traditional print media, the reproduction and distribution of texts serves to reinforce the perceived authority of the author. However, while a digital text may be "everywhere at once," Poster (2001) contends that the utilization of hypertext ultimately serves to diminish the author's importance. The following passage is instructive in this regard, since Poster is able to demonstrate that the unusual character of hypertexts and their ready co-optation and resignification by countless "Web authors" are directly attributable to their unique ontological status:

> But the temporal instantaneity of digital texts undermines their spatial stability. Embodied in computer files, digital texts subsist in space only at the whim of the reader. The author of digital texts loses the assurance of their spatial continuity. Pages of digital text have the stability of liquid. They may be altered in their material arrangement of the traces as they are read. They may be combined with other texts, reformatted in size and font, have sounds and images added to them or subtracted from them.
>
> . . . Digital texts thus have more permanence than paper in the sense that they may be distributed or copied without alteration. At the same time they have no permanence whatever. Digital texts are subject to a material regime fundamentally different from analogue texts. I contend that the author function of the analogue period of textual reproduction cannot endure the change to the technology of the power of bits. (Poster 2001, 92–93)

The ideas expressed above are highly relevant when considering the ways in which the Web may be exploited (simultaneously) by competing identities. They call attention not only to hypertexts as individuated digital objects, but also to the interlocking structures which constitute the WWW at any given point in time. Interestingly, the WWW may be understood as consisting of countless shifting, interconnected texts, or alternatively as a single, continually evolving text. In chapters 5 and 6 numerous examples will be given of the ways in which the Web's "authorless," interconnected character has been skillfully exploited by racist groups and other marginalized identities hoping to challenge common sense interpretations of reality. By contrast, chapter 4 will reveal how the same Web attributes—those which Poster (2001) claims diminish the centrality of the author—may just as readily be harnessed to enhance the authority of legitimating discourses.

Political Mobilization

The internet's greatest significance as an ICT arguably lies not in its ability to enable novel forms of "cyberculture," but rather in its potential to facilitate social and political change through the establishment or enhancement of activist networks, and its related capacity for dispensing information of the kind formerly monopolized by corporate and state-owned news agencies. Chapters 1 and 2 consider the ways this potential may be harnessed by social movements. Specifically, attention is directed to the uses to which the Net is routinely put by project identity organizations in the course of their attempts to alter U.S. foreign policy, and "educate" the public about realities in the Middle East. The specific network of interest is comprised of American-based groups associated with the Arab/Israeli "peace camp." However, in both chapters, consideration is given not only to the importance which the internet holds for this project identity and its representative organizations, but also the Net's value for those interests—including rival social movements and political lobbies of the resistance identity type—which actively oppose their agenda.

Considerable debate exists as to whether the "new" networked social movements, namely progressive movements which emerged in the 1990s and which rely heavily upon the use of internet technology, differ significantly from older movements in terms of their preferred mobilization strategies and chances of success in achieving political goals. This debate is driven largely by observations and speculation concerning the ability of states to cope with transnational activist networks potentially capable of circumventing governmental measures taken against them. For example, Ayers (1999) makes the case that processes associated with economic globalization have altered the terrain in which governments and social movements operate, providing contemporary activists with new opportunities when confronting state power:

> Contemporary globalization has thus had critical outcomes for the changing dynamics of contentious activity: it has weakened the mobilization potential of states and has created new opportunities for transnational mobilization and the diffusion of protest. International processes have straitjacketed the state's ability to perform many of the interventionist functions in the past. Global and regional trade pacts, investment firms, and multinational corporations are having important structural effects on a state's national political opportunity structure. At the same time, international processes have created new targets, new international alliances, new issues, and new and common strategic repertoires around which nonstate actors are rallying. This is where the Internet and its plethora of resources come into play in the cyber-diffusion of contention. (Ayers 1999, 137)

The passage cited above represents part of a larger attempt by Ayers to advance an approach to contentious politics and social movement mobilization which moves beyond the "state-centric" biases of earlier frameworks. In the course of his critique, Ayers (1999) draws specific attention to McAdam's (1996) assertions concerning the factors most likely to condition the success of activist mobilization efforts. McAdam cites the following political opportunity structures as those most widely recognized by social movement researchers as critical in this regard:

1. The relative openness or closure of the institutionalized political system.
2. The stability of that broad set of elite alignments that typically undergird a polity.
3. The presence of elite allies.
4. The state's capacity and propensity for repression. (McAdam 1996, 27)

Ayers (1999) contends that McAdam's framework is too state-centric to cope effectively with issues pertaining to transnational social movement activism, particularly in cases where the policies of a single state may not represent the primary source of political contention. However, while Ayer's arguments may hold importance with respect to social movement efforts designed to counter policies such as those surrounding international trade agreements, they are arguably much less relevant with respect to the agendas of the American-based social movements considered in the forthcoming chapters.

As previously indicated, it is the U.S. government's material and political support for the state of Israel which constitutes the central concern for the groups and organizations considered in this book. For example, both supporters and opponents of Israel's settlement practices in the occupied West Bank and Gaza recognize that the latter could never be sustained without massive American financial and military support. Furthermore, the United States has repeatedly proven itself to be all but immune to international pressure aimed at moderating its policies in the Middle East. Consequently, the political opportunity structures identified above by McAdam (1996) remain highly relevant for activist and lobbying organizations hoping to influence American Mid-East policies and/or public opinion. As will be made clear in chapters 2 and 3, their importance is directly reflected in the activist strategies promoted by relevant groups within their respective Web sites, and is equally apparent when considering the long history of grassroots mobilization surrounding U.S. policies towards Israel and Palestine.

In chapter 2, I consider the ways in which the internet has been exploited by leading Arab, Jewish, and international peace camp organizations to enhance their political mobilization strategies. Comparisons are made with the efforts of similar social movements prior to the appearance of internet technology. In chapter 3, this focus is narrowed to the Web's more specific capacity to serve as an alternative forum through which relevant organizations may address a mass audience. In both chapters, it will be emphasized that any attempt to assess the real benefits which the Net may offer contemporary activist networks must take into account both relevant historic precedents concerning successful social movement mobilization, and contemporary power dynamics and opportunity structures within the societies they hope to affect. Attention to these larger contexts is particularly important in light of a frequently raised argument, that internet technology provides relatively greater benefits for citizen-based groups traditionally lacking significant resources than it does for actors whom have long enjoyed access to dominant social and political institutions. I will highlight the limitations of this line of reasoning in chapters 2 and 3, where it will be demonstrated that any special advantages which the Net may offer to grassroots activists will likely evaporate in cases where contentious ideological issues are involved, and where dominant elites perceive a potential threat to their interests.

The Web as a Mass Medium

The Web's unusual hypertext structure, and related ability to provide a common "space" wherein diverse identities compete for attention, raises an important question. Do understandings of cultural hegemony and propaganda developed during the era of print and broadcast media provide a suitable basis for assessing the ideological character and authoritative status of information circulating online? As Urry (2000, 147) has observed, the internet has created conditions whereby states and corporations can no longer monopolize the information made available to the public. Instead, actors associated with a variety of social movements and non-governmental organizations may utilize the Net to challenge dominant messages and "subject states and corporations to suitable shaming" (Urry 2000). Unlike the case with more traditional mass media, news services providing information on the Web must operate within an environment where the competing claims of formerly marginalized groups circulate freely, and where their own products and services must compete with countless alternative sources of "news."

Castells (2004) suggests that both politicians and the dominant media must take account of the (frequently accurate) alternative sources of information put online by independent, politically motivated citizens and grassroots organizations if they hope to remain credible in the eyes of the public. Arguing that retaining credibility requires the appearance of evenhandedness, he states: "Without credibility, news is worthless, either in terms of money or power. Credibility requires relative distance vis-à-vis specific political options, within the parameters of mainstream political and moral values" (Castells 2004, 373).

While this argument doubtless holds some merit, it also glosses over a number of important realities. Most importantly, Castells ignores the fact that mainstream political and moral values are largely sustained and promoted through the workings of the mass media and not merely reflected within them. This is hardly a minor point, since the dominant, agenda-setting news media remain profit-driven enterprises positioned within larger networks of corporate and political power. That this reality has significant consequences in terms of how controversial issues and events are represented in the news, and hence understood by the public, has been well established in the work of numerous media researchers including Curran (2000), Golding & Murdock (2000), McChesney (2004), and Philo (2002). Whether or not mainstream media commentary occasionally takes the form of partisanship at the more superficial level of party politics is, in this sense at least, a much less significant issue. As Castells (2004, 375) himself admits, the media in democratic countries are "as plural and competitive as the political system is. That is not much."

What is understood as credible information by the public arguably has less to do with the perceived distance of the media from specific elements within the political system than it does with the media's ability to present information in accordance with prevailing myths and popular ideologies which have found support among dominant elites. Such reasoning is in line with Said's (1997) contention that media coverage of foreign conflicts and "alien" cultures reflects a politically and consumer-driven consensus among politicians, experts, and the media as to what is considered newsworthy. Said (1979; 1994; 1997) has argued convincingly that a tradition of imperialism continues to shape popular attitudes, influence art and literature, and guide Western perceptions of world events as depicted in the dominant mass media. He pursues this thesis most forcefully in relation to portrayals of the Middle East, drawing upon a Foucaultian conception of power and knowledge to affirm that "covering Islam from the United States, the last superpower, is not interpretation in the genuine sense but an assertion of power" (Said 1997, 150). This line of critique deserves to be taken seriously when considering the potential influence of "alternative voices" upon the mainstream media. It suggests that the issue of *how* such voices are acknowledged and integrated within a preexisting framework may be at least as important—if not more so—than *whether* they are taken into account.

Chapter 4 extends the discussion taken up in chapter 3 concerning the WWW's capacity to serve as an effective mass medium. However, the focus is no longer upon social movements, but rather upon the well-known news corporation, *CNN.com*. In the first section of the chapter, a thematic analysis is undertaken involving a series of background articles ostensibly provided to give this Web site's readership a more comprehensive understanding of the Arab/Israeli conflict. Here, I will show that dominant ideological frames which have long characterized reporting on this issue, and which ultimately serve to legitimate American policies in the Middle East, continue to shape news products online. The second part of the chapter extends the analysis by drawing attention to the ways in which other voices may be co-opted on the Web, and dominant narratives reinforced, through the use of the hyperlink. It will be demonstrated that while *CNN.com*'s designers have clearly perceived the need to engage with alternative sources of information existing online, they have been able to do so in a manner which has not led to a more "democratic" or impartial presentation of news. Nonetheless, the appearance of more balanced reporting is achieved, and so too is the impression that *CNN.com* represents an authoritative and disinterested purveyor of information.

War on the Web

Most studies of Web-based networks focus upon situations where the elements within a given "online community" hold interests, goals, and/or ideology in common. This is generally the case irrespective of whether the networks of interest correspond to e-businesses, work organizations, subcultures, political parties, social movements, diaspora communities, or any other social collectivity. By contrast, this book is primarily concerned with ideological struggles among competing groups and interests, and the ways in which the WWW may contribute to their transformation. This focus is most explicit in chapters 5 and 6, where attention is given to the Web strategies adopted by fringe elements claiming to represent the true interests of the greater white/Christian, Jewish, and Muslim communities respectively. Each of these identities has proven adept at exploiting the Web's underdetermined character, particularly when responding to the co-presence of both enemies and potential allies online. Within the Web environment, social actors long condemned by the political establishment and the mass media demonstrate a clear ability to challenge dominant ideologies, court allies, attract potential recruits, and confront enemies with a degree of flexibility and rhetorical sleight of hand impossible through the use of other media.

Unlike the project identity and "moderate" resistance identity organizations considered in chapter 3, the openly racist dogma and/or aggressive stance adopted by white separatists, Islamist militants, and Zionist fundamentalists makes it difficult (in varying degrees) for organizations representative of each to pursue their agendas through open protest, greater access to mainstream media organizations, or political lobbying campaigns. Nonetheless, the WWW may prove highly valuable for even the most marginalized social movements. Chapter 5 considers the Web medium's utility for identity building. Emphasis is given to the ways in which the Web has been utilized by relevant groups to exploit the co-presence of enemies online, engaging them in propaganda warfare while simultaneously reinforcing their own core doctrine and conspiracy theories. Chapter 6 considers the Web's capacity to aid the same identities in their attempts to extend their influence beyond their own social movement boundaries. In both chapters it will be demonstrated that the rhetorical, organizational, broadcasting, and narrowcasting potentials of the WWW can never be clearly separated; a fact argued to have significant consequences for the three identities under consideration.

Evidence suggests that the Web strategies pursued by socially marginalized resistance identity organizations may have contradictory results with respect to their long-term goals. On the one hand it will be demonstrated in chapter 5 that the sharing of Web space with countless other interests allows for the construction of propaganda at a level of sophistication unattainable through the use of other media. As will be made apparent, the world views and arguments put forward by competing racist and ethnic nationalist organizations often appear to gain greater force as a direct result of their potential interconnectedness on the WWW. On the other hand, paradoxically, the overlapping hypertext structures produced by countless resistance and project identities may simultaneously reinforce the perception that corporate media giants such as *CNN.com* represent the most reliable and disinterested sources of information online. Similarly, while it will be argued in chapter 6 that the Web may allow for greater cohesion among the SMOs loosely associated with a given identity movement and contribute to overall social movement growth, it will also be maintained that in most cases any such growth is unlikely to translate into political power.

Ideology and Civil Society

Contemporary models of civil society draw attention to the existence of a multitude of interconnecting public spheres, involving diverse but overlapping communities of discourse (Jacobs 2000). The social theorist Jürgen Habermas (1998) has raised the question as to whether these multiple public spheres might still be reconciled within a broader project of shared citizenship under the conditions precipitated by global capitalism. Significantly, the decline of the social welfare state has meant not only increasing disparity between rich and poor, but perhaps as well, any stable basis for a shared national identity and a common public culture. In the seventh and final chapter of this investigation, I consider evidence and arguments presented in chapters 2 through 6 in light of such larger issues as public opinion, identity politics, and the changing character of civil society. Here, several theoretical lines of argument are brought together to make the case that internet technology is likely contributing to processes of social fragmentation *and* ideological hegemony simultaneously.

The fact that the narratives and Web structures considered in this investigation were often found to be deeply interconnected might at first appear to bode well with respect to the WWW's capacity to serve as a public forum, one conducive to constructive exchanges and debate among competing social identities. In fact, however, considerable support has been found for Wilhelm's (2000) contention that:

> Rather than creating environments in which ideas and viewpoints can be challenged and contested, the Internet may well be reinforcing and accelerating the pace of balkanization, a phenomenon that erodes deliberative democracy and the working out of problems and issues in the public sphere. (Wilhelm 2000, 43)

Significantly, it will be shown that competing rhetorical and organizational networks on the WWW often—and quite literally—grow past and through one another in a manner which appears to reinforce the ideological barriers separating divergent groups and interests, while encouraging self-referential forms of identity-building on the part of each. At first, this finding might appear to be nothing more than a reflection of the specific research subjects under consideration. After all, many of these are self-proclaimed racists or other ideologues who consider their unwillingness to tolerate difference as a virtue. Nonetheless, research and theory from other important sources also suggest that the Web is contributing to processes of social/political fragmentation in pluralist, information-based societies such as the United States.

Wilhelm (2000, 43) makes the important observation that while individuals belonging to online networks may be widely separated geographically, they likely shared similar interests and understandings of reality *before* they became part of an online community. While this point might at first seem unremarkable, it holds importance when considering the Net's increasing popularity for "blogging" and other forms of social networking and information sharing within and among various segments of the public. Such practices have been encouraged by more than the novel character of the Web medium. For example, the withdrawal of the state's social welfare role has been linked to the rise of single issue lobbies and citizens' coalitions promoting the interests of specific communities (Castells 2004). And, as Bimber (2003) suggests, the eagerness with which the Web has been utilized by a multiplicity of cultural groupings and "issue publics" also reflects, at least indirectly, cognitive limitations shared by all humans. A growing body of psychological research suggests that there are strict limits to the amount of information that individuals can consciously process, let alone subject to critical evaluation.

One implication is that most people will remain dependent upon the mainstream mass media for the bulk of the information they receive about the world at large; information which could never be supplied via the narrowcasting channels favored by any individual or group.

The amenability of hypertext to rhetorical manipulation by virtually any interest group does not make the Web environment ideologically neutral territory. And neither the de-centered qualities of the Web medium, nor the Net's obvious usefulness to grassroots activists appear likely to pose any meaningful threat to established interests in pluralist societies. In fact, the Web's unique ability to provide a space wherein the doctrines and activist strategies of countless social identities may co-exist simultaneously appears far more likely to enhance rather than diminish processes of ideological hegemony which have long been visible within more traditional mass media. As will be seen, the unusual characteristics of hypertext, in combination with the networking practices of competing SMOs and information providers, may come to reinforce the logic and rhetorical force of legitimating discourses in a variety of ways. In the chapters which follow, it will become increasingly apparent that Ellul's (1965) insights concerning the character of propaganda, political pluralism, and social integration in modern technological societies continue to hold relevance in the age of global networks.

Chapter Two

Net-Based Activism and American Mid-East Policy

PART I: GRASSROOTS MOBILIZATION AND POLITICAL OPPORTUNITY

Wherever interests are vigorously pursued, an ideology tends to be developed also to give meaning, reinforcement and justification to these interests. And this ideology is as "real" as the real interests themselves, for ideology is an indispensable part of the life-process which is expressed in action. And conversely: wherever ideas are to conquer the world, they require the leverage of real interests, although frequently ideas will more or less detract these interests from their original aim.

(Otto Hintz 1931)[1]

A considerable body of research has accumulated concerning the various ways in which the internet has been utilized to enhance the mobilization efforts of activist networks. Most of the latter correspond to what were referred to in chapter 1 as "project identities": social movements dedicated to the politics of emancipation, egalitarianism, and inclusiveness. For example, there are now numerous accounts of internet use by feminist, human rights, anti-poverty, and environmentalist social movement organizations (SMOs), along with increasing attention to the anti-globalization movement. Many of these studies have proven highly valuable for revealing the ways in which internet technology has contributed to the shifting strategies and repertoires of action adopted by grassroots activists. In general, however, they have tended to provide less insight with respect to the Net's capacity to either reinforce or destabilize larger dynamics of political power. Moreover, when viewed in isolation such case studies risk creating the potentially misleading impression that the social movements under consideration are now better positioned to achieve *relatively* greater cultural/political influence than would have been possible prior to the appearance of internet technology.

In this chapter, I assess the Internet's potential to help one set of project identity actors, those associated with the Arab/Israeli peace camp, become more effective in their attempts to influence U.S. policies towards Israel/ Palestine. This focus will be complemented in chapter 3, where attention will be turned to the Web's usefulness to the same actors in their efforts to educate the public about relevant developments and issues. These are topics which I believe need to be addressed very carefully by social scientists. Many researchers continue to make strong claims concerning the Net's potential to alter the political status quo and/or to promote or reinvigorate grassroots democratic processes. For example, when considering political activism among citizen-based groups in America, Bimber (1998; 2003) suggests that the communication and information flows made possible by the internet will lower the obstacles to grassroots mobilization formerly experienced by many in American society. More specifically, he argues that, "Lower costs of organizing collective action offered by the Net will be particularly beneficial for one type of group: those outside the boundaries of traditional private and public institutions, those not rooted in business, professional or occupational memberships or the constituencies of existing government agencies and programs" (Bimber 1998, 156).

Similar assumptions about the strategic advantages which the internet offers to grassroots political activists have informed the work of various researchers leading some to suggest that a plethora of new parties, interest groups, and social movements may emerge to seriously challenge the status quo in politically open societies.[2]

Before considering the evidence for such assertions, more needs to be said concerning the particular actors considered in this chapter. First it should be noted that the network referred to here as the Arab/Israeli peace camp includes Arab, Jewish, and student-based organizations committed to what they perceive as a just resolution to the Arab/Israeli conflict; namely, one based upon relevant United Nations (UN) resolutions, human rights conventions, and international law. Relevant examples include Al-Awda, Tikkun, and the International Solidarity Movement. Two resistance identities will also receive attention: Christian fundamentalism and Jewish ethnic nationalism. Examples of representative organizations in the United States include the Christian Coalition and the American Israel Public Affairs Committee, respectively. The stance taken by these networks towards the Arab/Israeli conflict differs markedly from that of the peace camp, as both are committed to Israel's settlement policies on occupied Arab land. Ideological support for these policies derives primarily from literalist interpretations of religious scripture and/or from an understanding of Israeli expansionism as being necessarily commensurate with the survival and well-being of the Jewish ethnic nation. Hence, despite their mainstream status and close association with legitimating institutions, the ideologies of these collective subjects reflect their resistance identity character.

As Diani (2003) has observed, social movement networks are normally comprised of more than one type of identity-based actor. This point is important since it allows one to avoid the trap of equating a given identity network with a single activist organization, lobby group, or political party. An understanding of social movements as networks is also helpful when attempting to assess the factors most likely to affect their political success. Not least among these are the mobilization efforts of competing identity networks. As Diani (2003, 301) makes clear, social movement organizations engage in actions intended to harm other social actors who are either "denying them access to social resources (however defined) they feel entitled to, or trying to take away from them resources over which they currently exert control." Similarly, when identifying the factors most likely to condition the mobilization efforts of social movements, McAdam (1996) refers to the counter-mobilization potential of political interest groups and/or grassroots SMOs whose agendas overlap with those of other existing political elites. In this and the next chapter, Christian fundamentalist and Jewish Zionist organizations will be understood as constituting state allies and/or counter-movements, actively opposing the efforts of the Arab/Israeli peace camp.

I will argue that the status of the Arab/Israeli conflict as both a source of ideological contention at the populist level *and* as a central concern driving U.S. foreign policy in the resource rich Middle East, are the most decisive factors shaping the political opportunity structures confronting project identities concerned with this issue. Furthermore, the range and nature of the obstacles faced by project identity SMOs will likely preclude the possibility that the internet will provide them with any unique advantage or "edge" in their attempts to influence American foreign policy. Strong evidence in support of these arguments may be found when considering both contemporary instances in which the Net appears to have aided grassroots actors, and historic cases involving political mobilization efforts by relevant social movements prior to the development of digital technology. As will be demonstrated, critical attention to both types of precedent allows for a more sober assessment of the Internet's potential value to contemporary activists committed to altering U.S. policies towards Israel/Palestine.

Activism and the Net: Relevant Precedents

The "relative openness or closure of the institutionalized political system" is widely recognized within social movement theory as conditioning the success of citizen-based activist organizations (McAdam 1996, 27). This criterion is useful to keep in mind when considering an argument frequently made with respect to the new opportunities which the Internet ostensibly makes available to otherwise resource-poor activist networks in relatively open societies such as the United States:

> Because it is relatively inexpensive for them to operate online, they can spread their message, recruit new members, raise funds, lobby politicians, mount petition drives, and the like. Many of these familiar political strategies and activities would have been impossible even to attempt without the Web. (Margolis & Resnick 2000, 19)

As Bimber (1998, 156) points out, the success of citizen-based political efforts have traditionally hinged upon the existence of mechanisms needed to maintain both a stable membership and the financial support of patrons. Consequently, the decreased transaction costs and networking potential of the Internet should prove particularly attractive to "outsider" groups. The potential advantages offered to weak groups by the Net take on even greater significance when considered in light of the corollary to this line of argument; namely, that traditional political parties and interest groups probably will not increase their power and influence by going online. Instead they will most likely use the World Wide Web (WWW) to "prevent being outflanked by newer groups" and to "remain competitive in all areas of mass appeal" (Margolis & Resnick 2000, 18).

In his consideration of single issue politics in America, Bimber (1998, 156–157) refers to several examples in which the Internet has allowed citizen-based networks to lobby the government effectively with respect to their concerns. The first pertains to a grassroots response to a Congressional bill proposed in 1994 which would have put in place significant new barriers to the practice of home schooling. In this instance, citizens opposing the bill utilized the Net to locate allies across the United States, and then used electronic mail to urge them to contact Congress. Members of this newly formed activist network "flooded Capitol Hill with letters and phone calls, and managed to defeat the school bill amendment." Bimber (1998) also cites a similar case of successful Internet use by community activists in Santa Monica. Here, concerned citizens were able to persuade the city government to create a homeless shelter and other services after several years of unsuccessful attempts. It was the adoption of Internet technology which ultimately proved critical to achieving their goals. Previous attempts at organizing had been hampered by constraints imposed by face-to-face modes of interpersonal contact and activism. Perhaps most importantly, Net use by local activists allowed for the formation of a widespread lobbying group which extended beyond the confines of the immediate community and crossed socioeconomic lines.

What so impressed Bimber (1998) with respect to the examples cited above is that they involved cases of citizen-based responses to issues which did not receive widespread media attention; responses which took the form of ad hoc networks where participants often had few financial resources, little or no lobbying experience, and were often widely dispersed geographically. However, while these examples might at first appear instructive with respect to the potential benefits which the internet may offer to grassroots peace activists attempting to promote a just solution to the Arab/Israeli conflict, there are stronger reasons to believe that this is not the case. The importance which the U.S./Israeli strategic relationship holds to both dominant political elites and competing segments of the American public clearly sets it apart from less contentious issues such as homeless shelters or home schooling. The implications for project identity organizations hoping to set new conditions on U.S. support for Israel become clear when their political efforts are considered in light of relevant historic precedents, and when attention is directed to other major factors likely to condition the political opportunities available to them.

In addition to the relative openness or closure of the political system, three other elements are commonly cited in approaches dealing with the political opportunity structures confronting social movements. The first two include "the stability or instability of that broad set of elite alignments that typically undergird a polity" and "the presence or absence of elite allies" (McAdam 1996, 27). McAdam (1996, 28) notes that a final element, "the state's capacity and propensity for repression," has generally been treated as an extension of the other two criteria within most of the social movement literature. He also provides good grounds for viewing state repression as an independent variable in certain cases. However, for present purposes the issue of state repression—insofar as it holds relevance here—will be addressed in conjunction with attention to elite alignments and state allies for reasons which will become apparent.

Consideration of the crucial role played by political elites and state allies with respect to social movement mobilization allows for a useful comparison between the historic conditions which facilitated the political success of the Jewish and Christian Zionist movement(s) versus the opportunities and obstacles facing peace camp activists today. It is worth drawing attention to the fact that historically, Zionist activists working towards the establishment of a Jewish state in Palestine relied upon precisely those forms of grassroots mobilization and political action regularly argued to be enhanced, if not "made possible," through the use of internet technology. An extensive investigation by Stevens (1970) takes account of a wide range of tactics and strategies adopted by Jewish Zionist organizations in the United States between 1942 until 1947. Their methods included successful fund-raising drives in support of the settlement and military activities of Jewish immigrants to Palestine, the securing of radio time in 26 states, supplying major American newspapers with a continuous supply of Zionist press releases, lobbying the Senate and Congress to adopt policy positions favorable to Zionist interests, and organizing mass meetings, public petitions, and protest rallies for the purposes of winning greater public sympathy and pressuring the government to support Zionist goals (see Stevens 1970, chapters II and V).

The mobilization efforts of American Jewish Zionist organizations were complemented by the grassroots activism of Christian organizations such as the Christian Council on Palestine and the American Palestine Committee (APC), organizations which appeared in the late 1930s (Merkley 1999; Stevens 1970). The American Zionist Emergency Council (AZEC), a Jewish lobbying organization with close ties to international affiliates such as the World Zionist Organization, made a point of cultivating close ties with such groups. AZEC contributed substantial funds to the APC and helped the Christian organization to establish over seventy-five chapters and attain a membership of 15,000 by 1946. The membership of the latter quickly grew to include educators, clergymen, publishers, editors, writers, and civic leaders (Merkley 1999, 132). As early as 1942, two-thirds of the United States Senate were enrolled in the APC, as were 143 members of the House of Representatives and 22 governors (Merkley 1998). That same year, cooperation between APC and AZEC resulted in the passing of a declaration affirming support for the Zionist program in Palestine which bore the names of 68 senators and 194 Congressmen (Merkley 1998, 133). In 1944, lobbying by the APC in both houses of Congress led to the passage of a similar resolution affirming the need to support maximum Jewish immigration to Palestine.

Perhaps the most spectacular instance of Zionist mobilization occurred in the days preceding the United Nations General Assembly's recommendation to partition Palestine into separate Jewish and Arab States. The resolution in question was passed on November 29, 1947 by a majority of one vote. In the days preceding its passage, it was apparent to the Jewish Zionist leadership that had the resolution been put before the Assembly, it would have failed to secure the needed two-thirds majority. For this reason, a decision was made by Zionist leaders on November 25 to launch a major campaign designed to ensure that the necessary votes were secured. In a passage which brings to mind many of the examples of Net-based activism cited in recent literature, David Horowitz, a former member of the Jewish Agency Executive, recalls this dramatic mobilization effort:

> . . . The fighting spirit rose within us again. We met at the Agency offices and consulted on ways and means to turn the wheel of events once more. The struggle began again. The telephones rang madly. Cable-grams sped to all parts of the world.

People were dragged from their beds at midnight and sent on peculiar errands. And, wonder of it all, not an influential Jew, Zionist or non-Zionist, refused to give us his assistance at any time. Everyone pulled his weight, little or great, in the despairing effort to balance the scales in our favor. (Stevens 1970, 177)

Stevens (1970) also takes note of President Truman's remarks with respect to the same campaign:

The facts were that not only were there pressure movements around the United Nations unlike anything that had been seen there before but that the White House, too, was subjected to a constant barrage. I do not think I ever had as much pressure and propaganda aimed at the White House as I had in this instance. The persistence of a few of the extreme Zionist leaders—accentuated by political motives and engaging in political threats—disturbed and annoyed me. Some were even suggesting that we pressure sovereign nations into favorable votes at the General Assembly. . . . (Stevens 1970, 182)

The organizational skills and zeal which the Zionists brought to their mobilization efforts were clearly necessary factors contributing to their political success. Nonetheless, it is easy to overestimate the degree to which Zionist mobilization at the grassroots level was responsible for gaining first British and later American support for the goal of establishing a Jewish state in Palestine. As has already been indicated, Jewish Zionist organizations in America received considerable ideological support among political elites during the years leading up to the creation of the Jewish state. The same held true several decades earlier in Britain, where political support for the Zionist program led to the Balfour Declaration of 1917, a document which made Britain's commitment to the establishment of a Jewish national home in Palestine official. It should also be noted that while Jewish nationalist Zionism had its origins in the late 1800s, it did not become widespread within the European and American Jewish communities until the late 1930s (Akenson 1991, 152; Suzman 1999, 156). Significantly, Britain's adoption of the Zionist program was not the result of grassroots pressure from a broadly based social movement, but rather the product of a meeting of minds between the Jewish Zionist leadership and dominant political personalities concerning the desirability of establishing a European Jewish colony in Palestine.

Prior to the late 1800s, ideological support for the creation of a Jewish state in Palestine was more widespread among Christian Protestants, particularly in Great Britain, than among world Jewry (Akenson 1991, 152). Lloyd George, the British Prime Minister from 1916 to 1922, and Lord Balfour were both ardent Christian Zionists (Akenson 1991, 162; Merkley 1999, 48–50). The idea that a Jewish return to Palestine was biblically ordained was part of the childhood religious training of both men. Balfour regarded history as "an instrument for carrying out a divine purpose" (Mouly 1985, 17). Lloyd George, who had received more instruction in Hebrew history than in the history of England, apparently shared this view. When in attendance at the peace treaty of Versailles in 1919, an agreement which effectively divided the Middle East into British and French spheres of influence, Lloyd George expressed his belief that an opportunity had arrived to recreate the Holy Land of Scriptures and to draw the boundaries of Palestine from "Dan to Beersheba" (MacMillan 2001, 415; Mouly 1985, 17). However, neither the effectiveness of Zionist activism, nor elite support based strictly on ideological grounds can fully account for the fulfillment of Zionist goals in the Middle East.

Most historians and researchers concerned with the evolution of Zionism agree that the establishment of a Jewish state in Palestine would never have occurred were it not also for the fact that the goals of this social movement converged with great power interests in the region. As Suzman (1999, 157) has pointed out, the Balfour Declaration would not have been adopted "had the Ottoman empire not started to implode during the First World War, leading to a temporary congruence between British strategic interests and Zionist goals for a post-war order." During World War II, when Britain perceived the strategic need not to alienate the Arabs any further than it already had, its previous support for unlimited Jewish immigration to Palestine was withheld. The protests and lobbying efforts of the Zionist community ultimately proved unsuccessful in preventing the passage of a White Paper in 1939 designed to restrict the flow of Jewish refugees into Palestine. It was primarily the inability to secure adequate British support for Zionist goals after this period which prompted this resistance identity to concentrate its most vigorous diplomacy and lobbying efforts in the United States (Merkley 1999, 100–101; Stevens 1970, 1–3; Suzman 1999, 159). These efforts remain relevant to this day, with direct implications for American organizations associated with the Arab/Israeli peace camp.

Contemporary Peace Camp Activism

The historic circumstances which allowed for the fulfillment of Zionist goals should be kept firmly in mind when considering the markedly contrasting conditions faced by contemporary project identities hoping to bring about a more "just" resolution of the Arab/Israeli conflict. As Stevens (1970, 27) has pointed out with respect to the activities of American Zionist organizations during the 1940s, their considerable success in influencing the dominant media and in gaining the support of key public figures "was facilitated by the almost complete absence of any propaganda favoring the Arab cause." By contrast, contemporary organizations and lobbying groups dedicated to bringing American policies towards the boundary object in line with the international consensus have had virtually no support within the American political establishment and far less access to the mainstream media than that traditionally enjoyed by Zionist interests. A strong consensus across party lines has long existed with respect to the perceived necessity and wisdom of continuing America's massive financial and military support for the state of Israel. This consensus is reflected in a long record of successful U.S. attempts to shield Israel from international pressure with respect to its illegal settlement building practices and human rights abuses in the Arab territories it captured during the Six-Day War of 1967 (Quigley 2005).

The existence of an elite consensus lying in opposition to project identity goals does not in and of itself preclude the possibility that the Internet might provide organizations associated with the peace camp with greater advantages *relative* to those interests committed to upholding the political status quo. It is still possible that the internet may offer more to those with less access to traditional political and media channels than to those who have long enjoyed considerable influence in both of these areas. With this possibility in mind, it is useful to consider the most frequent uses to which the better known Palestinian rights and Mid-East peace organizations typically put the Internet. This will be done through brief reference to the forms of political action promoted within the Web sites of the Palestinian human rights organization Al-Awda, and the Jewish peace activist organization, Tikkun. The "direct action" tactics routinely engaged in by organizations such as the International Solidarity Movement will be exempted from the present discussion, but will receive attention in chapter 3.

Al-Awda represents the largest activist network concerned with Palestinian human rights. Its Web site, *al-awda.org*, describes the organization's character and mission under the heading *Who We Are:*

> The Palestine Right of Return (Al-Awda is Arabic for "THE RETURN") is a broad-based non-partisan global democratic association of thousands of grassroots activists and organizational representatives concerned for the Palestinian Refugees Right of Return. The purposes for which PRRC is formed are educational and charitable and relate to human rights of Palestinian Refugees. (Al-Awda [b])

The Web page from which this quote was taken also lists the organization's more specific goals. These include educating the U.S. public and international community and nonprofit human rights organizations with respect to relevant human rights conventions and UN resolutions, establishing social justice for Palestinians "beyond their defined geographic locations," and helping Palestinian refugees by means of empowerment projects and the provision of humanitarian aid.

On another page within *al-awda.org*, the following forms of activism are advocated under the heading *What You Can Do*:

GET EDUCATED
Visit our Resources and get additional info at *http://PalestineRemembered.com* and *http://www.mideastfacts.com*

ACT
Visit our *Action Alerts* page and act
Join one of our *Local Action Committees* see their websites at *Al-Awda Regional Sites*
Join one of our *Specialized Action Committees*
Organize and attend *Events* in your area
Contact and work with your local media, see *Media Activism*
If interested in reaching government officials, use
http://cflweb.org/congress_merge_.htm
Boycott campaigns: *http://www.BoycottIsraeliGoods.org* (Al-Awda [c])

The activist strategies promoted within *al-awda.org* are typical of project identity Web sites affiliated with the Peace camp, and are mirrored within the Web site *tikkun.org*. Tikkun is perhaps the best known American Jewish organization attempting to promote lasting peace between Israel and the Palestinians based upon recognition of Palestinian human rights and the implementation of relevant UN Security Council Resolutions. The name "tikkun" means "to transform, heal and repair" (Tikkun 2001, 5). It should be noted that in terms of its outlook, Tikkun lies at the boundary between "conservative" Zionist organizations and more "radical" Jewish organizations within the peace camp. For example, unlike Al-Awda, Tikkun does not advocate an unequivocal right of return for Palestinian refugees. Instead, it advocates a two-state solution to the Israeli/Palestinian conflict based upon Israel's return to the pre-1967 borders in conjunction with UN Security Council Resolution 242, and the creation of a fully sovereign Palestinian state within the West Bank and Gaza (Lerner 2001). At the same time, both Al-Awda and Tikkun qualify as peace camp organizations in the sense described at the beginning of this chapter. It is also worth noting that the two organizations have engaged in dialogue with respect to their key areas of disagreement.[3]

As with *al-awda.org*, emphasis is placed within *tikkun.org* upon the importance of education, political outreach, and fund-raising with respect to furthering its political objectives (Tikkun 2003a, 5–6). Its organizational strategies are also similar. For example, just as Al-Awda has formed "specialized action committees" for mobilization purposes, Tikkun has been working to develop "national task forces" to address its key areas of concern (Tikkun 2003a, 1). It should also be emphasized that the forms of political activism advocated within the Web sites of Al-Awda, Tikkun, and related organizations are similar in character to those traditionally pursued by a wide range of grassroots SMOs, including the Zionist organizations considered earlier. This may be seen clearly with respect to the activities recommended within *tikkun.org* under the heading *Education*. While these activities receive considerable elaboration within *tikkun.org*, it is sufficient merely to list them here:

1. set up meetings with leaders of local churches, synagogues, mosques
2. set up meetings with various professional groups
3. meet with leaders and activists in local unions
4. organize a series of house meetings
5. set up a meeting with the editorial board of your local newspaper
6. create a local teach-in on the Middle East
7. ask high school and college teachers to let you come and present to their students
8. use your imagination
9. create house or apartment parties and invite your friends and co-workers (Tikkun 2003a, 2–3)

As was the case with the early Zionist organizations active in the United States, Al-Awda and Tikkun both place considerable emphasis upon the need to encourage more "balanced" reporting with respect to events in the Middle East. Significantly, both organizations place emphasis on the importance of "rapid response media," the aim of which is to call mainstream media institutions to account when they misrepresent the facts or distort the historic record. Peace camp organizations also place importance on their own and other Web sites as alternative sources of information for use by the public. In addition, some organizations, such as the International Solidarity Movement, engage in dramatic and/or dangerous forms of activism which one would expect to gain considerable mainstream media attention. The potential importance which these and related forms of media activism may hold for the peace camp will be given closer consideration in chapter 3.

It should be noted that the Web sites of Al-Awda and Tikkun represent only two examples of the countless Web sites advocating greater recognition of Palestinian human rights and a solution to the Israeli/Palestinian conflict based upon relevant United Nations (UN) resolutions. For example, *al-awda.org* provides links to dozens of Arab/Muslim, Jewish/Israeli, and Christian Web sites with compatible political agendas. Many of these Web sites specialize in particular areas of activism. For example, some like *alnakba.org* and *palestineremembered.com* (much like *al-awda.org*) provide extensive information and resources concerning the Palestinian right of return. Others, such as *sustaincampagin.org* and *boycottisraeligoods.org* focus upon campaigns designed to make American aid to Israel contingent upon an end to the Israeli occupation of Arab territories. Still others, such as *againstisraeliwarcrimes.org* and *israel-state-terrorism.org*, are designed to draw attention to Israeli war crimes and human rights abuses. *Pmwatch.org* functions in the role of a media watchdog organization. Another Web site, *sabeel.org*, serves as a forum for the views of Palestinian Arabs of Christian descent; approaching questions of peace and social justice from the perspective of ecumenical liberation theology. These examples are far from exhaustive.

Whether they are considered individually or collectively, the Web sites of organizations associated with the Arab/Israeli peace camp now provide their membership(s) with what has become an indispensable information resource and organizational tool. However, while Internet technology has clearly become essential to the mobilization efforts of this project identity, care should be taken not to conflate the Internet's usefulness to Arab/Israeli peace activists with its potential to alter the (American) political status quo in their favor. As Margolis & Resnick (2000, 19) have observed, "any significant political movement in the future arising in the industrial world probably not only will have a strong presence on the Internet, but that presence will be one factor among many explaining its rise to prominence." They also note that most marginal movements making use of the Net will likely remain marginal. These points are important to keep in mind, particularly when the political activities of organizations hostile to the program of the Arab/Israeli peace camp are taken into account.

Were the difficulties faced by contemporary Mid-East peace organizations exclusively attributable to barriers imposed from above by powerful interests then there might be good grounds to accept the premise that from a relative standpoint, the Internet does offer more to peace activists than to political and corporate interests committed to upholding current U.S. policies in the Middle East. However, the reality is that the peace camp's agenda is also opposed by an extensive network of Zionist organizations which continue to rely upon their own ability to mobilize grassroots support. It is worth noting that the Web site of the American Israel Public Affairs Committee (AIPAC) promotes similar forms of activism to those advocated within *al-awda.org* and *tikkun.org*. However, unlike the latter, AIPAC represents a highly influential lobbying organization. The *National Journal* ranked AIPAC as the second most powerful lobby in Washington after the National Rifle Association and it is widely understood to be the most important lobby influencing foreign policy (Massing 2006; Hanley 2003). Consequently, the strategies it adopts—

whether on or off-line—will be almost certainly be backed by considerably greater financial and political resources.

AIPAC's entrenchment within the mainstream political system contrasts starkly with the status of organizations belonging to the peace camp. Al-Awda would not likely be able to arrange for "a private dinner at the home of Vice President and Mrs. Gore," "briefings with the State Department and receptions with U.S. Senators," or provide an "in-depth resource center" for use by Hill Staff; accomplishments listed by AIPAC within its Web site *aipac.org* (AIPAC 2004a-b). Likewise, Rabbi Michael Lerner of Tikkun has commented to the effect that many politicians view meetings with members of his organization as "politically dangerous" due to the overwhelming presence of AIPAC on Capitol Hill (Kaplan 2004, 24). At the same time AIPAC's ability to mobilize a substantial grassroots base of support is impressive. Each year it hosts a policy conference in Washington, during which it can count on a substantial political celebrity and grassroots turnout; as occurred for example, in March of 2003, when 5,000 activists converged on Washington to express their reservations about George Bush's Road Map for Peace (Brownfeld 2003).

That the interests most strongly opposed to the goals of Middle East peace activists frequently take the form of both political elites *and* populist grassroots social movements is perhaps most apparent with respect to Christian fundamentalism. As Lienesh (1993, 229) has observed, "in the eschatology of the New Christian Right, Israel is the key." More specifically, Christian fundamentalists believe that the creation of modern Israel represents the fulfillment of biblical prophecy, and that the Arab territories it captured during the 1967 Six-Day War belong to Israel by divine right. In February 2002, Senator James Inhofe gave a speech before the Senate in which he defended Israel's right to retain and settle these territories, arguing that "This is not a political battle at all. It is a contest over whether or not the word of God is true."[4] Significantly, the belief system upheld by this resistance identity cannot be dismissed as the doctrine of a disempowered religious fringe. "Christian conservatives" are now a dominant force within the Republican Party, and political lobbying groups such as the Christian Coalition (CC) represent an enormous grassroots constituency. The CC presently claims an organized membership of roughly 1.5 million (Castells 2004: 24).

Christian fundamentalist support for Israel's expansionist policies has been recognized and encouraged by successive Israeli governments. In 1977, after President Carter expressed an interest in securing some form of autonomy for Palestinians in the occupied West Bank and Gaza, Israeli Prime Minister Menachem Begin sent a special emissary to the U.S. to gain the support of fundamentalist leaders. A few weeks later, full-page advertisements appeared in large circulation newspapers including the *New York Times* and the *Washington Post*, affirming that these territories belonged exclusively to God's "Chosen People" (Mouly 1985, 27). More recently, the readiness of Christian Zionists to mobilize on Israel's behalf has been demonstrated through the activities of a relatively new organization known as the Jerusalem Prayer Team (JPT). The JPT's board members include Christian Coalition founder and 700 Club host, Pat Robertson, and former Moral Majority leader, Jerry Falwell. The organization has grown to include 2 million members, and has invested millions of dollars in Israel since its inception in the mid-1990s (Brownfeld 2003).

In May, 2003, shortly after a meeting was held between JPT representatives and Israeli Tourism Minister Benny Elon, the JPT initiated a new fund-raising drive under the banner "Adopt-a-Settler." Elon had asked if there was anything the organization could do in support of Israel's settlers (Gross 2003). In response, the JPT initiated its new campaign with the goal of raising enough funds to provide $55 apiece to 14,000 settlers. The dependency of these efforts upon traditional grassroots mobilization practices is reflected in the comments of a JPT spokesperson interviewed by *Forward* (Gross 2003). Here it was affirmed that the drive was being successfully undertaken through the use of newsletters, sermons, fliers, and parlor meetings around the country. It is worth noting that while the Internet will almost certainly aid in this and similar efforts, mobilization practices such as those listed above have a long history of use by social movements. As was mentioned with respect to Al-Awda and Tikkun, the JPT and other Zionist organizations appear to be using the internet primarily to complement traditional forms of activism. This is apparent when visiting the JPT's Web site, where "calls to action" consist primarily of requests to sign online petitions supportive of various Israeli occupation practices, and/or condemning the practices and statements of various Arab and Muslim governments and organizations (JPT 2004).

A good illustration of the range and nature of interests prepared to mobilize in defense of the Israeli occupation was provided by the Interfaith Zionist Leadership Summit for America and Israel. The event, which was held on May 17–18, 2003, at the Omni Shoreham Hotel in Washington, was prominently advertised within the Web site of the Christian Coalition (CC). The expressed purpose of the summit, which was sponsored by Zionist House and the National Unity Coalition for Israel, was to derail President Bush's Road Map for Peace. If implemented, the Road Map would require Israel to return at least some of the territory it captured in the Six-Day War of 1967, a possibility deemed unacceptable to the CC and the summit's twenty-one co-sponsors. The latter consisted primarily of Zionist Christian and Jewish political action committees, media watch organizations, and neo-conservative think tanks. Its twenty guest speakers included the presidents of the Christian Coalition and the Zionist Organization of America, Michael Ledeen of the American Enterprise Institute, former U.S. Ambassador to UNESCO Alan Keyes, Alan Safian of the Committee for Accuracy in Middle East Reporting in America (CAM-ERA), and two prominent Zionist academics: Prof. Louis Rene Beres, and Prof. Daniel Pipes of The Middle East Forum (Christian Coalition 2003).

The fact that pro-Zionist interests span the spectrum from elite political institutions and powerful political lobbies to countless grassroots religious and cultural organizations means that their attempts to counter the activism and mute the voice of the peace camp will be particularly formidable. This may be seen in relation to ongoing efforts by Zionist and neo-conservative efforts to restrict academic freedom on American college campuses. For example, on October 31, 2003, Congress passed a bill (H.R. 3077) that could require university international studies departments to show greater support for American foreign policy, or risk losing their federal funding (Goldberg 2003; Roy 2005). Of particular concern to those behind the bill was the political and media critique of Palestinian scholar Edward Said whose work is widely recognized as central to the development of postcolonial theory. Prior to his death in 2003, Said remained an outspoken advocate of Palestinian human rights and a harsh critic of U.S. peace initiatives in the Middle East. After 9/11, Said and numerous other academics critical of U.S. foreign policy were accused by neo-conservative politicians and scholars of having lowered America's guard to the threat posed by Islamist terrorism (Roy 2005).

The Congressional bill mentioned above is part and parcel of a much larger effort to curtail academic criticism of Israeli policies towards the Palestinians, the ongoing war in Iraq, and U.S. foreign policy more generally. These efforts have involved coordinated actions on the part of both off-campus groups and lobbies such as AIPAC, the Washington Institute for Near East Policy and the David Project, and student organizations such as Hillel, Israel on Campus, and Students for Academic Freedom (SAF). These and other groups have attempted to vilify numerous professors critical of present U.S. policies—particularly those within International and Middle East studies programs—deliberately conflating criticism of Israel with the defense of terrorism and the promotion of anti-Semitism (Roy 2005; Scott 2006). A major force behind this campaign was and remains Daniel Pipes's Campus Watch Web Site (*campus-watch.org*), with its motto "Monitoring Middle East Studies on Campus." Campus Watch, which is an extension of the think tank Middle East forum (cited above), at one time listed the names of individual professors deemed to be too critical of Israeli policies. One result was that many individuals were barraged with hate mail and spam on such a scale that their e-mail accounts were rendered practically useless. In response to heavy criticism, Campus Watch now only lists relevant institutions and programs. A similar Web site run by SAF—which has branches on 135 American campuses—continues to list professors by name (Mearsheimer & Walt 2006; Scott 2006).

The developments discussed above draw attention to a fourth criterion widely cited in the social movement literature as likely to limit the success of political activist networks: the state's capacity and propensity for repression (McAdam 1996, 27). While state repression may be far less pronounced within liberal democracies such as the United States than under other forms of government, it is still an issue of some relevance here, particularly in relation to state and/or police surveillance practices. As noted by Lyon (2003, 4), the terrorist attacks of 9/11 provided a clear opportunity for those with an interest in expanding the state's surveillance capacities to integrate and exploit existing ideas, policies, and technologies in the name of the War on Terror. Official attempts to make new and expanding surveillance practices—such as the mass monitoring of e-mail messages and computer data-mining of personal information—both legal and routine remain ongoing. And it is certainly worth observing that the two segments of the American public which have arguably received the greatest police and/or state surveillance since (at least) 9/11 have been Arab and Muslim Americans on the one hand, and anti-war activists on the other (Goldberg 2004; Scott 2006). These two groups which overlap considerably in the case of the peace camp.

The issue of surveillance is highly salient when considering questions of relative advantage. Just as there are aspects of internet use which may benefit grassroots activists disproportionately when compared to more powerful actors, the reverse may sometimes also hold true. Clearly, surveillance represents one area in which the state may exploit internet technology, along with countless additional resources, more effectively than SMOs. At the same time, the watchdog and (counter)mobilization efforts of organizations such as Campus Watch, SAT, or CAIRwatch[5] may converge with state surveillance practices, further contributing to an atmosphere of intimidation and harassment experienced by those critical of America's present stance on such issues as Iraq or Palestinian human rights. It is no secret that the same political forces most supportive of an expansionist Israel and an open-ended U.S. War on Terror have also been among the most vigorous advocates for increased state surveillance powers at home (Castells 2004; Greenwald 2007). Numerous cases have come to light in which anti-war and pro-Palestinian activists have found themselves under surveillance and/or subject to harassment from both state authorities and organizations such as Campus Watch (Massing 2006; Scott 2006).

The intent here is not to suggest that present U.S. policies towards Israel/Palestine are unassailable or that the political forces behind them are invincible. However, it does appear likely that insofar as dissent on this issue does become more open and visible with respect to mainstream political and media debate, that internet activism will not be a major contributing factor. If the historic record is any indication, changes in government policy will likely be driven much less by the grassroots efforts of SMOs concerned with international law and human rights, than by changing perceptions among political elites regarding the practical wisdom—in terms of costs versus benefits—of relying upon Israel as a key ally in the Middle East.[6] Irrespective of any such development, the existence of pro-Zionist elements at virtually every level of social and political organization in American society appears to guarantee that any advantages which the internet makes available to them will likely either match or surpass those accruing to their opponents in the peace camp.

Closing Remarks

The factors most likely to advance or hinder the mobilization efforts of any particular activist network are not always readily apparent, and may only be discerned clearly through ongoing empirical research. Certainly, cases have been documented in which the Net does appear to have played a key role in helping grassroots actors achieve their political goals. However, as suggested earlier in this chapter, such successes may be largely attributable to the relatively non-contentious nature of the issues in question. And other studies suggest that social movement networks which routinely confront powerful interests will likely experience challenges similar to those faced by the Arab/Israeli peace camp. For example, Dordoy & Mellor (2001) maintain that despite its ongoing involvement with Net-based activism, the environmental justice movement is fighting an increasingly downhill battle with industry. Notably, the difficulties faced by this social movement include a lack of positive media attention, heavy lobbying by industry, and the counter-mobilization efforts of anti-environmentalist groups.

The analysis undertaken in this chapter worked largely from the premise—supported by the calls to action highlighted within relevant Web sites—that activists typically approach the internet as an information resource and toolbox which may be used to enhance the effectiveness of more traditional mobilization practices. When internet technology is approached in this light, it is perhaps unsurprising that the political opportunity structures which have historically conditioned the political mobilization efforts of SMOs continue to play a crucial role in the information age. As Margolis & Resnick (2000, 18) observe, political activists typically use the internet to "locate and disseminate information, to contact and organize political sympathizers, and to lobby government officials and political representatives." However, it must also be recognized that internet technology may be employed as a means of *bypassing* traditional political and media channels. This is perhaps most apparent with respect to the Web's capacity to provide an alternative route through which less powerful actors may directly or indirectly address and attempt to educate the public. The possibility that relatively weak actors such as those fighting for Palestinian human rights will gain significant advantages when attempting to utilize the Web in this manner is the subject of the next chapter.

NOTES

1. As quoted in Habermas (1984, 188).

2. For further discussion see Margolis & Resnick (2000) Ch. 1.

3. Transcripts of a relevant debate between Rabbi Michael Lerner of Tikkun and Dr. Abu Sitta of Al-Awda concerning the rights and future status of Palestinian refugees are available within *al-awda.org* under the heading "Debate with Tikkun on Refugees" http://www.al-awda.org/?page=Debate%20wth%20Tikkun%20on%20...

4. See Inhofe, James. 2002. Seven Reasons Why Israel is Entitled to the Land. *CBN News*, March, 4.

5. An organization dedicated to monitoring the alleged terrorism-related activities of the organization, Council on American-Islamic Relations (CAIR).

6. There are at least some tentative signs that such a shift may be in its early stages. Recent critique of U.S./Israel relations by former President Carter (2006) and by other relatively conservative sources such as Mearsheimer & Walt (2006) are noteworthy in this regard. There has also been increasing media attention to the role of the Christian right in supporting Israel's occupation practices.

Chapter Three

Net-Based Activism
and American Mid-East Policy

PART II: PUBLIC OPINION

Backdrop: The Mainstream Media as a Legitimating Identity

Pro-Palestinian rights activists have long insisted that Western, and particularly American, news media coverage of events in the Middle East is unfairly biased in a manner favorable to the state of Israel. Exactly the opposite claim has been made by Israel's supporters, particularly those sympathetic to Israel's expansionist policies in the occupied territories. Attempts to assess the seriousness of these charges and counter-charges are complicated by the potential difficulty of clearly defining just what constitutes pro-Israel, pro-Arab, or pro-Palestinian reporting. For example, many organizations belonging to what was referred to in chapter 2 as the peace camp believe that more just American and Israeli policies would benefit Israel as much as the Palestinians. In this sense, Jewish project identities such as Tikkun or Rabbis for Human Rights could be considered as both pro-Israel and pro-Palestinian. Nonetheless, if pro-Israeli bias is taken to mean news reporting which directly or indirectly serves to legitimate Israeli policies towards the Arabs and which highlights Israeli suffering—even as Arab/Palestinian suffering and regular Israeli violations of human rights and international law go largely ignored—then there can be no doubt that Western news reporting has long been tilted in Israel's favor. In fact, this is precisely what one would expect given the history of Western policies in the Middle East on the one hand, and the large body of research dealing with the political economy of news on the other.

That the mainstream news media of print and television continue to play the role of legitimizing identities in democratic societies cannot seriously be contested (see pgs. 9–10). Even Schudson (2000, 180), a strong critic of Herman &

Chomsky's (1988) "propaganda model" approach to news content, concedes that in virtually all political and economic systems "news coincides with and re-inforces the definition of the political situation evolved by the political elite."[1] It is widely accepted among media researchers that in democratic societies this sit-uation arises indirectly rather than as the result of government decree; a situation which makes news bias harder to detect, but no less pervasive. In countries such as the United States, Canada, and Britain the ideological character of news and its relative invisibility are primarily attributable to several closely related factors. Foremost among these are the profit orientation of the mass media as corporate enterprises, the media's heavy reliance on advertising revenue, its vulnerability to discipline from government agencies and corporate bodies, and its depen-dence upon government bureaucracies, corporate public relations firms, experts, think tanks, etc. for a continuous supply of readily accessible and dependable in-formation (Curran 2000; Herman & Chomsky 1988; McChesney 2004).

The news media's position within the larger political economy has produced an interesting phenomenon. While debate in the media surrounding controver-sial issues may be both vigorous and highly visible, it tends to take place within a relatively narrow range of "permissible" debate (McMurtry 1998). That is to say, the underlying assumptions and accepted premises which set the parameters of media discourse are rarely questioned. At the same time, the very presence of media criticism (within this range) makes the press appear far more "free" in terms of its willingness and ability to play the role of watchdog than is indicated by its actual ties to, and dependence upon, state and corpo-rate goodwill. News reports dealing with the War on Terror provide an excel-lent case in point. As Lustick (2006, 14) observes, the American media con-tinue to be filled with arguments and criticism concerning how the War on Terror is prosecuted, "which nonetheless establish its rationale and scale as un-questionably appropriate." Hence, rather than being the target of penetrating media critique, the War on Terror has become the background narrative against which definitions of problems, categories of analysis, and the boundaries of acceptable opinion are framed (Lustick 2006, 8–28).

Research suggests that elite conceptions of the world are most closely ad-hered to by the media in the case of foreign news reporting (Chin-Chuan et. al 2000; Schudson 2003). Ironically, this tendency may be exacerbated by a gen-uine commitment on the part of journalists to high standards of professional-ism and objectivity. For example, a study conducted by the Center for Inter-national and Security Studies at Maryland, which investigated news reporting on weapons of mass destruction (WMD) for the periods May 5–26, 1998, Oc-tober 11–31, 2002, and May 1–21, 2003, revealed a persistent distortion of key facts and general lack of balance in coverage of this issue (Moeller 2004). Much of this imbalance was attributed to the "inverted pyramid" approach to news writing, a convention whereby greatest weight (in terms of words in print) is given to the statements of "key players" such as political leaders, with any criticism left to rival politicians or establishment experts. The underlying rationale for this practice is that facts and statements should be presented "just as they are," without interpretation by journalists. In the case of reporting on WMD, the result was that the White House set the news agenda (Moeller 2004). For example, the media followed the administration's lead by lumping together unrelated forms of weaponry and warfare under the broad category of weapons of mass destruction, and even more significantly, by consistently associating WMD with terrorism.

The tendencies cited above are readily apparent with respect to the specific case of news reporting on the Israeli/Palestinian conflict. In a thorough study of British television coverage of the first and second Palestinian intifadas (uprisings), Philo & Berry (2004) note that virtually all news reporting operated from the implicit premise that Israeli violence was defensive or retaliatory in character. This approach served, at least indirectly, to justify ongoing Israeli military actions in the West Bank and Gaza. By contrast, drawing attention to Palestinian and Israeli violence within the context of an illegal occupation— as opposed to an Israeli war on terror within which Palestinian violence is ostensibly motivated by an irrational hatred of Israel—would necessarily draw attention to the refugee status, living conditions, and human rights violations of those under military rule. A related tendency concerned news coverage of relations between Israeli settlers and Palestinian Arabs. The two groups were generally portrayed as mutually hostile communities with (implicitly equal) claims to the same territory, engaged in sporadic tit-for-tat violence. Almost no attention was given to the role played by armed settlers as an extension of the military occupation, to the fact that settlers (illegally) utilize a disproportionate share of scarce resources in the territories, that they live on confiscated Palestinian land, or to the fact that settlers are able to attack Palestinians and their property with relative impunity.

Given Israel's status as America's most favored client state, it should come as little surprise that pro-Israel media coverage has been even more pronounced in the United States than in most other Western countries. The Middle East has long been a major preoccupation of the United States, both as a vital arena of strategic interest, and an ongoing source of crises requiring "expert management." The ideological apparatuses which perpetuate U.S./Arab relations along these lines are extensive. As Said (1997, 153) observes, both Britain and France produced a class of colonial experts during their many decades of administering Islamic colonies. However, this class of experts never had a counterpart comparable to the vast network of the "Middle-East studies-government-corporate alliance" which has coalesced in the United

States since the end of WWII. In this regard, it bears mentioning that most of the experts currently relied upon as information sources by journalists are supplied by think tanks which have consistently proven friendly to Israeli expansionism, and which have also been highly influential in the formation of U.S. Mid-East policy. The latter include such organizations as the American Enterprise Institute, the Brookings Institute, the Heritage Foundation, the Hudson Institute, the Center for Security Policy, the Foreign Policy Research Institute, and the Institute for Foreign Policy Analysis, among others (Mearsheimer & Walt 2006).

It is important to recognize that the media's profit orientation and close ties to (other) corporate and state interests are not the only factors affecting news content, which is also influenced by such phenomena as the work routines and ethical standards of news professionals, prevailing cultural currents in society at large, and the media advocacy of citizens' groups. However, as suggested earlier with respect to the issue of news professionalism, such factors may serve to reinforce dominant ideological frames at least as often as they promote more open media. This is readily apparent in the case of citizen-based attempts to influence news coverage of Israel/Palestine. As was mentioned in chapter 2, engaging the news media remains a priority for both Zionist organizations and their project identity adversaries. Turning first to the latter, media activism ranks chief among the calls to action listed in the peace camp Web sites of Al-awda and Tikkun. Within *tikkun.org*, the following comments appear under the heading *Rapid Response Media*:

> Eventually, we'd like journalists in a given town who write a balanced story, and who quote people from the Tikkun Community perspective, to be receiving phone calls of appreciation, and their editors or publishers similarly getting those calls. Conversely, we want the television news anchors and reporters, assignment desk editors, newspaper editors and journalists and publishers to be getting a barrage of complaints every time the story minimizes or misunderstands or misrepresents the peace perspective. . . . (Tikkun 2003a, 5)

The achievements of peace camp organizations have often been impressive. For example, in April 2001, Rabbis for Human Rights took out a full-page advertisement in the *New York Times* to draw attention to Israel's ongoing destruction of Palestinian homes and crops in the West Bank (Solomon 2001). The Palestinian organization Al-Awda has had successes as well. Some of these are listed under the heading *Media accomplishments 2003* within its Web site *al-awda.org*. They include the submission of over 8,000 letters and op-ed pieces to mainstream newspapers and magazines, 200 of which were published (Al-Awda [a]). Furthermore, independent news monitoring organizations such as Palestine Media Watch (*pmwatch.org*) have been created to serve the needs of the peace camp by detecting cases of bias in the mainstream media. These may prove important when activists attempt to call news organizations to account.

While not insignificant, such accomplishments must be weighed against the efforts of counter-movements. For example, Palestine Media Watch has a Zionist watchdog counterpart, Palestinian Media Watch. As will be commented upon shortly, the latter organization has had a significant influence on U.S. decision-making. And much like Al-Awda and Tikkun, major American Zionist organizations such as AIPAC and the Christian Coalition promote letter writing and e-mail campaigns aimed at disciplining the media. One executive at CNN has claimed that he sometimes receives as many as 6,000 e-mails in a day from Zionist sources complaining about a story (Mearsheimer & Walt 2006). Such activism can be intimidating, particularly when it receives backing from members of the political establishment. For example, in May 2003, CAMERA organized demonstrations outside National Public Radio (NPR) stations in thirty-three cities to protest reporting deemed overly critical of Israel. NPR's Boston station reportedly lost over $1 million in contributions as a result (Mearsheimer & Walt 2006). Further pressure came from members of Congress who asked for an internal audit of NPR's Mid-East coverage (Mearsheimer & Walt 2006). Ironically, a thorough content analysis of NPR's reporting undertaken by FAIR (Fairness and Accuracy in Reporting) in 2003 revealed a marked pro-Israel bias in the NPR's news coverage, a point which will be returned to later in this chapter.

The issues raised above draw attention back to the conundrum faced by peace camp activists discussed in chapter 2. Namely, the existence of both established political elites and populist social movements rallying to the cause of greater Israel appears to guarantee that these actors will have the upper hand when attempting to exploit the various communication and mobilization potentials enhanced or made available through use of the Net. Similarly, it would appear that for the time being at least, attempts by peace camp organizations to lobby the media—with or without the help of the internet—will continue to be outmatched by the efforts of their equally committed and more resource-rich opponents. Still, given the multi-faceted character of Internet technology, this need not be the end of the story. What if the Web itself is utilized as a news medium, rather than as simply one more means for harassing the corporate media? What about its capacity to serve as an information resource readily accessible for use not only by Mid-East peace activists, but also by mainstream journalists and members of the general public seeking a fuller account of developments in the Middle East and/or alternative points of view concerning those developments? Even if peace camp organizations cannot outperform their enemies by exploiting the Web as a broadcast medium, can they not perform just as well? If so, is it not inevitable that they will create a significantly more even playing field in the contest to influence public opinion? It is to these and related considerations that we now turn.

The Web as an Alternative Mass Medium

The argument that the internet may play an equalizing role with respect to relatively powerful versus relatively powerless actors in society has perhaps been made the most forcefully with respect to the WWW's capacity to serve as an alternative forum through which any individual or group may address the broader public. Affirmations to the effect that less influential groups will likely have more to gain when using the Web for representational purposes than will well-established interests with more access to the traditional mass media are commonplace. As Margolis & Resnick (2000, 19) remark, "a presence on the Web could greatly increase the exposure of a narrow interest group to its own constituency and to the public at large." They note further that "no matter how obscure or outré the cause, if it has a home page, it can be located by employing a search engine." However, while there is clearly truth in these statements, the obstacles faced by marginal actors attempting to use the Web effectively as a public platform have generally been underestimated.

The frequently voiced notion that the Web may provide an alternative medium for use by social movement organizations (SMOs), or others outside the political mainstream, is both appealing and highly suggestive. The very term "alternative" implies that control over one's own Web logs and/or "news broadcasts" should make concerns about the forces serving to shape the products of the corporate news media irrelevant. As will be demonstrated in the remainder of this chapter, this assumption is not valid. Traditional influences on mainstream news content may have profound implications for social movements hoping to influence public opinion through use of the Web. This is largely because the political economy issues raised above are inseparable from the types of obstacles to activist mobilization efforts considered in chapter 2. In that chapter, it was argued that while the Net may provide marginalized political activists with a tactical edge relative to established interests in certain cases, this is more likely to prove to be the exception rather than the general rule. Likewise, evidence suggests that SMOs, such as those associated with the peace camp, will remain at a disadvantage irrespective of whether they employ the Web to lobby the mainstream media directly, use the Web to help gain media attention through the exploitation of shocking events, supply news reporters with alternative Web-based information, and/or whether they attempt to address the public directly by the same means.

The true nature of the challenges faced by weak actors attempting to utilize the WWW as a representational medium cannot be fully appreciated unless a clear distinction is made between the Web's capacity to serve as an information resource and source of inspiration for those belonging to a particular social identity, versus its potential to function as a mass, or broadcasting medium. That this distinction has often been either blurred or overlooked in case studies of internet use by social movement organizations, is apparent in the passage below which draws attention to the importance of computer-mediated communication (CMC) for environmental activists:

> In particular CMC use will affect the need to gain media attention. Trying to gain media attention is particularly difficult, primarily because actions are not newsworthy, yet extreme acts will be condemned and, even when coverage is given, actions are often represented without explanation of the proposed message. The use of CMC could radically alter this search for media representation, by enabling self-representation to a large audience. Traditionally many choices of repertoires of action have been based on the assumption that their actual action will be mediated by the media and more powerful actors. The use of CMC challenges this assumption as it enables the activists themselves to mediate their message. (Pickerill 2001, 149)

While Pickerill (2001) has clearly identified a central problem faced by many activist organizations, namely the difficulty in gaining positive media coverage, evidence suggests that the internet does not provide a satisfactory solution. The most important difficulties facing project identities hoping to exploit the WWW directly as a public forum stem from the fact that "alternative" Web sites will most likely be visited and utilized by those already holding views compatible with the perspectives expressed therein. Wilhelm (2000, 43) has referred to this phenomenon in terms of "homophily" or "the propensity to gravitate to persons with similar viewpoints"; a tendency which he argues is encouraged by the internet. The resulting "balkanization" of cyberspace into competing identity-based enclaves may have a number of negative consequences for project identities, some of which will be discussed here, while others will receive attention in chapters 4, 5, and 6.

The most obvious problem holding relevance here is that relatively few members of the general public will ever be directly exposed to the alternative sources of information put online by peace activists and other project identity actors. Even when members of the public do desire to know more about a specific topic which they had previously only heard about through the mainstream media, considerable confusion may arise with respect to which Web sites offer the most pertinent or accurate information. This was implicitly acknowledged in Taylor's

(2000) investigation of the Web-based information campaigns mounted by both combatants and civilians on different sides of the 1999 Kosovo conflict. Noting the extensive amount of "Web reporting" conducted by individuals and groups directly involved in those events, Taylor observes that:

> The difficulty, of course, was in checking authenticity—both of the senders and of the information itself. And whereas it can be argued that one has the same difficulty with reporters and newspapers, the point is that the *profession* of journalism has a tradition of values and responsibilities to such issues as 'the truth' that simply does not, as yet, exist on the Web. Thanks to the internet, therefore, the fog of war in Kosovo merely got thicker. (Taylor 2000, 200)

Taylor's comments highlight the fact that the alternative sources of information made available through Web logs or "blogs" are generally not the neutral purveyors of raw information they often claim to be. As is the case with the mainstream media, the presentation of facts and information within SMO Web sites reflect the ideologies and framing practices dominant within the communities for whom they claim to speak, even when the identity of the latter remains unclear. This fact raises particular difficulties for Mid-East peace activists, whose own Web sites must compete with countless pro-Israel sites also claiming to dispel important myths about the Arab/Israeli conflict prevalent in the mainstream media. The fact that the Web sites of these and other identities may draw upon the same facts or matters of record to support highly divergent points of view is a phenomenon which will receive close attention in chapters 5 and 6. For now, it is merely worth noting that individuals seeking alternative sources of information through the use of search engines may end up feeling confused or disappointed. In addition to the Web sites of online news services, travel agencies, and mainstream Arab and Israeli institutions, a *Google* search based on such terms as "Arab/Israeli conflict," "terrorism," "Holy Land," or "Palestinians" may well lead the Web surfer to information put online by white supremacists, Black Muslim groups, Christian fundamentalists, or Jewish militants, to name only a few possibilities.

While members of the public may be either unwilling or unable to navigate competing sources of Web-based information adeptly, some argue that project identity Web sites such as those put online by Palestinian human rights organizations may yet serve the interests of both activists and the public. Various researchers have suggested that seasoned reporters and journalists, who are better able to assess the quality and origin of Web-based information, will inevitably make use of the Web to bypass earlier constraints on their journalistic freedom. This practice will in turn result in more balanced media coverage of important issues. For example, Castells (2004, 371–375) contends that if the mainstream media fail to take advantage of the alternative information flows made available online, their credibility in the eyes of the public could be seriously undermined (also see Alterman 2007). The logical corollary of this argument is that the potential for greater journalistic creativity and freedom on the part of media workers will be encouraged by the owners and managers of the corporate media, who will wish to ensure that their industry remains viable.

It is worth noting that the line of argument referred to above has been cited specifically with regards to the potential opportunities which the Web now affords Palestinian rights activists. Writing in the *Christian Century*, professor of religion Fred Strickert (2001) considers the usefulness of the Web to Palestinians both in terms of spreading information among their community and organizations, and in terms of its capacity to provide a resource for journalists. Included in his discussion are references to photographs and information put online by various Palestinian groups, along with criticisms of the Israeli occupation put forward by Rabbi Michael Lerner, the main organizer behind Tikkun. Also mentioned is an incident which involved the shooting of a 12-year-old Palestinian boy named Mohammed Al-Dura, a topic which will be returned to shortly. For present purposes it is sufficient to observe that there is little evidence suggesting that the existence of blogs promoting Palestinian and/or peace activist perspectives are having any meaningful impact upon reporting in the mainstream news media.

Writing in the Canadian newspaper, the *Toronto Star* (January 8, 2004), Antonia Zerbisias draws attention to the almost complete media blackout surrounding Israel's siege of Nablus, the largest Palestinian city in the West Bank, during December 2003:

> We're looking at perhaps two dozen Palestinian dead and maybe 250 more injured since mid-December when the town came under a virtually uninterrupted Israeli military blockade. A 5-year-old was gunned down just before Christmas. This week, a 15-year-old was shot dead because, as IDF troops said, he was hurling concrete blocks from a rooftop. His 17-year-old cousin was killed during the burial because, as the Jerusalem Post reported, "soldiers spotted an armed Palestinian participating in the funeral." (Zerbisias 2004)

After discussing these and related events, news of which she gathered from such peace camp Web sites as *palestinemonitor.org* and *palsolidarity.org*, Zerbisias observes:

> Mostly the "operation" on the town, where homes have been dynamited and civilians confined to quarters, has merited a few sentences in the back pages of North America's newspapers, including this one. Not even the CBC, the network that stands accused of a systemic anti-Israeli bias, has given the siege more than a few seconds of airtime. (Zerbisias 2004)

Zerbisias also notes that during the same period as the siege, considerable media attention was directed to events in Israel/Palestine which appeared to reflect favorably upon Israel. This concerned Israeli declarations that it would dismantle unauthorized (by the Israeli government) settler outposts in the West Bank. As Zerbisias noted, many of these outposts "consisted of nothing more than a hilltop trailer and a flag" (Zerbisias 2004).

The argument that the plethora of identity based information resources made available online will contribute to a more open mass media might appear to find at least indirect support in the quotes above, since Zerbisias utilized Web-based Palestinian media sources. Nonetheless, it is an argument which rests upon a highly questionable premise. The key assumption is that there was previously a general lack of readily available alternative news sources which was responsible for the ideologically narrow range of viewpoints expressed in the media with respect to contentious issues such as the Arab/Israeli conflict. However, as discussed at the beginning of this chapter and confirmed in the work of numerous media researchers, the issue of preferred journalistic sources cannot be isolated from other questions of political economy. In light of Zerbisias' comments concerning the Canadian Broadcasting Corporation (CBC), it is worth considering the importance of "flak" in this regard. This term was coined by Herman & Chomsky (1988, 26) to refer to the ability of various interests to bring pressure to bear on the media when the latter report in ways deemed unfavorable by the interest(s) in question. Significantly, "the ability to produce flak, and especially flak that is costly and threatening, is related to power (Ibid)."

As noted earlier in this chapter, evidence suggests that Zionist organizations worried about "news bias" can generally draw upon more extensive resources than their project identity counterparts; a reality in no way diminished by the proliferation of project identity Web sites. By contrast, the peace camp's ability to produce flak remains relatively limited. That much was apparent in a recent case involving two of Canada's largest newspapers, the *Globe & Mail* and *Toronto Star*. On February 15, 2006, an editorial entitled "See Hamas for What It Is" appeared in the *Globe & Mail*. The piece was written by Marcus Gee, a long-time apologist for Israel's occupation policies. In it, Gee claims that the recent Hamas election victory is a grave cause for concern, arguing that the organization remains committed to Israel's violent destruction. As evidence, he cites statements made by suicide bombers in video footage allegedly provided on a Hamas Web site. Writing in the online newsletter *Counterpunch*, Palestinian activist Samah Sabawi (February 23, 2006) revealed that Gee had not actually visited any such Web site. Instead, Gee was relying upon information provided by *Palestinian Media Watch* (PMW), a site hosted by a right-wing Israeli settler named Itamar Marcus. Since then, Sabawi, with support from journalist Antonia Zerbisias (quoted above) of the *Toronto Star*, has initiated letter campaigns and petitions to have Gee disciplined by his employers. So far, these efforts have proven futile; the *Globe & Mail* continues to back Gee, refusing to take any punitive measures against him.

The events referred to above suggest a strong connection between an organization's ability to produce flak on the hand, and a related ability to provide alternative information on Web sites which is likely to be perceived as both credible and attractive for use by journalists, politicians, and the general public on the other. They also draw attention to the linkage between the media access barriers considered here, and the political action dilemmas discussed in chapter 2. For example, it deserves mention that in addition to running the Palestinian Media Watch Web site (see above), Itamar Marcus also writes for *Frontpagemag.com*, a Web site run by neo-Conservative David Horowitz. Horowitz has been a central figure in the campus reform campaigns described in chapter 2, and has close ties to *campuswatch.org*. Marcus is also the founder of the Center for Monitoring the Impact of Peace (CMIP). The latter organization is dedicated to proving that Palestinian violence towards Israel is primarily attributable to negative messages in the Palestinian media as opposed to the economic depravation, land thefts, and violations of human rights suffered by Palestinians living under Israeli military occupation since 1967.

In 2000, the CMIP gained notoriety by releasing a study concerned with the content of textbooks approved by the Palestinian Authority (PA) for use in Palestinian classrooms. The study found that the school materials in question were characterized by volatile anti-Israel and anti-Semitic messages. The study soon became the basis for repeated condemnations of the Palestinian Authority by Hillary Clinton and other American politicians, who uncritically accepted the CMIP claim that Palestinian textbooks incited violence. Since its publication, the study has come under attack from a number of academics — including Dr. Nathan Brown of George Washington University and Dr. Ruth Firer, the head of a research team from the Harry S. Truman Advancement of Peace — for being politically motivated, intentionally misleading, and methodologically flawed (Moughrabi 2001). Somewhat ironically, the PA's efforts to improve the Palestinian curriculum were lauded in the Israeli newspaper Ha'aretz, which also criticized the CMIP study. Nonetheless, the study has had a very real impact on the lives of Palestinians. In December 2000, the Italian government directly referred to it when announcing its decision to cut funding for the new Palestinian school curriculum. And the same time, the World Bank notified the PA that money allocated for the development of school texts and teacher training would be diverted to other projects (Moughrabi 2001).

The general lack of sympathetic media attention to the conditions faced by Palestinians in the occupied territories also holds implications with respect to the direct action tactics engaged in by some project identity organizations. As Ayers (1999, 134) has observed, social movements may be understood as "sustained interactions between those with power and those without it" and in the course of these interactions SMOs may utilize non-institutional tactics which create disruption to promote social and political change. Various organizations associated with the peace camp, including Rabbis for Human Rights and the International Solidarity Movement (ISM) have regularly utilized non-institutional tactics to protect the lives and homes of Palestinians in the occupied territories. For example, individuals belonging to both of the aforementioned organizations have served as human shields in a variety of situations. These have included regular attempts to prevent armed settlers from harassing Palestinian farmers trying to harvest their olives, and the creation of human barriers between Israeli soldiers and unarmed Palestinian protesters.

The emphasis which the ISM places upon non-violent demonstration is apparent in the mission statement within its Web site, *palsolidarity.org*. Here, this SMO describes itself as . . .

> . . . an international citizen's peace-making campaign formed in August 2001, using the proactive direct action epitomized by Gandhi, Archbishop Tutu, Dr. Martin Luther King and other practitioners of non-violent resistance. (International Solidarity Movement 2001)

From a humanitarian perspective, the actions engaged in by the ISM and allied organizations may be considered important in their own right. The documentation and reporting of relevant human rights activity within project identity Web sites such as *palsolidarity.org* may also provide an important source of pride and inspiration for activists. However, if the actions of peace activists are to have any impact with respect to America's continued funding of the Israeli occupation, they must first have the desired effect upon U.S. public opinion. Ironically, the main obstacle faced by the ISM in this regard is highlighted within a newspaper article featured within its own Web site under the heading, *ISM in the News*. Writing in the Lebanese *Daily Star*, Laila al-Haddad begins her report on the ISM with the following remarks:

> GAZA CITY: They leave their comfortable, safe environments to live in one of the most volatile areas in the world often putting themselves in the direct path of danger. In the US and many parts of Israel they are considered traitors to the fight against international terrorism human shields defending dangerous criminals. Elsewhere they are thought of as unsung heroes. Either way, their work usually goes unnoticed. (al-Haddad)

Even when ISM practices do receive attention in the mainstream American media, there is no guarantee that this coverage will reflect favorably upon the actions of this or similar organizations. A good example concerns the case of 23-year-old college student Rachel Corrie, an American ISM activist who was twice run over by an Israeli bulldozer after she attempted to stop it from demolishing the home of a Palestinian physician. While the incident did receive brief attention in the American media, the extent and nature of the coverage, combined with a general lack of concern on the part of the U.S. government, made it unlikely that the incident would inspire widespread public outrage. Writing in *The Guardian*, Naomi Klein (2003) observed that Corrie's death "made the papers for two days and then virtually disappeared" having met with "almost total official silence." As noted in *tikkun.org*, reporting in the *Washington Post* did not even raise the possibility that the bulldozer driver's actions were deliberate, despite considerable evidence including eyewitness accounts suggesting that this was in fact the case (Tikkun 2003b, 1).

The relative lack of American media attention to Corrie's death is significant in light of the fact that such stark events or tragedies have frequently been argued to provide activists with ammunition in the form of sensational or morally shocking incidents. Such events, it is often claimed, will necessarily attract the attention of a sensation-seeking, profit-driven media establishment, and may also serve to galvanize an otherwise apathetic or ill-informed public.[2] The reality, at least for activists belonging to the peace camp, is less straightforward. The obstacles faced by those attempting to draw attention to the plight of Palestinians living under Israeli military occupation through use of this tactic are considerable; a reality underscored during the "image war" which ensued after the dramatic shooting death of a Palestinian boy in Gaza was captured on film. The events in question deserve exposition since they draw attention to the inseparability of the most central issues addressed in this and the previous chapter. In particular they highlight the linkage between the under-reporting of Palestinian suffering in the mainstream media, the obstacles presented by the counter-mobilization practices of grassroots elements tied to dominant elites, the importance of framing practices in mainstream media reporting, and the inadequacy of project identity Web sites as vehicles for addressing a mass public.

On September 30, 2000, the second day of the second Palestinian intifada, 12-year-old Mohammed al-Dura and his father were killed after being caught in crossfire between Israeli soldiers and Palestinian gunmen in the occupied West Bank. A Palestinian news crew working for French television took footage of the events in question, which showed the terrified boy huddled against his father in front of a wall before being shot, apparently by Israeli soldiers. Palestinian rights activists attempted to draw public attention to the incident by entering an image taken from this footage into an online photo contest sponsored by *MSNBC.com*'s "Year in Pictures 2000" (MSNBC 2000). At first, it appeared that the attempt would prove successful. For the first three weeks of the contest, the photograph remained well in the lead, looking to be the clear winner. However, it quickly fell to sixth place after a widespread e-mail campaign was launched by Israel supporters urging people to vote for other photos. According to the Associated Press (2001), the pro-Israel campaign in turn led to an additional flood of votes by Palestinian supporters attempting to push the image back to first place. The latter attempt proved unsuccessful, however, and the photograph remained "behind five animal pictures, including one showing a puppy with maimed legs and one showing a dog peeking its head through a fence unable to reach a fire hydrant" (Associated Press 2001).

In light of the issues raised so far, it should be (re)acknowledged that dissenting viewpoints which stray from the normal range of news discourse do occasionally appear in the mainstream media. As a rule, however, their relative infrequency and general incongruity with dominant media frames generally makes them appear quixotic or unrealistic (McMurtry 1999). Such is likely to be the case even when dissenting arguments have more to back them up in terms of demonstrable facts or matters of historic record than do less "radical" perspectives. By contrast, media frames which directly or indirectly serve to legitimate the agendas and outlook of powerful interests tend to remain invisible to both the reporters who adopt them and the public who read or listen to their stories. As Couldry (2003) observes, media power is symbolic power, and to challenge it is to contest the way social reality itself is defined or named. This puts project identities challenging accepted wisdom at a severe disadvantage. Not only do they typically lack the resources to lobby the media effectively, but even when their messages are heard they are unlikely to sound convincing. It is easy to overlook that fact that the same logic is likely to apply in the case of the sensational or shocking story, often seen as a sure bet for provoking public outrage.

Even had the Al-Dura photograph won the *MSNBC.com* photo contest, there are good reasons to believe that this contingency would not have had a lasting impact upon the perceptions of the American public. The mainstream media do not generally depict the killing of Palestinian civilians, international peace activists, or journalists by Israeli soldiers against the backdrop of an illegal and/or brutal military occupation, but rather within the context of a "tragic conflict," in which Israelis constitute the only "victims of terror" (see chapter 4, 106–107). Within such a discursive framework, drawing brief media attention to the shooting death of a Palestinian boy would appear unlikely to have any significant impact upon public attitudes and might even serve to reinforce official Israeli arguments concerning the depravity of Palestinian parents who willingly martyr their children as part of a single-minded campaign to destroy Israel. The latter explanation was in fact put forward by the Israeli diplomat who initiated the e-mail campaign to prevent the al-Dura image from winning the photo contest, and was promoted by the Israeli Foreign Ministry.[3]

As previously indicated, the substantial amount of alternative information made available online by anti-occupation activists does not appear to have affected earlier trends with respect to media reporting of the Arab/Israeli conflict. This may be seen in a recent study conducted by FAIR (Fairness and Accuracy in Reporting). In response to complaints of both pro-Palestinian and pro-Israel bias on the part of National Public Radio (NPR), FAIR conducted a study of the NPR's news coverage of Israeli/Palestinian violence during the first six months of 2001 (Ackerman 2001). The study revealed that during this period, in which 77 Israelis and 148 Palestinians had been killed, the NPR reported the deaths of 62 Israelis and 51 Palestinians. Notably, Israeli civilian victims were more likely to have their deaths reported than members of the Israeli security forces; 84 percent versus 69 percent respectively. The opposite held true for Palestinians. Seventy-two percent of Palestinian security forces deaths were reported, versus 22 percent of civilian deaths. Of the 112 Palestinian civilians killed during the period studied, 26 were reported by the NPR. Of the 26 Israeli civilians killed, most of whom were settlers, 21 were reported. More importantly in light of present considerations, only 22 percent of Palestinian civilian deaths among minors under the age of 18 received coverage versus 89 percent in the case of Israeli victims (Ackerman 2001).

Recent studies conducted by "If Americans Knew," an organization based in the San Francisco Bay area, point to even greater distortions in the case of the corporate media. Two prominent local daily newspapers, the *San Francisco Chronicle* and the *San Jose Mercury*, were subjected to quantitative analysis with respect to their reporting of Israeli versus Palestinian deaths in headlines or first paragraphs of relevant reports during the period of September 29, 2000–March 31, 2001. In the case of the *San Jose Mercury*, front page coverage was given to 71.5 percent of Israeli deaths, and 4.3 percent of Palestinian deaths at a time when Palestinians were being killed at three times the rate of Israelis (Weir 2003). A similar trend was found in the case of the *San Francisco Chronicle*, and was reflected most strongly with respect to the deaths of children. During the period in question, 93 Palestinian children were killed, the majority by gunfire to the head, along with 4 Israeli children. Nonetheless, a total of six headlines were generated in each case. Overall, children's deaths were reported by the newspaper at a rate 25 times greater for Israelis than Palestinians. In both newspapers, America's connection to the conflict via aid to Israel was almost never mentioned; 1.2 percent and 1.1 percent of the articles of each newspaper respectively (Weir 2003). A third study of the *New London Day*, during the period of March–June 2003, showed similar results. In the case of Palestinians, 62 percent were reported in headlines or first paragraphs of articles on the topic, compared to 159 percent of Israeli deaths, which were two-and-a-half times more likely to be reported than Palestinian deaths (If Americans Knew, 2003).

In light of the data cited above, it is worth noting that one lengthy and involved report of Mohammed Al-Dura's death did appear in the mainstream media. This took the form of an investigative report which appeared in the *Atlantic Monthly* magazine in June 2003. However, rather than drawing sympathetic attention to the circumstances faced by Palestinians living under Israeli rule, this report aimed to cast doubt upon the authenticity of the events surrounding the incident in question. Admissions of guilt on the part of the Israeli military were dismissed as irrelevant by the article's author, James Fallows, who chose to focus instead upon the conspiracy theories of several Israelis who claimed that the entire incident was engineered by Palestinian activists. According to Fallows's sources, Al-Dura was either intentionally killed and "martyred" by Palestinian militants in the name of their cause, and/or had only appeared to be shot before being driven off by those who orchestrated the incident. What is most noteworthy about the article is not so much the strength or weakness of the evidence cited by Fallows, but rather its appearance during a period in which the routine killing of Palestinian civilians, and particularly of Palestinian children by Israeli soldiers, had been grossly and systematically underreported. It bears mentioning that by the second day of the Intifada, the date on which Al-Dura was killed, 15 Palestinians had already been shot dead by Israeli forces, four of whom were minors. Four more Palestinian minors, including another 12-year-old boy, were killed on the following day (Rose 2003).

When left with the choice of addressing the American public by means of either traditional or Web-based media channels, activists belonging to the Arab/Israeli peace camp face a classic "catch-22" situation. On the one hand, identity-based Web sites such as *al-awda.org*, *tikkun.org*, or *palsolidarity.org* allow activists to frame their actions and present their messages in their own terms, without fear of media distortion. As indicated throughout this section, however, such Web sites represent an inadequate means for addressing the general public, whether they are employed directly as broadcasting media, or indirectly as a journalistic resource. This reality was implicitly acknowledged by the activists who chose to enter Al-Dura's image in a photo contest promoted within the Web site of the major online news outlet *MSNBC.com*. However, when project identity actors do attempt to convey their concerns through dominant media channels, their intentions and actions are unlikely to be reproduced either faithfully or consistently enough to have any meaningful or lasting impact on public opinion.

By contrast, mainstream Zionist SMOs are much better positioned than their project identity rivals to enjoy the best of both worlds with respect to both Web-based representation and the mainstream media of print and television. They may readily utilize the Net as an identity-based information and communication resource, while worrying less about the Web's ability to serve in the additional capacity of a broadcasting medium. While organizations such as AIPAC or the CC are clearly not always happy with the media's portrayal of events surrounding the Arab/Israeli conflict, they are in a much better position to exert pressure on media institutions when they deem it necessary. In chapter 4, it will be demonstrated that coverage of the Arab/Israeli conflict in *CNN.com* is indeed much more compatible with Zionist interpretations of recent Mid-East history, than of those belonging to the Arab/Israeli peace camp. It will also be argued that processes of media framing may be enhanced through the strategic use of hypertext, a fact which has allowed *CNN.com* to co-opt the ideological territory of human rights and international law—the very basis of project identity claims to legitimacy—on behalf of the U.S. government.

NOTES

1. The main criticism of Herman & Chomsky's (1988) propaganda model, leveled by researchers such as Schudson (2003) and Golding & Murdock (2000), is that their model is too rigid and not sensitive enough to account for influences on media content, besides top down (government and corporate) pressures. Nonetheless, they readily concede that the political economy forces cited by Herman & Chomsky remain critical influences on news framing practices.

2. A good example of a case where such a strategy has resulted in a measure of success involves the issue of "blood diamonds" or "conflict diamonds" as discussed by Gaber & Willson (2005).

3. For example in an article made available online by the Israel Foreign Ministry entitled, "Palestinian Child Sacrifice" by Gerald Steinberg (2000).

Chapter Four

The Voice of Legitimacy: *CNN.com* and the Arab/Israeli Conflict

Public opinion forms itself around attitudes and theoretical problems not clearly related to the actual situation. And the symbols most effective in the formation of pubic opinion are those most remote from reality. Therefore, public opinion always rests on problems that do not correspond to reality.

(Jacques Ellul 1965, 101)

In this chapter, I address the issue of ideological competition between weak and powerful actors differently than in chapters 2 and 3. Previously, attention was given to the goals and strategies of social movement organizations (SMOs) in their attempts to influence government policies and public opinion. By contrast, the focus in this chapter is on the influential media giant *CNN.com* in its dual role as a major news provider on the World Wide Web (WWW), and legitimating institution vis-à-vis American foreign policy. The present chapter differs from the previous two in another important way as well. The emphasis is no longer upon the internet's value as an information/communication "toolbox" for use by activists, but rather upon the unique character of hypertext as a medium within a medium. While hypertext represents only one possible form of computer-mediated communication, it is through this means of disseminating information that the internet most closely resembles those print and broadcast media which have traditionally served to inform public understandings of social, cultural, and political reality. The chief concern here is with whether a leading news corporation such as CNN can maintain its status as an *authoritative* source of information within the crowded and potentially chaotic medium of the WWW.

Like other major news outlets, *CNN.com* faces competition from an expanding array of commercial, governmental, and grassroots disseminators of "news" online. These include social movement organization, and citizen-based groups and lobbies such as those considered in chapters 2 and 3. Without a doubt, the gate-keeping capacity of the traditional press is seriously undermined in an environment where information can develop and circulate with fewer conventions or editorial filters, and where numerous pathways exist for information to flow from micro to mass media (Bennett, 2004). One potential implication is that the very presence of countless alternative voices on the WWW may induce a "trickle up effect" whereby the dominant media themselves become more porous and open to a broader array of influences emanating from something akin to a global civil society. Nonetheless, as was argued in chapter 3, the expectation that a profusion of new voices online will inevitably lead to a more democratized news media appears unduly optimistic. Furthermore, the Web may provide mainstream news outlets not only with alternative sources of information, but also with the means to position themselves strategically in relation to them.

The arguments presented in this chapter proceed from the premise that *CNN.com* has in fact perceived the need to respond to the presence of alternative sources of information made available by a broad range of online actors. It will be demonstrated, however, that strategic use of hypertext has allowed *CNN.com* to acknowledge such voices in a manner which appears to reinforce, rather than call into question, dominant interpretations of social and political reality. As will be made apparent in this chapter, as well as in chapters 5 and 6, both the relative political power and the world views upheld by various identities operating online may have a direct bearing upon their rhetorical strategies. In the case of *CNN.com*, this organization's twin role as a legitimizing identity and "objective" disseminator of news has left it with the ideological task of portraying the Arab/Israeli conflict in terms of a direct correspondence between U.S. Mid-East policies and universal moral/legal principles. At the same time, the very sources of authority repeatedly invoked within *CNN.com* to support hegemonic interpretations of reality may readily be used to discredit, in full or in part, the validity claims underlying these same interpretations. The last point is important since the media's credibility with the public has often been equated with its ability to present information "truthfully."

A number of researchers have called attention to the "colonization of cyberspace." They point to the flooding of the Web with commercial propaganda, as well as the sophisticated use of portals, search engines, and modifications to Web architecture imposed by Internet Service Providers (ISPs) such as AOL/Time/Warner (e.g. Chester and Larson 2005; Winseck 2003).

These developments are clearly significant, having direct implications for the ways in which the WWW is likely to be used and navigated. However, they have often received attention at the expense of more micro processes of hypertext manipulation which may also be utilized in the service of powerful interests or dominant ideologies. It should also be noted that when hypertext has received attention from researchers, it has often been treated as inherently antithetical to modern notions of authority and/or to established relations of power (e.g. Landow 1992; Poster 2001). By contrast, I will show that it is precisely the "anarchic" qualities of this medium which may be harnessed to reinforce the authority of legitimizing identities such as *CNN.com*. Hegemony is a process whereby dissenting voices are not only crowded out, but also co-opted and integrated within dominant frameworks, and the Web is uniquely conducive to such co-optation.

The arguments outlined above are based upon findings corresponding to a sample of texts extracted from a portal internal to *CNN.com*, and made accessible to the reader under the banner *Special Report: Mideast Land of Conflict* (henceforth referred to as S-R). This portal was specifically designed to provide greater political and historic context for *CNN.com*'s "up to the minute reporting" of issues and events surrounding the Israeli/Palestinian and broader Arab/Israeli conflicts. While the majority of texts (and links) made available within S-R have remained essentially unchanged, with only minor additions and changes to sub-headings since the portal's appearance in 2001, the sample in question was obtained during the month of December 2002. It consisted of all "print-based" articles made available within S-R which were also amenable to reproduction in hard-copy form.[1] A total of 56 separate articles—consisting of texts one paragraph or more in length—were identified within the portal and collected for analysis. The significance of a number of additional texts located within S-R, including the transcripts of various United Nations resolutions, is also taken into account.

Analysis of the sample referred to above is undertaken in two main sections. In part I, a cluster of interrelated ideological themes are identified as pervasive within S-R. These themes are shown to serve as framing devices with respect to *CNN.com*'s treatment of the Arab/Israeli conflict. They are then considered in light of the text-based—as opposed to link-based—rhetorical devices which reinforce their logic and give them the appearance of common sense understandings of reality. The initial analysis of content also includes a critical assessment of the validity claims which underlie interpretations of relevant events and policy developments presented in the portal. Because these claims relate directly to American military and diplomatic interventions in the Middle East, and because the rhetorical strategies employed within S-R depend in part upon the systematic exclusion of information needed to assess them critically, it was necessary to devote some attention to the actual historic record concerning the U.S. government's involvement in the region.

In part II of the analysis, consideration is given to the ways in which the ideological themes and validity claims identified in the initial examination of text content have been expanded and reinforced rhetorically through use of the hyperlink. Implicit attention to some inter-textual structures, particularly those involving the presentation of Web pages in chronological sequence, was necessary in part I. However, it is in the second part of the analysis that Web structures are considered which do not merely imitate text formats existing in other print media. Here, attention is given to the relationship between content versus inter-textual structures within the S-R portal, as well as to the rhetorical significance of hyperlinks leading from the portal to Web sites external to *CNN.com*. As will be seen, *CNN.com* has proven able to integrate internal and external sources of Web-based information in an ideologically consistent manner; one likely to enhance its status as a legitimizing identity on the WWW.

CNN.com's "Land of Conflict":

Part I: *Dominant Themes and Validity Claims*

A number of closely interrelated ideological themes were found to characterize portrayals of the Israeli/Palestinian, and broader Arab/Israeli conflicts within *CNN.com*'s *Special Report: Mideast Land of Conflict* portal (S-R). These include minor myths surrounding key events and players in the region, as well as broader discourses concerning the larger historic role played by the United States in relation to the Arab/Israeli conflict. The latter include the most pervasive as well as the most significant ideological themes with respect to the present focus on CNN as a legitimizing identity which may ostensibly serve to cast American foreign policy objectives in a favorable light. The most central theme corresponds to America's alleged role as a well intentioned peacemaker and champion of democracy in the Middle East. This guiding theme or "grand narrative" provides the ideological backdrop against which a number of more minor narratives and myths take on their meaning.

Two central lines of rhetoric are relied upon within S-R to reinforce the impression that America represents a player in the Middle East whose intentions are honorable, even if its goals in the region are sometimes frustrated. The first concerns the U.S. commitment to the creation of the modern, democratic state of Israel in 1948 and its ongoing support for the Jewish state thereafter. The second concerns America's equally firm dedication to bringing about a just settlement of the Arab/Israeli conflict. These commitments are presented within S-R as mutually reinforcing and as matters of moral principle. This understanding of U.S. policy is supported by repeated reference to a narrow range of facts, events, legal documents, and myths, and through the consistent omission or sidelining of other equally relevant information. The logic behind this form of "enlightened propaganda" is thus very difficult to detect, especially for those unfamiliar with the modern history of the Middle East, and serves to deflect what are arguably more realistic interpretations of American motives, interests, and policies in the region.

The portrayal of America as both a committed supporter of the state of Israel and as an honest peace-broker in the Middle East, is most explicit in a series of articles made available for viewing within *CNN.com*'s S-R portal under the main heading *Camp David Accords: Framework for Peace*. This material will henceforth be referred to as the Peace Exhibit. The Peace Exhibit's constituent texts were authored and/or compiled by Terry Sullivan, Associate Professor of Political Science at the University of North Carolina. All texts within the Peace Exhibit are made available to the viewer by following links within S-R, and through the use of the *CNN.com*'s browser window. However, as stated in its general introduction, the Peace Exhibit was "produced by PRESIDENT and the Jimmy Carter Library," and is not the product of *CNN.com*'s own staff of writers (Sullivan [a]).[2] This compilation of texts may be argued to be simultaneously "internal" and "external" to the S-R portal, a phenomenon which will be given attention in Part II of the analysis.

As will be demonstrated, a seamless thematic and rhetorical continuity exists between the content of texts made available within the Peace Exhibit and those found elsewhere in the S-R portal. The Peace Exhibit's constituent texts deal primarily with events surrounding the Camp David Peace Accords facilitated by former president Jimmy Carter, which led to a formal peace treaty between Israel and Egypt in 1979. Also included are more general background articles dealing with the Arab/Israeli conflict and the related diplomacy of previous and subsequent American administrations. The Peace Exhibit is divided into four "exhibit areas" under the headings *Prelude*, *Preparations*, *Negotiations* and *Legacy*. Each of these areas is in turn sub-divided into smaller sets of articles, most about a page in length. A brief description of the four exhibit areas is provided on a Web-page headed *The Tour*, as follows:

Prelude, briefly outlines the diplomatic history leading up to the Camp David meetings. *Preparations*, describes the physical setting of meetings and the government preparations necessary for hosting such negotiations. *Negotiations*, describes the day by day bargaining between the three delegations, using President Carter's memoirs and those of others who were there. *Legacy* discusses the impact of Camp David on modern history. (Sullivan [b])

The main themes and narrative structure which characterize the Peace Exhibit are readily made apparent not only in terms of textual content, but also in relation to the various headings and subtitles used to guide the reader through a chronological account of relevant events, conflicts, and diplomacy. The most colorful of these accounts are located within the *Negotiations* exhibit area, and deal specifically with the Camp David peace talks. Here, the efforts of the Carter administration to bring about peace between Israel and its most formidable enemy, Egypt, are recounted within collections of texts under the headings *The Situation, The First Few Days, Gathering Gloom,* and *Triumph!* The general content of Peace Exhibit is framed within its accompanying introductory statement as follows:

> The history of Arab-Israeli relations is one of bitter conflict. A history with roots deep into the past and whose progeny have entangled the entire modern world. Every generation since World War II has witnessed the violence and terrible suffering endemic to this region. And often the region's suffering has spilled over. Recent history, however, has promised hope. The beginning of that promise, the framework for peace, was built at Camp David in 1978. (Sullivan [a])

Significantly, the region's problems are misleadingly framed within the Peace Exhibit as both ancient and "endemic" to the region. Few would contest the fact that the Middle East, and particularly the "holy land," has been a repeated site of conquest and conflict for many centuries. It is important to emphasize, however, that the modern state of Israel, and hence the Arab/Israeli conflict itself, would not exist at all were it not for the policies of the region's former colonial masters, particularly Great Britain. The Zionist goal of establishing a Jewish state in Arab Palestine would never have been realizable without first British, and later American, support (Merkley 1998; Suzman 1999). It is also worth noting that acceptance of the Zionist program did not become widespread within the European Jewish community until *after* Britain officially committed itself, in 1917, to the establishment of a national Jewish home in Palestine (Akenson 1991, 152). It was largely big power support for Zionism which made it appear more realistic to the broader Jewish community, allowing it to become the basis of a genuine grassroots movement. In a very basic and fundamental sense, therefore, the Arab/Israeli conflict represents a relatively recent product of Western intervention in the Middle East, a reality which does not sit easily with the guiding themes of the Peace Exhibit and other commentary found within S-R.

Western domination of the Middle East was consolidated after the Arabs provided assistance for the British and French military effort against Turkish forces during World War I (MacMillan 2001, 366–426). Arab support proved invaluable in bringing about a relatively speedy and low-cost (to the British and French) end to over 400 years of Ottoman rule in the region. This support had been given with the understanding, based upon promises from the British and French, that the Arab world, including Palestine, would be granted political independence as a reward for Arab war efforts (see Hadawi 1967; Khouri 1985; MacMillan 2001). These promises were not kept, and in a series of undertakings beginning with the signing of the Sykes-Picot agreement of 1916, the Middle East became effectively divided into British and French spheres of influence. Britain's authority in the region included the Palestine Mandate, the geography of which corresponds to what has historically been referred to as Palestine, and which today includes the territory encompassing Israel and the occupied West Bank and Gaza. The Palestine Mandate also included the territory associated with the modern state of Jordan.

As numerous scholars and historians have recognized, the breaking of wartime promises to the Arabs, and subsequent division of the Arab world, was driven by French and British strategic and commercial interests in the region. As Knightly (1991, 8) has commented, "oil concessions would be easier to negotiate with a series of rival Arab states lacking any sense of unity, than with a powerful independent state in the Middle East." In addition to a growing preoccupation with oil, Britain also had a long-standing commercial interest in maintaining its links to India via the Persian Gulf and Egypt's Suez Canal (MacMillan 2001, 384–385). In fact, it was largely due to the efforts of Chaim Weizmann, then leader of the English Zionist community, in convincing the British government that a European Jewish colony in Palestine would give them a loyal ally in a strategically important area, which led Britain to support the Zionist goal of creating of a Jewish national home in Palestine (MacMillan 2001, 416; Suzman 1999, 79). Britain's official commitment to this goal was formally laid out in the Balfour Declaration of 1917.

The Balfour Declaration is "discussed" twice in the S-R portal. The first reference appears within an article entitled *On Israel's 50th, the glass is half full*, which includes a brief, point form summary of relevant historic incidents leading to Israel's declaration of statehood in 1948. The other article entitled *The Balfour Declaration* consists of a one-page text. Both references essentially take the form of apologies for British colonial practices in Palestine. The first reference consists of the following statement: "In 1917, Britain promised the establishment in Palestine of a national home for the Jewish people. No explicit political promises were made to the local Arabs" (Stein 1998, 1).[3] Presumably, the latter part of this statement is designed to deflect potential arguments concerning the earlier promise of independence made to Arab leaders by Britain and France. The earlier commitment is not mentioned in this article, however, although the discrepancy between the two promises is referred to as a "misunderstanding" between Britain and the Arabs in the article entitled *The Balfour Declaration*. In the latter text, the evenhandedness of British policies is emphasized:

> The British did lay the foundation of a separate Arab state in 1921. They reserved lands east of the Jordan river—or Transjordan, three quarters of the Palestine mandate exclusively for Arabs and transferred control to the Hashemite royal dynasty. Now Jordan, the region gained full independence from Britain in 1946. (CNN 2001a)

In this text, an illusion of fair play—if not outright favoritism towards the Arabs—was created by drawing attention to the fact that more territory was designated for the Arabs under the British mandate than for a Jewish state. Attention is drawn away from the fact that since virtually all of the territory in question had been inhabited and/or owned by Arabs for centuries, the Arabs were not being "given" anything by the British that wasn't already theirs. Conversely, the Palestinian Arabs were clearly expected to give up most of their homeland for the establishment of the proposed Jewish state. This same article states that "British Foreign Secretary Arthur Balfour . . . endorsed the idea of a Jewish homeland in Palestine (but not, the declaration stipulated, at the expense of the Palestinian Arabs)." It is difficult to imagine how a Jewish state could have been created in Palestine without this being done at the expense of an indigenous population actively opposed to the idea.[4] The point is moot, however, since the British quickly made it clear that the concerns of the Palestinian Arabs were irrelevant. Not mentioned in this article, or anywhere else within S-R, is a memorandum written by Lord Balfour in 1919, which included the following statements:

> In Palestine we do not propose even to go through the form of consulting the wishes of the present inhabitants of the country . . . The four great powers are committed to Zionism. And Zionism, be it right or wrong, good or bad, is rooted in agelong traditions, in present needs, in future hopes, of far profounder import than the desires and prejudices of the 700,000 Arabs who now inhabit that ancient land. (Hart 1984, 50)

British and French policies in the Middle East are referred to as colonial practices only once within any article in *CNN.com*'s S-R portal. Significantly, however, with regards to this single reference, these practices are not presented as in any way commensurate with American policies in the region initiated after WW II. The reference in question appears within an article in the *Prelude* section of the Peace Exhibit entitled *Arab-Israeli Conflict*. It consists of a two-page summary of the three major Arab/Israeli wars fought after Israel's declaration of statehood in 1948 (i.e. 1956, 1967, and 1973). Here, French and British commercial interests in the Suez Canal and the creation of the state of Israel under the British Mandate are described as "linked to the colonialism of the area that the Arab states had long fought" (Sullivan [c]). References to these colonial practices are then connected to events surrounding the Suez Crisis of 1956, and ultimately to the more enlightened policies of the United States:

> Egyptian independence inevitably led to a renewed interest in the Canal. In 1956, the new Egyptian government of Gamal Nasser nationalized the Canal, thus depriving the British and French of revenues they had enjoyed for almost a century. In a coordinated assault, the Israelis, British and French attacked Egypt in an effort to recover the Canal by force. The British and French concentrated on the Sea end of the Canal, while the Israeli army swept across the Sinai.
>
> Eventually, intervention by the US government forced the British and French to withdraw and give up on the idea of repatriating the Canal. Continued diplomatic pressure on Israel forced its eventual withdrawal from the Sinai, as well. (Sullivan [c])

The passage cited above leaves the reader with the distinct impression that American policies in the Mid-East represent a departure from those previously pursued by Britain and France. It is important to keep in mind that the central theme running through the Peace Exhibit, the collection of texts in which this article is embedded, is one of "hope for the region" made possible by the United States. However, subsequent events have demonstrated that American opposition to the attack on Egypt during the Suez Crisis was not motivated by a desire to end foreign domination in the region. Instead, it was almost certainly intended to put the British and French on notice that their role as the dominant powers in the Middle East had come to an end, a role which would now be filled by the United States (Hersh 1991, 41–42). Likewise, if Israel intended to pursue expansionist policies in the region, it would do so with American backing or not at all. In the decades which followed, such backing would be forthcoming, a topic to which we will return.

It is difficult, if not impossible, not to recognize continuity between the concerns driving British and French policies in the Middle East prior to WWII and those adopted by the United States as it came to replace the former states as the regional imperial power. In 1953 for example, the United States aided in the overthrow of the democratically elected government of Iran, after Mossadegh nationalized the British-owned Anglo-Iranian oil company. One consequence of this operation was that 40 percent of Iranian oil was transferred from British to American hands (Ahmed 1991, 11). When President Carter spoke of his government's role in bringing about peace between Egypt and Israel, he affirmed that Arab/Israeli peace was "intimately tied in with the Persian Gulf's stability" and with "energy supplies for our country" (Meyer 2004, 91). In his State of the Union address in January 1980, Carter stated that any "attempt by an outside force to gain control of the Persian Gulf region will be regarded as an assault on the vital interests of the United States" and that "such an assault will be repelled by any means necessary, including military force" (Draper 1991; Stork & Wenger 1991).

Beginning in the 1980s, construction began on a massive system of bases in the Gulf, particularly Saudi Arabia, for use by American forces (Stork & Wenger 1991). Clearly these efforts, which were undertaken with the aid of decidedly non-democratic governments, were intended to maintain U.S. hegemony in the Gulf and not to instill democratic reform in the host countries. However, if America's goals in the Middle East are to appear truly laudable, its material interests must be played down in favor of a vision which holds that U.S. policies are guided by a concern for peace, democratic government, and regional stability. Hence, U.S. support for the state of Israel, regularly portrayed in the Western media as the region's "only democracy," is to be understood not as part of a larger strategic arrangement for continued regional domination, but rather as an expression of solidarity with a country which shares America's most fundamental values. One article found within S-R entitled *U.S. and Israel: such good friends*, deserves special mention in this regard, since it was the only text within the portal devoted specifically to the topic of the U.S./Israeli "special relationship." In this four-page text, American support for the Zionist cause is accurately portrayed as preceding the creation of the Jewish state in 1948:

> Ties between the countries go back to the 1940s, when the United States pressured Britain and the United Nations to partition Palestine and create a Jewish homeland. (Christensen 1999)

American pressure at the United Nations (UN) was in fact very real, and allowed for the General Assembly's 1947 recommendation to partition Palestine into Jewish and Arab states. Thanks to direct American pressure on a number of member states including the Philippines, Haiti, Liberia, and France (which had been threatened with a total cutoff in U.S. aid), the resolution passed by the necessary one-vote majority (Cockburn 1991, 27; Hadawi 1967, 92–94). At the time, many countries were reluctant to support the proposed recommendation since it posited that roughly 56 percent of the country, including its most fertile land, be reserved for a Jewish state at a time when Jews owned only 7 percent of the land, and represented about one-third of Palestine's population (Kimmerling 2003, 26). These facts are not raised in the article, or elsewhere in S-R. Instead, America's support for the establishment of a Jewish state in the heart of the Arab world is framed in a manner which confirms its inherent morality:

Reasons for American support ranged from horror at the Holocaust and a penchant for rooting for the underdog to a desire to have a stable democracy in a volatile region. The United States also wanted a strategically situated military partner as the Cold War unfolded. (Christensen 1999)

Here, the *only* reference within *CNN.com*'s S-R to the strategic role played by Israel on America's behalf, is ranked last among the concerns driving American foreign policy, and is only mentioned in relation to Cold War politics. Even this single reference is arguably misleading, since the historic record suggests that indigenous forms of Pan-Arab nationalism and populist social movements such as those associated with Nasser during the 1960s, with Ba'ath socialism as manifested in Iraq and Syria, with the Islamic revolution in Iran, and more recently with Islamist movements throughout the Middle East, have and continue to be viewed by America as the greatest obstacles to its continued influence in the region.

Evidence suggests that a desire to maintain control over Middle East oil reserves is the primary reason for America's staunch support for the state of Israel. However, as discussed in chapters 2 and 3, ideology and domestic politics have played an important role as well. Most notably, the political lobbying efforts of political action committees (PACs) espousing Christian and Jewish variants of Zionism have had a particularly marked effect upon both American policy formation and popular understandings of events in the Middle East. Nonetheless, only one reference is made within S-R to pro-Israel PACs, and this reference is not in any way critical of the role played by such groups in relation to U.S. policy formation. The article cited above entitled *U.S. and Israel: such good friends* continues to delineate the motives behind U.S. support for Israel by quoting a spokesperson for the American Israel Public Affairs Committee (AIPAC):

"For sheer volume and depth it's quite an extraordinary relationship," says Howard Kohr, executive director of the American Israel Public Affairs Committee, a U.S. lobby group. "Family is not a bad characterization either. Israel shares U.S. values on democracy, freedom of the press, the treatment of women and so on." (Christensen 1999)

No further attention to the activities or influence of AIPAC, one of the most powerful political lobbies in the United States, is provided in this or any other text within *CNN.com*'s S-R portal. Regardless, AIPAC is implicitly recognized as an authoritative source of information concerning the U.S./Israeli special relationship rather than being identified as powerful pressure group whose role in influencing American foreign policy might deserve scrutiny from the media.

The lack of any critical attention within S-R to the nature of the U.S./ Israeli special relationship, and/or to the role played by lobbying groups in strengthening it, is particularly striking in the wake of 9/11. American support for Israel was a primary motivation for the attacks in question, as interviews with Bin Laden and numerous statements by Al-Qaeda have made abundantly clear. There is also no doubt that real American pressure on Israel to end its illegal occupation of the West Bank and Gaza would aid in reassuring large portions of the Arab world that the United States is not their enemy (regardless of the reality) and would make it far easier for the governments of America's Arab and other Muslim allies to cooperate with the United States in its War on Terror. However, at no point in the S-R portal is America's massive material support for Israel ever explicitly connected to that country's expansionist practices in the occupied territories; practices which are directly responsible for much of the growing anti-American sentiment throughout the Middle East and the larger Muslim world. Ironically, numerous anti-Semitic groups have not hesitated to incorporate this line of reasoning within their Web sites; a fact which could potentially serve to discredit and/or further marginalize an otherwise valid line of inquiry (see chapter 6).

While Israeli democracy is celebrated throughout the S-R portal, attention is never directed toward the inherent contradiction between Israel's existence as a Jewish state and its presumed status as a democracy. Such uncritical attention to Israeli democracy is particularly prevalent within two past "Special Reports" made available within S-R entitled *Israel at 50,* and *Israel elections 1999.* One article in the latter compilation entitled *Expatriate finds Israelis very much involved in Politics* begins with the sub-heading "*I have few friends in America who vote. Practically everyone I know in Israel votes.*" The article in question was written by an American woman holding dual U.S./Israeli citizenship. She comments on her experiences in Israel as follows:

As an Israeli citizen—I have dual US and Israeli citizenship—I have always felt an obligation to follow the events that shape the country.

On a recent visit, I was particularly interested by the current political and social turmoil as elections approach.

With five candidates running for prime minister and 33 parties fighting for 120 seats in the Knesset, keeping up with the elections is an arduous task.

In Israel's democratic system, many political parties are allowed to form. To be considered an official candidate for Knesset, one needs only a few thousand supporters. The result is a multitude of parties.

There is a saying in Israel that says when two Israelis meet, there is a political argument. When three Israelis meet, it is a new political party. (Rosenblatt 1999)

The article concludes on an upbeat note with the writer commenting, "In the few weeks I spent in Israel, I was exposed to a multitude of political debates, issues and opinions."

While Arab citizens of Israel are allowed to vote and form political parties, few outside of Israel are aware that no party which openly opposes the principle of a "Jewish state," or proposes to change its character by democratic means, is allowed to participate in elections to the Knesset (Shahak 1997, 3). The Israeli government is committed to the principle that Israel remains a Jewish state rather than a state of its citizens, over 20 percent of whom are non-Jewish (mostly Palestinian Arabs). Its refusal to allow Palestinian refugees to return to their homes, as demanded repeatedly by the United Nations General Assembly, is based largely upon the fear that Jews will eventually come to constitute a minority in "their" country. Given present demographic trends, however, Arabs inside of historic Palestine (Israel, the West Bank, and Gaza) will soon outnumber Jews unless Israel either expels large numbers of Arabs, as it did in 1948 and 1967, or is able to bring about massive Jewish immigration (Ahmad 1999; Kimmerling 2003, 17). Israel continues to search desperately for new pools of Jews to settle in Israel in line with its "law of return" whereby any Jew entering Israel automatically becomes an Israeli citizen.

In fundamental ways, Israeli democracy is at odds with principles underlying conceptions of democracy and citizenship held in countries such as the United States or Canada with whom Israel supposedly shares "core values." This is clearly the case with regards to Israeli policies concerning the use of state land. Once Arab land has been confiscated for settlement purposes it belongs to "the land of Israel." This land, which constitutes over 92 percent of land in Israel, is reserved for the exclusive use of Jews. Even those Palestinians serving in the Israeli army do not have the right to use such land (Said 1997, 129). Israel Shahak, a holocaust survivor and harsh critic of Zionism, comments that this "institutionalized racism exceeds in importance the robbing of land from the Palestinians." Drawing a comparison with the takeover of First Nations land in North American he notes that "there are many states which have systematically robbed land. The U.S., for example, robbed Indian land, transforming most of it into state land. Nonetheless, such land is now available for use by any U.S. citizens."[5]

In the decades following the Suez Crisis of 1956, the U.S./Israeli relationship became increasingly close. In particular, American aid to Israel rose substantially after Israel launched attacks on Syria and Egypt during the Six-Day War of 1967, effectively removing the threat to American interests in the region posed by Nasser's Pan-Arab nationalism. Increases in American aid also followed Israel's interference in Jordan's internal conflict with Palestinian nationalist guerrillas, and during and after Israel's invasion of Lebanon in 1982 (Butterfield 1991; Haddad 1991). In fact, America's material support for the Jewish state is unprecedented. Israel, a country with a total population of roughly 7 million inhabitants, has been by far the largest cumulative recipient of U.S. financial and military aid since World War II (McArthur 2003). It possesses one of the most formidable military forces in the world, and is the only Middle Eastern state with a known nuclear weapons capability (Cohen 1998; Hersh 1991).

Throughout the decades of the U.S./Israeli special relationship, the bulk of American financial aid to Israel, roughly three billion dollars a year, has taken the form of direct grants (McArthur 2003). Israel is free to spend this money as it chooses, and since 1967 it has funneled a great deal of American aid towards its illegal settlement building practices in the West Bank, Gaza, and East Jerusalem; the remnants of historic Palestine which it wrested from Jordanian and Egyptian control during the Six-Day War. This fact is significant in light of the themes and rhetoric pervading commentary throughout S-R. Within the collection of texts referred to as the Peace Exhibit, the credibility of America's "peacemaker" image hinges largely upon the use of repetitive, but highly selective, references to international law. Conversely, in the case of reports dealing with the more recent (1993–2000) American-sponsored Oslo Peace Accords between the Israelis and Palestinians, relevant legal and human rights documents are systematically ignored. The rhetorical common thread is that relevant agreements and documents are invoked only when it is possible to frame these as compatible with American policy, even when this apparent compatibility is largely spurious.

Within the Peace Exhibit, numerous references are made to United Nations (UN) Security Council Resolutions 242 and 338. In fact, their complete texts are made available as documents within the exhibit. The first of these resolutions was passed immediately after the Arab/Israeli Six-Day War of 1967, and was intended to lay the groundwork for a comprehensive peace between Israel and its Arab neighbors. Resolution 338 was passed after Egypt and Syria launched the Arab/Israeli war of 1973, in an attempt to recover territory captured by Israel in the previous conflict. It called for an immediate cessation of hostilities and the implementation of resolution 242 in all its parts. The following excerpt, which links the passing of 242 with the diplomacy of the Johnson administration, was taken from within the *Prelude* section of the Peace Exhibit under the sub-heading *American Diplomatic Efforts*:

> The Johnson Administration set out to pursue a five point program which offered a comprehensive solution to the Arab-Israeli conflict. After considerable debate on these principles, the UN adopted a comprehensive statement on peace—UN Resolution 242. The resolution called for the end of belligerency,

the withdrawal of forces from occupied territory, acknowledging the territorial integrity of every state in the area, creation of demilitarized zones, settlement of the refugee problem, and the creation of a special envoy to negotiate peace. (Sullivan [d])

Security Council Resolution 242 is referred to thirteen times within the Peace Exhibit. Most of these references appear in the *Negotiations* section, and all of them appear within a narrative of U.S. peacemaking. The clear implication, frequently made explicit, is that American diplomatic efforts to bring about a comprehensive resolution of the Arab/Israeli conflict are in accord with relevant international law, and hence with the consensus of the international community. The passage cited above continues as follows:

The diplomatic efforts initiated to carry out UN-242 failed when the Israelis made it clear they would not withdraw and when the Arab states, taking advantage of a new found cold war relationship with the Soviet Union, began to rearm themselves with more weapons. (Sullivan [d])

The above statements are misleading. As early as 1970, and again in 1971, Egypt, Israel's most powerful Arab neighbor, indicated its willingness to make peace and recognize Israel, provided that the latter comply with 242 and withdraw from the Arab territory it captured during the Six-Day (1967) War. Essentially the same position was adopted by Jordan in 1971 and by Syria in 1972 with the condition that Palestinian "rights" must be recognized (Chomsky 1999, 41–64). Egypt and Syria launched the Arab/Israeli war of 1973 in an attempt to regain these territories only after numerous peace initiatives on the part of Egyptian President Anwar Sadat were rejected by Israel and ignored by the United States (Cockburn 1991; Hersh 1991, 221). Furthermore, despite the Carter administration's declared commitment to 242 during its successful efforts to negotiate peace between Israel and Egypt, America's willingness to honor this UN resolution has arguably been weak or non-existent with regards to the other Arab territories occupied by Israel.

It is widely believed in the Arab world that the primary purpose of the Camp David accords was to neutralize Israel's only significant enemy, allowing Israel to pursue its expansionist policies unhindered (Haddad 1991).[6] This belief is supported by considerable evidence. Only three years after the signing of the accords, Israel launched a full-scale invasion of Lebanon without fear of military opposition from the Arab states, aside from limited resistance from Syrian forces already in that country. A U.S. veto at the Security Council prevented the imposition of economic sanctions on Israel, and aid to Israel increased during and after the invasion (Butterfield 1991). In addition, Israel's practice of land confiscation and settlement building in the Palestinian territories accelerated after the signing of the Camp David Accords, as it did again during the duration of the more recent U.S. sponsored Oslo Peace Accords (Bird 2000; Kimmerling 2003, 36; Marshall 1995). These developments are significant in light of the fact that since at least the mid-1970s, every Arab government bordering Israel—along with the Palestine Liberation Organization (PLO)—had agreed in principle to make permanent peace with Israel, provided that the latter comply with relevant international law.[7]

It is perhaps unsurprising that neither the tactical aspects of the Carter administration's efforts to bring about peace between Egypt and Israel, nor basic principles guiding American foreign policy in the Middle East since the Second World War, are critically examined within a document produced in cooperation with the *Jimmy Carter Presidential Library*. However, as already indicated, America's goals and policies in the region are consistently depicted as benign, not only in the Peace Exhibit, but in virtually all relevant reports produced by *CNN.com*'s own staff of writers and regular contributors. In particular, the impression that the United States represents an unbiased mediator between Arabs and Israelis is reinforced in those sections of S-R which deal with America's sponsorship of the Oslo Peace Accords.

As with the Camp David Accords initiated by President Carter, unconditional U.S. support for the state of Israel is not presented within S-R as in any way problematic with regards to America's more recent sponsorship (1993–2000) of the Oslo Peace Accords involving the Israeli government and the Palestinian Authority. Following the lead of consecutive American administrations, Israeli violations of international law are *never* directly addressed as such anywhere within *CNN.com*'s S-R portal. Instead, such issues as Israeli settlement building in the occupied territories and the status of Palestinian refugees are viewed not as legal or human rights issues to be dealt with by the international community through the enforcement of relevant UN resolutions, but rather as points of disagreement to be worked out in peace negotiations between Israel and the Palestinians. This is a useful strategy as it serves to deflect attention from, or present as unrealistic, Palestinian/Arab grievances which have a solid legal basis, when these conflict with U.S./Israeli policies.

The complete conformity between the foreign policy positions adopted by the U.S. government and commentary within S-R may be seen clearly in a set of three articles for which direct links are provided on the portal's main page. These deal with the issues of Israeli settlement building, the status of Jerusalem, and the plight of Palestinian refugees respectively. The question of Israeli settlement building is addressed in conjunction with the issue of Palestinian statehood in an article entitled *Palestinian Borders and Jewish Settlements*. Like virtually all articles within the portal, this "background" piece is very brief; a fact which itself holds rhetorical significance since inconvenient matters of record may easily be excluded for considerations of "space." The article is worth quoting in its entirety, since it is the only article in S-R devoted specifically to the issue of Israeli settlements. It is also illustrative of a trend within S-R to frame legal issues which reflect unfavorably on Israel— and by direct implication the United States—in terms of "differences of opinion" between the disputants:

> The Palestinian side has insisted that its state should include all the Palestinian territory occupied by Israel in the war of 1967—in other words, Gaza and the West Bank, including East Jerusalem. The Israelis disagree, saying that Israel's security needs require a presence in strategic parts of the West Bank and that some of the Jewish settlements built during the years of occupation be incorporated into Israel.
>
> A fact-finding committee led by former U.S. Sen. George Mitchell recommended on May 21, 2001, that the Israeli government freeze all settlement activity, including the natural growth of existing settlements. The committee also called on the Palestinian Authority to "make a 100 percent effort to prevent terrorist operations and to punish perpetrators."
>
> *Israeli Viewpoint*
> Israel's settler community, which numbers some 200,000 in the West Bank, as well as its conservative and religious supporters see the territory as part of the biblical land of Israel and have vowed to resist ceding control. The settlements are seen as essential for Israel's security—as a first line of defense from the east. The Gaza settlements, while also flash points in the conflict are less populated, and the land does not carry as much biblical significance for the Israelis.
>
> *Palestinian Viewpoint*
> The Palestinians are suspicious of any attempts to maintain an Israeli presence in territories occupied in 1967. The territory controlled by Yasser Arafat's Palestinian Authority is dispersed and intersected by 144 Israeli civilian and military installations, diminishing the validity of that administration's control. The settlements are seen as an instrument of the ongoing occupation, the aim of which is to divide any future Palestinian state into noncontiguous portions. (CNN 2001b)

Never mentioned in this or other articles within S-R is the fact that the "Palestinian viewpoint" concerning Israeli settlement building is consistent with the position held by the international community as put forward in numerous General Assembly and Security Council resolutions of the United Nations. Resolutions of the Security Council are particularly important since they are legally binding, potentially allowing UN member states to apply economic sanctions, or in extreme cases, deploy military force against the non-compliant party.

The existence of Israeli settlements in the Palestinian territories of the West Bank, East Jerusalem and (formerly) the Gaza Strip, along with those built on Syria's Golan Heights, represent a clear violation of international law (Quigley 2005). Clause 55 of the 1907 Hague Convention states that the creation of permanent "facts on the ground" by the occupying power is not permitted; population transfers from the occupying country to occupied territories provide an example (Kimmerling 2003, 77–78). Numerous Security Council Resolutions have specifically affirmed the illegality of Israeli settlement building. For example, in 1979 the Security Council passed Resolution 446 which stated that Israeli settlement building practices had "no legal validity and constitute a serious obstruction to achieving a comprehensive just and lasting settlement in the Middle East." That position was reaffirmed in 1980 with the passing of Security Council Resolution 465 which determined that "Israel's policies and practices of settling parts of its population and new immigrants in the Palestinian and other Arab territories occupied since 1967, including Jerusalem, constitute a flagrant violation of the Fourth Geneva Convention" (United Nations [a]).

No text within the S-R portal discusses, or even mentions the fact that the United States could easily put an end to Israeli settlement building practices if it so desired. Israel could not afford to lose the massive amounts of financial and military aid which it receives from the United States. This amount has been estimated to total $94.458 billion between U.S. fiscal years 1949 through 2002 (McArthur 2003). However, according to the Israeli Committee against House Demolitions, during the eight years that the United States sponsored the Oslo peace negotiations between Israelis and Palestinians, the number of Israeli settlers in the occupied territories actually doubled, even as American financial and military aid continued to flow freely. As was the case concerning the diplomacy of the Carter administration, bringing such awkward facts to light would directly conflict with an understanding of the United States as a neutral and fair-minded arbiter between the relevant parties.

The rhetorical pattern established in *Palestinian Borders and Jewish Settlements* reappears within texts dealing with Jerusalem. This may be seen clearly in the concluding paragraphs of an article entitled *Status of Jerusalem*, the only text within S-R devoted specifically to this issue. Once again, emphasis is placed upon Israeli and Palestinian "perspectives" while ignoring relevant human rights and legal conventions:

Israeli Viewpoint
   Ceding control even over the Palestinian neighborhoods of East Jerusalem, or the Old City, is a red line for many Israelis, who consider Jerusalem to be the heart of Zionism and an integral part of Jewish identity. They want to ensure that they maintain access to sites they consider sacred, and they are not willing to negotiate on this point.

Palestinian Viewpoint

Besides Palestinians' historic territorial claims on Jerusalem's Old City, the presence there of the Islamic holy sites makes the issue a red line not only for Palestinians but for the entire Arab and Muslim world. Palestinian Authority President Yasser Arafat was unable to compromise at Camp David on his demand for sovereignty over the sites and the eastern portion of the city. (CNN 2001c)

By focusing upon the "emotional significance" which this city holds to the relevant parties, this article neatly bypasses the awkward fact that Israel's annexation of Arab East Jerusalem is every bit as illegal as its ongoing land confiscation and settlement building practices in the West Bank. However, drawing attention to the illegality of Israeli practices in Jerusalem would destroy the illusion of "equal, competing claims" to the Eastern, primarily Arab half of the city, which needs to be resolved through negotiations in which both sides must "compromise." This is the line which the U.S. government has adopted since the Clinton administration's sponsorship of Oslo. More ominously, pressure has been mounting from within the U.S. Congress to officially recognize Jerusalem as Israel's capital. Such a move which would violate relevant international law including those resolutions cited above, along with Security Council Resolution 242 which recognizes the inadmissibility of acquiring territory through the use of force.

It is significant that an article devoted to the issue of Jerusalem's status makes no reference to those Security Council resolutions, including 252 (1968), 267 (1969), 298 (1971), 476 (1980), and 478 (1980), passed specifically for the purpose of declaring Israel's attempts to alter the status of that city "null and void" (United Nations, 18). Instead, one article within S-R entitled *At-A-Glance: Facts and Figures on the state of Israel* actually describes Jerusalem as Israel's capital:

Capital: Jerusalem, population 600,000. (Jerusalem is the seat of Israeli government and its self-declared capital, although Jerusalem's status is disputed by several countries that do not recognize Jerusalem as Israel's capital) (CNN 1998)

This text directly misrepresents the facts, the actual situation concerning the views of other countries being the inverse of what is presented. Only a few countries have ever recognized Israeli sovereignty over any part of Jerusalem, which was designated in the UN partition plan of 1948 as an international zone, and no states presently have embassies there. The U.S. maintains consulates in Jerusalem, but at present these are not in any way accredited to Israel (Williams 2000). As indicated above, however, this situation may change if continued American congressional attempts to override relevant international agreements in a manner favorable to Israel succeed. Similar efforts to dismiss UN proclamations and human rights conventions relating to the issue of Palestinian refugees have already borne fruit, a point which will be returned to shortly.

The third article for which Palestinian and Israeli "viewpoints," rather than relevant legal documents and international understandings provide the focus, concerns the status of Palestinian refugees. Over two-thirds of Palestine's native Arab population fled or were forcibly expelled from their country at the time of Israel's creation in 1948. The positions of the "two sides" with respect to the fate of Palestinian refugees are summarized in an article entitled *Palestinian refugees and the right of return*:

Israeli viewpoint

Israeli leaders have held to the position that the right of return is nonnegotiable. It would create a demographic problem for Israel, making it unable to continue as a Jewish state. Israel has suggested it would accept a proposal for some 10,000 Palestinian refugees to rejoin their families inside Israel as a "humanitarian gesture" and financial compensation for refugees, to be funded by Western donors.

Palestinian Viewpoint

The displacement of Palestinians cuts to the core of Palestinian national identity. Many Palestinians say their right to return goes beyond the U.N. resolution, stemming from a right of a people to live in their homeland. For Palestinians, it's a matter of principle and historical rapprochement—Israel acknowledging the wrongs it has caused to the Palestinian people. (CNN 2001d)

Only two other articles within S-R discuss Palestinian refugees, and these do not even mention the existence of any relevant UN resolution on the matter. This fact is noteworthy given the frequent attention given within S-R to the UN's 1947 recommendation to partition Palestine into Jewish and Arab states. In fact the complete text of General Assembly Resolution 181, which corresponds to this decision, is made available for viewing within the S-R portal. UN resolution 194, which affirmed the right of the Palestinians to return to their homes and/or receive compensation if they chose not to return, was passed in December 11, 1948, one day after the ratification of the Universal Declaration of Human Rights (Chomsky 1999). Article 13(2) of the Declaration states that "Everyone has the right to leave any country, including their own and return to his country." Israel's admission as a member state of the UN was based upon the understanding that Israel would honor resolution 194 (United Nation [b]).

Since the Palestinian refugee issue lies at the heart of the Israeli/Palestinian conflict, and hence at the center of the larger Arab/Israeli conflict, one might expect 194 to receive considerable attention within S-R. As mentioned above, however, the resolution is referred to only once within S-R and unlike UN Resolution 181 its text is not made available for viewing within the portal. Once again, discourse within *CNN.com* parallels official U.S. policy positions. At the December 1993 UN session, the Clinton administration changed official U.S. policy and opposed Resolution 194. The resolution had been reaffirmed regularly since its passing, but on this occasion was reaffirmed by a vote of 127-2, with the United States and Israel casting the dissenting votes. As a result, the U.S. position is now more consistent with a well-established pattern in which Israel and the United States vote together in opposition to relevant UN resolutions. Since 1982, the United States has vetoed 32 Security Council resolutions critical of Israel, exceeding the total number of vetoes cast by all other Security Council members (Mearsheimer & Walt 2006).

To sum up, an array of closely interrelated ideological themes and supporting rhetorical devices are deployed within *CNN.com*'s *Special Report: Mideast Land of Conflict* (S-R) portal to present American policies as morally and legally legitimate. Most notably, partial and misleading appeals to authority are invoked in a manner which suggests that American Mid-East policy is compatible with universally recognized (i.e. by member states of the United Nations) principles of justice and human rights. At the same time, various devices are used to position the voice of *CNN.com* as a neutral and authoritative source of information on the Arab/Israeli conflict. In this sense, *CNN.com* fails to adopt any meaningful watchdog stance towards the policies of the state, essentially taking on the role of the "Voice of America." The complete compatibility between reporting produced by *CNN.com* and commentary originating from the *Jimmy Carter Presidential Library* (and made available *within* the S-R portal) underscores this point. Attention will now be turned to the ways in which the legitimating function of the dominant media may be significantly enhanced within the network environment of the World Wide Web through strategic utilization of the hyperlink.

Part II: *Anchoring Authority in a De-centered Medium*

In this section, I argue that the hegemonic principles referred to above have been extended and reinforced vis-à-vis the strategic use of hypertext. As noted by Shields (2000, 152), appraisals of hypertext often fixate on the "disassociative" powers of the hyperlink. However, the Web link may best be understood as a *synthetic* device, "a tool that brings multifarious elements together into some kind of orderly unit." This point is particularly salient when examining a Web site as extensive as *CNN.com*. This news site contains an enormous number of texts and also provides extensive links to Web pages beyond its own internal network(s). In the forthcoming analysis, I will make extensive references to the *Special Report: Mideast Land of Conflict* (S-R) portal's internal structure, as well as to its positioning within the larger *CNN.com* Web site, and/or its linkages to Web-based texts external to *CNN.com*. As will be made clear, internal (to S-R) and external Web links may both play a variety of rhetorical functions. All of these functions relate in one way or another to the potential incorporation of disparate Web-based sources of information within the narrative logic upheld within the S-R portal.

As indicated in this chapter's introduction, *CNN.com*'s, *Special Report: Mideast Land of Conflict* banner appears within a window next to all reports dealing with the Israeli/Palestinian conflict and wider Arab/Israeli conflict. Clicking on this banner takes the reader within the S-R portal. Once within the portal, the S-R main page allows the reader to access three main collections of texts. The most prominently displayed of these correspond to the heading, *Mideast Land of Conflict* (CNN 2001e). This collection contains the most up-to-date material concerning the ongoing Israeli/Palestinian conflict, and related U.S. attempts at mediation. Listed in a column beneath this general heading, links pertaining to various interrelated topics are made available under the sub-headings *Issues, Resources*, and *History & Culture*. For example, a link listed as *key players* under the sub-heading *Resources* leads to a series of texts providing profiles of various politicians involved in the Israeli/Palestinian conflict. Another link under the *Issues* sub-heading entitled *Palestinian Refugees* leads to an article devoted to that topic. Fifteen such links are provided in the column below the *Mideast Land of Conflict* header (CNN 2001e).

In addition to the collection of articles subsumed under *Mideast Land of Conflict*, two additional collections of articles, designated *Mideast 101* and *CNN.com Mideast Archives* (henceforth referred to as Mideast Archives) are listed on the S-R main page. These appear in the form of links at the bottom of the page along the horizontal axis. *Mideast 101* is a relatively insignificant compilation of texts consisting (at the time of data collection) of only four articles. *Mideast Archives* is much more extensive, consisting primarily of articles taken from two past "special reports." The first, entitled *Israel at 50*, initially appeared within *CNN.com* in 1998, and celebrates Israel's existence and achievements on its 50th anniversary of statehood. A smaller collection of articles within the network entitled *Israel Elections 1999* is largely concerned with the fate of the Oslo Peace Accords. All of the articles examined in Part I of this chapter were taken from within the three collections of reports identified above, along with the series of texts dealing with the Camp David Accords and referred to in Part I as the Peace Exhibit. While the latter is not listed directly on the S-R portal's main page, it may be accessed by following one of two link pathways originating therein. The rhetorical significance of this feature will be addressed in due course.

Before delving further into the matter of S-R's internal structure and its relationship to external networks of Web pages, it is important to emphasize that the four collections of texts identified above complement one another thematically. The *Peace Exhibit* was given special attention in Part I due to the fact that it originates from PRESIDENT and the Jimmy Carter Library, and was therefore useful for highlighting the similarities between official/governmental versus media discourses pertaining to the Arab/Israeli conflict. Its central narrative, which concerns America's role as a fair and well-intentioned peacemaker between Israel and Egypt, is reinforced throughout the texts comprising *Mideast 101*, which deal mainly with the Arab/Israeli wars, and within *Mideast Land of Conflict*, which looks uncritically to the U.S.-sponsored Oslo Accords as the appropriate framework for achieving peace between Israelis and Palestinians. Articles found within *Mideast Archives* deal largely with the democratic character and political challenges faced by the state of Israel, and with the "fulfillment of hope" that the creation and maintenance of that state represents to the Jewish people. Rhetorically, the content of *Mideast Archives* serves to reinforce both the moral correctness of the American/Israeli special relationship, and the right of Israel to exist in the form of an ethnic democracy.

Mideast Land of Conflict, *Mideast Archives*, *Mideast 101* and the Peace Exhibit are best understood as representing four separate, but interconnected Web page networks held within the *Special Report: Mideast Land of Conflict* (S-R) portal. The central characteristic of Web networks is interconnectedness (Poster 2001), or connectivity (Shields 2000). The latter term will be employed here. The key idea in relation to connectivity is that elements "turn toward" various other elements within the network they share. This is readily apparent within S-R, where articles within each of the four networks listed above are frequently accompanied by a short list of links which connect them to other texts within their own network dealing with closely related topics. The four networks are in turn interconnected through links on the S-R main page. As emphasized in much of the literature on hypertext, elements within a network take on much of their identity in relation to the other elements to which they are directly linked, as well as to the larger networks within which they are embedded. In the case of the four networks of Web pages identified above, the ideological themes pervading texts within each one are reinforced both by their internal network configuration, as well as by the relationship of each network to the others.

Differences in Web structures often reflect differences in organizational agendas (Jackson 1997). The overall Web configuration within the S-R portal may best be characterized as constituting a *satellite* structure. Such structures posses a dominant node or nodes (in this case networks) with other nodes performing an ancillary function. Jackson's (1997) assessment of the satellite configuration is highly instructive when considering the internal structure of S-R:

> This would encourage the user to move often from center to periphery, giving the site a dynamic "pushing" feel. A satellite structure might be used strategically by a designer to differentiate "primary" from "secondary" or supporting information or to focus the user's attention on a small number of "central" documents. It is also a typical structure used by news organizations in presenting an online news product. (Jackson 1997, 14)

In the case of S-R, the dominant node is represented by the *Mideast Land of Conflict* network, the main texts of which are made directly available by links on the S-R main page. These texts deal primarily with "the recent conflict" and U.S. mediation attempts, and are supported by the contextual information provided in the other three networks. It is important to stress, however, that the S-R portal is not entirely self-contained. Rhetorical techniques enabled by links leading from within the portal to external networks greatly reinforce the ideological logic established within it, a point which will be returned to shortly.

While the emphasis in this part of the chapter lies with Web structure, it is important to reiterate that the rhetorical uses of the hyperlink can never be meaningfully considered in isolation from Web page content. This is apparent when considering both the associative logic by which messages are reinforced within the S-R portal, and also when assessing communicative techniques present within the larger *CNN.com* Web site. One advantage of disseminating messages on the WWW is that rhetorical devices made possible via hypertext may be complemented by more traditional techniques of juxtaposing information. For example, throughout the duration of this case study, additional portals characterized by themes ideologically compatible with those revealed within S-R appeared regularly in *CNN.com's* World section. These included "special reports" such as those entitled *War on Terror*, and *Target Iraq*. While these portals were not connected to S-R through use of the hyperlink, their windows, or portal entrances, frequently appeared immediately above or beneath the former much in the same manner as relevant photographs or captions may be placed on the contents page of a magazine.

One portal which began to appear regularly beneath S-R in the months following 9-11 was designated by the banner *In-depth Special: Victims of Terror* (CNN 2002a). Interestingly, the portal's content deals entirely with Israeli victims of Palestinian terror attacks. It consists of an extensive gallery in which these victim's photographs are presented alongside personal information including their age, and the circumstances under which they were killed. Palestinian civilians, international peace activists, and foreign correspondents shot by Israeli soldiers within the context of an illegal occupation do not qualify here as "victims of terror" (CNN 2002a). This point is noteworthy when one considers the fact that since the signing of Oslo, Palestinian civilians killed by the Israeli military have greatly outnumbered Israeli civilians killed by Palestinians. Similarly, ongoing Israeli practices of house demolitions, crop destruction, land confiscation, and other occupation measures recognized by the UN as violations of the Geneva Conventions are not described as instances of state terror anywhere within *CNN.com*.

The points raised above lend credence to Herman & Chomsky's (1988) arguments concerning the treatment of "worthy" versus "unworthy victims" in the news. In their landmark book *Manufacturing Consent* (1988), the authors argue that those in the former category typically consist of American citizens or the citizens of her allies. They receive extensive attention in the press and are described in sympathetic, personalized and emotionally charged terms.[8] Victims in the unworthy category—who tend to be the direct or indirect victims of U.S. policy—receive much less attention, most of which is statistical and depersonalized. The treatment of Israeli versus Palestinian victims of violence clearly fits with this pattern. The accompanying understanding of Israelis as a civilized democratic people "like ourselves" is clearly consistent with themes within S-R concerning the correctness of America's material and moral support for the state of Israel. It should also be emphasized that *CNN.com*'s reporting is hardly unique in this regard; the tendency noted above is consistent with the findings of other recent studies of the conflict (see chapter 3).

Much of the thematic continuity evident within *CNN.com*'s World section is facilitated by means of external links to other "authoritative" sources of information. On September 19, 2002, on a Web page entitled *CNN.com presents new online look*, *CNN.com* announced a list of new features designed to enhance the ease of site navigation and information access for its visitors. The six new features listed included "Partner Content," as described herein, "We've made it easier to access stories, games and analysis from CNN/Sports Illustrated, CNN/Money, Time, Entertainment Weekly, People, In Style, Fortune and Business 2.0, sites that offer content complementary to CNN.com's core news coverage" (CNN 2002b). *CNN.com*'s partner content is often relevant in relation to the boundary object. For example, the *World* section regularly provides links to stories concerning the Israeli/Palestinian conflict appearing in *Time.com*. These "partner" links may be contrasted with those leading to the Web sites of non-affiliated organizations containing information of "related interest." The latter are not endorsed by *CNN.com*, a point which will be returned to shortly.

At the time of data collection, *CNN.com*, along with its Internet Service Provider (ISP) America Online (AOL), were owned by the global media giant *Time/Warner/AOL*.[9] The same held true for the media outlets identified as contributors to *CNN.com*'s "partner content." In conformity with global trends of media concentration and convergence, which have already affected the content and availability of other media, AOL has become one of a shrinking number of ISPs dominating the Internet. While the broader strategies adopted by Internet Service Providers to control patterns of Internet use are not the focus of this investigation, it is important to at least recognize the increasing levels of control being exercised by ISPs over Web architecture and content. As Winseck (2001) observes:

> . . . the evolution of new media is being biased away from the open systems model of telecommunications and the Internet toward a closed model, where in house content is favoured over other sources, either in a heavy-handed manner, such as by refusing access to networks altogether (the history of the cable industry and specialty channels), or subtly through network design, acceptable user policies, user menus, search engines, portals, and so on in ways that give priority access to some sources of content and not others. (Winseck 2003, 181)

In addition to the ways in which ISPs may attempt to constrain the surfing habits of Web users, it is also worth noting that Time Warner possesses the world's largest library of music, films, TV shows, and cartoons, and arguably has more recognizable media brand names than any other firm in the world. As McChesney (1998, 34) emphasizes, branding is considered "the most crucial determinant of market success and the one factor that can assure success in the digital world with its myriad of choices, albeit controlled by a small number of owners." It is also worth mentioning that *CNN.com* now presents its news products in numerous languages including Arabic. As suggested throughout this chapter, however, even the relatively free access to the WWW which is arguably still available to less powerful social actors does not appear to pose a serious challenge to the authority of legitimating identities online. One reason is that they may readily be subsumed within legitimating narratives.

As stated earlier, the S-R portal is not a self-contained entity. Links have been put in place by its designers which connect some of this portal's Web pages to networks outside the domain of *CNN.com*. It is worth keeping in mind, however, that designations such as "inside" and "outside," and even the terminology of "networks" are helpful, but purely metaphorical ways of talking about relationships among texts online. Shields (2000, 151), has drawn attention to the double function of the link as both "a sign that is a seamless part of a page or text and as an indexical sign that flags and indicates." He argues further that links should not be understood simply as thresholds or passages to other pages:

> The link is both part of the text and an index caught on the threshold of departure, signaling to another page or text. It is paradoxical because it appears to be another gateway. To indulge in an architectural metaphor, it is less a portal to the outside and more like a hidden passageway in a building—a door to the inside, which leads out somewhere else, reinforcing a sense of self-sufficient totality. (Shields 2000, 151)

Importantly, the hyperlink allows both Web pages and Web sites to exist "within" more than one network simultaneously, a phenomenon which may readily be exploited for rhetorical purposes. For example, the link makes it possible to incorporate a text belonging to an outside network within the narrative structure of the home site, while taking advantage of any symbolic association between the text in question and the other network of which it is simultaneously a part. If incorporating a particular text in this manner is not advantageous from a rhetorical standpoint, then said text may simply be reproduced within the home site as it might be within a printed text such as a book or newspaper. Both strategies have been artfully employed within the *Special Report: Mideast Land of Conflict* portal.

In Part I, it was affirmed that while numerous United Nations (UN) documents are relevant for a clear understanding of the international consensus concerning the boundary object, only three UN resolutions received consideration within S-R. These consist of General Assembly Resolution 181—dealing with the 1947 recommendation to partition Palestine into Jewish and Arab states—along with resolutions 242 and 338, which were intended to provide a comprehensive framework for a resolution of the Arab/Israeli conflict. In each case, the relevant texts are made available for viewing within the portal. A link on the S-R homepage allows the reader to access the full texts of 242 and 338, plus an additional three other "key documents" (2001e, 1). The latter correspond to the Oslo Peace Accords, the Israel-Palestinian Interim agreement (or Oslo II), and the Wye River Accord. Each of these agreements concern peace talks between the Israeli government and Palestinian Authority recently (1993–2000) sponsored by the United States.

A link labeled *Key Documents* is provided under the *Resources* subheading of the *Mideast Land of Conflict* network (2001e, 1). The *Key Documents* link may also be accessed indirectly through another link labeled *Timeline*. The latter appears under the *History & Culture* subheading. Clicking on *Key Documents* takes the user to a pop-up window display wherein links to three brief summary texts are provided on the left hand margin. These three links are labeled *Oslo accords*, *Wye accords* and *U.N resolutions 242 and 338*.[10] Activating any of these three links calls up a one-page summary text providing background with regards to the corresponding document(s). At the bottom of each summary page, direct links are provided to the actual documents discussed above.

Two links are highlighted at the bottom of the Oslo accord summary page. These are designated *U.S. State Department: Israeli-Palestinian Declaration of Principles* and *Israeli Government: Israeli-Palestinian Interim Agreement*. The Wye accord summary text includes a link entitled *The White House: The Wye River Memorandum*. All of these documents were negotiated within the framework of the U.S.-sponsored Oslo Accords. Activating any of the links listed above will automatically "transport" the reader into the official Web domains of the U.S. State Department,[11] Israeli government,[12] or the White House (Office of the Press Secretary)[13] respectively. It should be recalled that an aura of legitimacy for the democratic institutions and policies associated with both the American and Israeli governments was established within the Web pages constituting S-R. So, too, was the importance of those documents most closely associated with U.S. foreign policy in the Middle East. Making the documents most closely associated with American foreign policy available within their "home" networks thus performs a dual rhetorical function. It gives these documents an increased aura of authority and authenticity, while simultaneously serving to reinforce dominant narratives within S-R, and hence the legitimating voice of *CNN.com*.

In contrast to those documents signed within the framework of the U.S. sponsored Oslo Accords, making the texts of UN Resolutions 242 and 338 available for viewing within their home network on the World Wide Web (WWW) would be much more problematic when taking considerations of rhetoric into account. Visiting the UN's official Web site, *domino.un.org*, by means of links leading from S-R to the texts in question, would almost certainly draw the reader's attention to the extensive list of Security Council and General Assembly Resolutions condemning Israeli practices in the occupied territories and elsewhere, as well as those recognizing the legitimate aspirations of the Palestinians, including their right to return to their country of origin. Indeed, it is the identity associated with the documents in each case, namely U.S./Israeli versus UN, which appears to have been the deciding factor with regards to their placement within "appropriate" networks of Web pages.

At the bottom of the summary page dealing with UN Resolutions 242 and 338, two links labeled *U.N. resolution 242* and *U.N. resolution 338* are provided. Activating either one of these links takes the user to the text in question. At the same time, the user moves out of the dominant *Mideast*

Land of Conflict network, and directly into the network identified in this chapter as the Peace Exhibit. As noted earlier, Web pages are defined as much by their relationships to other Web pages and networks as they are by their content. In this instance, S-R has made UN resolutions 242 and 338 available to the viewer as nodal points embedded within a larger network; one designed to uphold a narrative in which the U.S. plays the role of Mideast peacemaker and bearer of universal values. The incorporation of these UN documents within the Peace Exhibit reinforces the illusion that American foreign policy in the Middle East is guided primarily by universal standards of justice and human rights, a theme already well established in the reports produced by *CNN.com*'s own staff. When considered in this light, the informational content of these documents is less important than their semiotic value as signifiers of American moral leadership within the community of nations.

The radial or satellite structure of S-R was described earlier in this section. The network of texts associated with *Mideast Land of Conflict*, which focus upon the most recent U.S.-mediated attempts at resolving the Israeli/Palestinian conflict, was identified as the dominant node, or network. The other three networks of texts, *Mideast 101*, *Mideast Archives*, and the Peace Exhibit, perform an ancillary or supporting function. In addition to the latter networks, another display serves to reinforce the centrality of messages and themes prevalent throughout S-R and upheld within *Mideast Land of Conflict*. Listed alongside the links provided to the *Mideast 101* and *Mideast Archives* networks, at the bottom of the S-R main page, is a link designated *Related Sites*. Unlike the former links, however, activating the *Related Sites* link does not take the user beyond the confines of the central *Mideast Land of Conflict* network.

Activating the *Related Sites* link brings a Web page under the same heading within the S-R main page, and hence within the dominant *Mideast Land of Conflict* network. The page lists a total of nineteen links under the subheadings *Palestinian Sites*, *Israeli Sites*, and *General Sites*. Six links correspond to each of the former two headings, with seven links provided under *General Sites* (CNN 2001f). Each link is accompanied by a short, one-sentence description. For example, a link labeled *Palestinian Central Bureau of Statistics* is accompanied by the statement "This site contains demographic and economic information on Palestinians living in disputed lands."[14] *General Sites* provides links to Web sites hosted by the U.S. State Department Near Eastern Affairs Bureau, U.S. Secretary of State, Egypt State Information Service, Jordan National Information System, President of Lebanon, and the Syrian Ministry of Information, as well as to the United Nations: Question of Palestine Web site.

As noted earlier, links to these non-partner Web sites are accompanied by a disclaimer with respect to their content. This appears immediately beneath the Web page's heading and reads "Note: Pages will open to a new browser window. External sites are not endorsed by CNN Interactive" (CNN 2001f). In this instance, the designers of S-R are clearly not interested in incorporating the Web page content of these competing sources of information within the portal's own narratives. Web pages accessed by means of these links do not become part of networks internal to *CNN.com*. Instead, the identification of these Web sites within *Mideast Land of Conflict* in the form of a list of links is best understood *as* the intended message. As with the UN documents held within the *Peace Exhibit*, the primary importance of these links is rhetorical or semiotic. Providing a list of links to related sites for the benefit of the user is best understood as a magnanimous gesture; a tolerant, fair-minded acknowledgment of "other points of view" from an online actor confident of its own authority.

The presence of the United Nations Web site within the list of links provided under *General Sites* might at first seem to negate the argument raised earlier concerning the rhetorical inappropriateness of providing a link to this Web site. Additionally, the access provided by *CNN.com* to Web pages hosted by Palestinian as well as Israeli interests does appear to be a genuine expression of fairness on the part of S-R's designers. Once again, however, it is important to emphasize that from a rhetorical standpoint, these links function within S-R primarily as signs. Since these and other Web sites might just as easily be accessed by means of a quick key word search on *Google*, taking "ownership" of these competing Web sites through their identification within the portal has rhetorical advantages.

Through means of the narrative structures and rhetorical techniques present within the S-R portal, *CNN.com* has already laid claim to the ideological territory of universal norms and values which might otherwise be associated with online actors such as the UN, or the project identity actors considered in chapters 2 and 3. Likewise, those documents identified within S-R as the most relevant for a clear understanding of the Arab/Israeli conflict have already been incorporated within its central narratives. It should also be recalled that the rhetorical strategy identified in Part I of this chapter as dominant within the *Mideast Land of Conflict* network involved the repeated juxtaposition of Palestinian versus Israeli "points of view." While the necessary context needed to assess the validity of their competing claims was lacking, an illusion of disinterested objectivity was produced nonetheless. This illusion is reinforced, rather than diminished, by the display of Israeli and Palestinian Web sites on the *Related Links* Web page. The mere act of providing such links reinforces the perception that *CNN.com* represents an authoritative and disinterested center of gravity around which partisan viewpoints circulate.

Closing Remarks

Throughout this chapter, a broad range of communicative strategies were identified within *CNN.com*, and more specifically within its *Special Report: Mideast Land of Conflict* portal. While some of these clearly entail rhetorical techniques long utilized within traditional print media, others depend upon the unique features of the World Wide Web. Perhaps most significantly with respect to the concerns driving this investigation, *CNN.com*'s designers appear to have risen to the challenge of disseminating news effectively in a medium "populated" by countless other identities attempting to broadcast messages of their own. Through skillful manipulation of the hyperlink, the voices of various online sites were acknowledged by *CNN.com* in a manner which appeared to reinforce, rather than call into question, the integrity of dominant narratives within this major news site.

In the next two chapters, it will be demonstrated that legitimating identities are not the only online actors capable of exploiting the peculiarities of hypertext for rhetorical and organizational purposes. Here, the Web strategies of three resistance identities widely understood as extremist and militant in outlook will be examined. It will be argued that while the WWW has served the membership of these social movements in a variety of ways, the ability of representative organizations to propagandize effectively to the public at large remains severely limited. Furthermore, their Web-based networking and propaganda warfare activities may actually reinforce the perceived authority of online information providers such as *CNN.com*.

NOTES

1. A small number of articles and graphics within the portal take the form of "pop-up" windows, the contents of which are not amenable to reproduction in hard-copy form, and which do not have separate Web page addresses. Some of these receive attention in part II of this chapter due to the fact that they provide hypertext pathways between some of the key texts under consideration in Part I.

2. PRESIDENT (2004) is "sponsored by LIA, a consortium managed by the University of North Carolina at Chapel Hill, which includes Sun Microsystems and Cisco Systems—the partners in UNC's Metalab Project, the Presidency Research Group of the American Political Science Association, and the National Archives and Records Administration and its Presidential Libraries." Presidential Libraries (2004) makes available "the papers, records, and other historical materials of U.S. Presidents since Herbert Hoover" (Presidential Libraries 2004). The Presidential Library system is made up of ten presidential libraries, each of which includes a museum. The Web site of the *Jimmy Carter Library & Museum* (2004) provides a link to *Camp David Accords: Framework for Peace*.

3. It is worth noting that the author of this text, Dr. Kenneth Stein, was the first director of the Carter Center (1983–1986) where he remained a fellow until December 2006, when he resigned to protest the publication of Carter's book *Israel: Peace Not Apartheid*. Stein is a professor of Contemporary Middle Eastern Mystery and Israeli Studies at Emory University.

4. That the Palestinian Arabs were opposed to the idea is beyond dispute. The American King-Crane commission of 1919 reported that the Palestinian Arabs "were emphatically against the entire Zionist program" (MacMillan 2001, 423; Tillman 1982, 12). During the 1930s, the Palestinian peasantry partook in a "great revolt" against the British occupation and accompanying Zionist colonization of Palestine. The revolt was eventually crushed with nearly 20,000 Arab casualties (Swedenburg 1999, 157).

5. Quoted in Said 1997, 129–130.

6. According to Kimmerling (2003, 80–81) this strategy was pursued by the Israelis, and particularly by former Prime Minister Menachem Begin and General Ariel Sharon, who believed that peace with Egypt would be necessary before the Palestinians could be destroyed as a political force in Lebanon, and before Israel could lay permanent claim to the West Bank.

7. Chomsky (1999, 67) notes that in January 1976, the United States vetoed a UN Security Council Resolution designed to guarantee "the sovereignty, territorial integrity and political independence of all states in the area and their right to live in peace within secure and recognized borders." The states in question included Israel and a Palestinian state in the occupied territories. The resolution had been backed by Egypt, Syria, Jordan, and the PLO.

8. Notable exceptions may include American human rights workers, missionaries, or others whose activities often conflict with U.S. foreign policy imperatives.

9. Time Warner and AOL merged in 2000. After suffering significant losses, the two corporations broke their merger in 2003.

10. These pop-up displays and their contents do not represent separate Web pages within the portal but are superimposed upon/within the S-R homepage http://www.cnn.com/SPECIALS/2001/mideast/.

11. http://dosfan.lib.uic.edu/ERC/briefing/dispatch/1993/html/Dispatchv4

12. http://www.israel.org/mfa/go.asp?MFAH00qa0

13. http://state.gov/www/regions/nea/981023_interim_agmt.html

14. It is worth noting that frequent use of the term "disputed lands" or "disputed territories" by CNN and other news services is highly misleading. It implies that the status of territories captured by Israel in 1967 remains unclear and has yet to be resolved, when in fact there is broad international agreement that the territories in question are *occupied* and that Israel must end its rule over them (Quigley 2005).

Chapter Five

Hate and Holy War on the WWW

PART I: CONFRONTING THE OTHER

The cyberculture exists only in terms of self-referentiality: it simply communicates with and within itself; and it is the endless circuit of communication—of connections and interconnections—that provides the rationale for its existence.

(Robins & Webster 2001, 226)

It should perhaps come as little surprise that the WWW, with its ease of accessibility, networking capabilities, mass audience, and potential for avoiding censorship, has proven irresistible to groups and individuals notorious for their "extremist" views. And yet, it remains unclear just how much importance this technology ultimately holds in terms of furthering the political agendas of groups such as those belonging to the racist far-right. Chapters 5 and 6 explore this issue by examining the Web-based communication, propaganda, alliance building, and organizational strategies adopted by three resistance identities. This chapter will begin by considering the beliefs and goals of each identity—which correspond to ideological variants of white supremacism, Zionist fundamentalism, and Islamist militancy, respectively—using representative Web sites as a key point of reference. Attention will then be extended to the various ways in which the WWW has been utilized by representative groups for purposes of identity building and propaganda warfare. This focus will be complemented in chapter 6, where attention will be directed to additional, complementary strategic uses to which the same identities have put the Web, and their implications for the long-term success of each movement.

The internet offers a diverse array of options for those seeking new means for protest, and the Web strategies favored by some social movements may hold less appeal to others. This point should be kept in mind when considering the socially and politically marginal status of the groups considered here. Significantly, the racist doctrines and/or militant programs advocated by organizations such as the Ku Klux Klan or the Jewish Defense League make it very difficult for them to pursue their agendas openly within the American political system, or to gain sympathetic coverage from the mainstream media. The obstacles faced by organizations widely understood to be promoting hate or violence are even greater in these respects than those confronting the project identity organizations considered in chapters 1 and 2. It is worth noting, for example, that relatively less emphasis is placed upon political lobbying and (mainstream) media activism within the Web sites of the identities considered here. Nonetheless, it will be demonstrated that relevant social movement organizations (SMOs) actively exploit the WWW's capacity to serve as an informational and ideological resource in what are often creative and intriguing ways.

The "sharing of space" within the Web environment presents a major challenge for any resistance identity attempting to utilize this medium for political purposes; namely, that use of the Web medium provides similar benefits for one's enemies and ideological rivals. While such is arguably the case with respect to any online actor, this situation is particularly vexing for those groups already relegated to the political margins. It will be demonstrated in the forthcoming case studies that each of the three resistance identities has acted resourcefully to ensure that its voice is not drowned out by those of rival social movements, anti-racist organizations, or any other interests which might seek to marginalize them further. In particular, each has proven highly adept at exploiting the Web's interconnected and underdetermined qualities (see chapter 1, 10–12). People define who and what they are through reference to what they are not, and construction of the "political self" is closely bound to the discovery of threats posed by the other. Significantly, the WWW provides fringe movements with a particularly effective vehicle for identifying and exploiting the ideologies, goals, and rhetoric of enemies when attempting to affirm and demarcate the parameters of their own identities.

When discussing that form of social solidarity exemplified by resistance identities, Castells (1997, 9) refers to "the building of defensive identity in terms of dominant institutions/ideologies, reversing the value judgment while reinforcing the boundary." Challenging and discrediting the practices and discourses associated with dominant institutions and organizations is essential for resistance identities if they hope to promote their own agendas as legitimate alternatives. It is the dominant, hegemonic interpretations of reality reproduced through the workings of the mass media which clearly represent the most relevant authority in this respect. Hence, as Billig (1991) has emphasized, racists, ultranationalists, and others on the political fringes must employ all of their rhetorical skills to exploit the contradictory and dilemmatic nature of common sense beliefs if they hope to gain greater credibility for their own views. At the same time, the particular propaganda strategies they adopt reflect not only their marginality, but also their specific convictions, fears, and historic experiences. As will become apparent, these and other predispositions may be further evoked and attenuated within the Web environment.

"Extremist" resistance identities must also be prepared to challenge the authority of "moderate" resistance identities whose leadership role within a given religious/ethnic community they hope to supplant. In fact each of the identities considered here clearly hopes to usurp the status of their more mainstream counterparts—which include some of the resistance and project identity organizations described in chapters 1 and 2—as the "legitimate" representatives of the same ethnic/religious communities. Many of the latter are closely affiliated with the political establishment, and represent legitimizing identities in their own right. Doubt must therefore be cast upon the judgment and/or the true intentions of such competitors. Their naivety, hypocrisy and and/or ineptitude must be contrasted with the purist program of the resistance identity challenger, which must in turn be shown to flow seamlessly from core identity doctrine. Hence, establishing the authority of resistance identity ideology requires the presentation of arguments which are both emotionally appealing and logically coherent. Basic tenets must be supported by appeals to appropriate alternative authorities, and the presentation of convincing evidence.

The concerns touched upon above will be considered in three main sections, followed by a short discussion. Each section deals with the goals and Web strategies of one resistance identity, and also provides an introduction to the doctrines and political agendas dominant within each identity network. The section headings correspond to three Web sites: *stormfront.org*, *kahane .org*, and *radioislam.org*. The selection of these Web sites was not random. Each one exemplifies the ideological outlook and political ideals most central to the identity it represents, and each was either created or inspired by relevant charismatic leaders. They also exhibit high levels of connectivity in terms of links to and from other Web sites affiliated with their own and other identities. Consequently, they provide useful vantage points for considering not only the ideological frameworks they represent and promote, but also the ways in which the Web strategies and hypertext networks produced by the three sets of actors have become conflated. It should be noted that while

the specific content visible within the Web sites and Web rings of each identity has not remained static, the strategies and techniques discussed here remained essentially unchanged during a four-year period (1999–2003) of regular observation. The examples cited should be understood as illustrative of
these strategies and techniques, rather than as attempts to prove that specific
actors have relied exclusively upon their use over a given time-frame.

Stormfront.org: Promoting the Cause of "White Nationalism"

The Web site *stormfront.org* first went online in 1995, and is often cited as the
Web's first major hate site (Goldman 2001, 2). Its creator, Don Black, has
been involved with racist organizations since his teens. In 1980, Black suc-
ceeded his mentor, David Duke, as leader of the Knights of the Ku Klux Klan
(Kinsella 1995, 203). *Stormfront.org* has received considerable attention from
both the mainstream media and from assorted "hate watch" organizations.
This is due in part to this site's relatively long history and its sophistication,
as well as to some of its more sensational features such as a children's Web
page which is maintained by Black's teenage son (McKelvey 2001). Significantly, Black has designed his Web site to function as a resource for use by
anyone interested in the beliefs and goals of the white nationalist movement,
rather than as a front for a specific racist organization.

Stormfront.org provides an extensive amount of free resource materials in
the form of multimedia texts originating from a wide variety of racist individuals and organizations. It also markets identity-based books, tapes, and
other materials to anyone interested in the movement. All Web site materials
are designed to promote a white separatist or "white nationalist" political program in the United States, and to encourage cooperation with like-minded
racist organizations elsewhere in the Western world. The long-term goal of
the white separatist movement, as presented within various texts within
stormfront.org, is to establish a state for "Euro-Americans" within those areas of the United States where whites have become increasingly concen-
trated, allegedly as a result of "anti-white persecution" and/or racial upheaval
in America's major urban centers. In *stormfront.org* and other racist Web
sites, the exact geography of any future white state or states is often left
vague, viewed as flexible (depending upon contingency), and/or remains a
matter of debate within the movement.

The home page of *stormfront.org* is visually striking. A large standard consisting of a cross through a circle takes up roughly the top quarter of the page.[1]
The motto "White Pride World Wide" appears within this icon. Directly beneath, the heading "White Nationalist Resource Page," is followed by the Web
site's mission statement: "Stormfront is a resource for those courageous men

and women fighting to preserve their White Western Culture, ideals and free-dom of speech and association—a forum for planning strategies and forming political and social groups to ensure victory" (Black [a]).

If the statements and symbols on the homepage succeed in holding the vis-itor's initial attention, he or she will soon be directed to two articles designed to familiarize the reader with the most fundamental ideological premises in-forming the white separatist program. On the left margin of the homepage, in-ternal links are provided to the main resource areas within *stormfront.org*. These links are labeled as follows: *White Nationalist Community Discussion forum, Press Coverage, What is Racism?, Who Rules America?, Text library, Graphics library, Women's Page, Kids page, Comments, Home*. The fourth and fifth headings refer the reader to texts which are also made available within the Text library through several link pathways. Links to *What is Racism?* and *Who Rules America?* are also frequently highlighted elsewhere on the homepage. These texts are clearly intended to function both as "hooks" designed to capture the attention of new visitors to the site, as well as pro-viding useful points of reference in the reader's education.

Much like the internal text links highlighted on the main page within *CNN.com*'s *Special Report: Mideast Land of Conflict* portal, the articles *What is Racism?* and *Who Rules America?* provide the reader with a means for con-textualizing commentary, humor, and information made available elsewhere within the larger Web site (and Web rings) of which these texts are a part. Sig-nificantly, they introduce the reader to the two most fundamental beliefs driv-ing the white separatist program. The first belief is that Americans of Euro-pean descent constitute a persecuted minority whose rights and culture are threatened by the presence and growth of other racial groups in the United States. The second, closely related belief is that the American government is being manipulated by ZOG, an acronym for the Zionist Occupation Govern-ment. ZOG is argued to be in the process of consolidating Jewish control over the world's most powerful governments and institutions, a task it has all but completed within the United States. The latter premise is particularly impor-tant since it has acted not only to shape white separatist attitudes towards the Arab/Israeli conflict, but also the hopes and energies which movement lead-ers such as Black have invested in the internet. The latter point will be re-turned to shortly.

The text *What is Racism?* (Jackson) relies heavily upon seductive rhetoric to instill a sense of moral outrage in the (white) reader. Visitors to *storm-front.org* are made aware of the hypocrisy and "anti-White racism" which al-legedly permeates American society. Governmental policies concerning affir-mative action and immigration are cited as evidence of white persecution, as is official indifference to minority crime and the anti-white hate practices of other "racial groups." The author argues that while racial minorities are encouraged to organize and lobby for their political rights, similar efforts on the part of "Euro-Americans" are invariably branded racist. The text *Who Rules America?* (National Vanguard Magazine) is also intended to provoke white anger, but relies more heavily upon persuasive arguments intended to appeal to the reader's common sense. Most importantly, it provides a general explanation which might help account for the pervasiveness of anti-white racism within a country governed primarily by whites. Such an explanation is essential in light of the fact that most of this racism is argued to be systemic, with its roots in the American political establishment.

Interestingly, *Who Rules America?* and numerous other texts within *stormfront.org*, attribute much of the blame for the existence of anti-white racism in America to the "racial irresponsibility" of "white liberal elites." The reader is informed that when racial minority groups—which originally provided these elites with a cheap pool of labor—came to demand more and more from the political system, white elites were willing to grant them endless concessions. In so doing they hoped to safeguard their privileged status in society while maintaining public order. However, it is also maintained that this corrupt and short-sighted strategy will backfire for a number of reasons, most of which concern racial differences. The reader is informed that minority races instinctively compete both with whites and with one another for dominance, that they will never be satisfied by the concessions and special privileges granted them by the establishment, and that they are inherently incapable of coexisting peacefully and productively with whites.

The blindness and racial irresponsibility of white elites is argued to have been successfully exploited by ZOG, the real agent attempting to bring about the demise of American civilization. The Jews are depicted as relentlessly pursuing a strategy which involves the buying out of institutions formerly under the control of white elites, while inserting themselves into key positions of influence in government and commerce. This line of argument is pursued most forcefully with respect to the mass media. *Who Rules America?*, which is subtitled *The Alien Grip on Our Media Must Be Broken*, provides numerous facts and figures to demonstrate that Jews either own, or hold key positions within, virtually all of America's major media institutions. The "Jewish takeover" of CNN receives special attention within this text, with media tycoon Ted Turner cited as a classic example of an influential, but irresponsible white willing to sell out to ZOG (National Vanguard Magazine, 3).

Alleged Jewish control of the media is used to explain how the "Zionist establishment" has been able to brainwash the American masses with anti-racist propaganda and to stifle resistance to and awareness of ZOG. However, the reader is warned that this so called anti-racism is not accepted by the Jews themselves. The latter employ anti-racist doctrine as part of a divide and rule strategy designed to promote race mixing and ensure the destruction of white/Christian American civilization, while allowing for ZOG's consolidation. The "truth" of this doctrine is demonstrated by the fact that while the Jews rail against racial inequality in America, they defend racial segregation in the case of Israel. Israel's right to exist is equated with the Jewish right to self-determination, a right denied to American whites. It is this reasoning, combined with the belief that American support for Israel threatens America's national interests, which drives the white separatist preoccupation with the Arab/Israeli conflict; a preoccupation which is ubiquitous within the Web sites of this resistance identity.

In recent decades the larger white separatist movement has become increasingly influenced by the "Christian Identity" sub-movement, the doctrine of which provides an additional impetus for racist concern with the events and players in the Middle East.[2] Central to Christian Identity doctrine, which bears scant resemblance to orthodox versions of Christian faith, is the belief that western Europeans constitute the true descendents of biblical Israel. Conversely, the Jews are believed to be descended from Satan, who is claimed to have seduced Eve in the Garden of Eden, resulting in the "Jewish seedline" (Barrett 1987, 335; Dobratz 2001, 289). Present-day Israelis are thus understood as impostors whose claim to Israel/Palestine is fraudulent. It is also believed that ultimately the Jews, or "House of Judah," which is often equated with modern Israel, will eventually be destroyed by God on Judgment Day (Kinsella 1995, 109). Christian Identity adherents also believe that non-whites, whose ancestry predates Adam, are "mud people" who lack souls and hence are not fully human. While "white nationalists" such as Don Black and David Duke generally prefer to express their racist beliefs in "scientific" terminology, it should be noted that white separatist Web sites frequently combine "scientific" and "religious" arguments. For example, numerous documents within *stormfront.org*'s Text library stress the necessary relationship between the greatness of Christian civilization and "whiteness."[3]

Unlike many other groups on the political margins, the communicative barriers confronting stigmatized social movements such as white separatism often have less to do with a lack of economic resources or easy access to the Web, than with the nature of the messages they hope to convey. As Billig (1991) has observed, racist organizations such as the Ku Klux Klan or the National Alliance promote beliefs and lines of argument which directly contradict dominant understandings of reality and which clash with widely held sentiments concerning acceptable public discourse. Despite the relatively large size of the white separatist movement and its long history in America, its core beliefs are rarely reflected in the mainstream media or in the statements of politicians today. While systemic forms of racism may be alive and well, there is currently a strong taboo within liberal democracies against explicit statements of ideological racism.[4] Nonetheless, white separatists have shown themselves to be proficient at exploiting the peculiarities of hypertext to enhance the rhetorical force of arguments such as those described above. Significantly, the Web allows them to highlight the origins and authorship of messages widely understood as credible, while carrying the rhetorical battle into their own home (Web) territory.

An extensive collection of mainstream media texts are made available to visitors to *stormfront.org* through its *Press Coverage* link. Most of these texts, which typically take the form of newspaper and magazine articles critical of *stormfront.org*, serve as targets to be discredited by the "superior" reasoning put forward elsewhere within the Web site. However, they also serve a more compelling propaganda function. As products of the "Jewish controlled media" these texts were ostensibly produced either by corrupt or brainwashed whites associated with an oppressive liberal establishment, or by Jews more directly connected to the shadow government argued to lie behind it. As such, they may be presented as direct evidence in support of the tenets put forward in *Who Rules America?* For example, one Web page, which bears the general heading, *Stormfront Press Coverage*, is accompanied by the sub-heading, "What the controlled media has to say about Stormfront (Black [b])." Similar framing techniques are also used to introduce specific news articles. The following statement is placed above a news piece which first appeared in the *Fort Lauderdale Sun-Sentinel* on May 11, 1995 entitled *Since the Oklahoma City bombing, some Internet sites featuring hate materials shut down, others flourish* (Lorek 1995): "*Six weeks after the Stormfront website went online, the media finally has to come to grips with the fact that they now have competition. They no longer have a monopoly on information –DB*" (Black [c]).

In addition to media texts obtained from the Western press, an extensive collection of cartoons taken from Arab newspapers are used within *stormfront.org* to reinforce white separatist arguments concerning both the "controlled media" and the Arab/Israeli conflict. Here, attention is drawn to the fact that the texts in question, most of which involve the demonization of various Israeli politicians, have been described as anti-Semitic by "ZOG-affiliated" organizations such as the Anti-Defamation League (ADL). This fact is in turn used to reinforce two lines of propaganda pervasive within *stormfront.org*. First, they direct attention to "Jewish hypocrisy" concerning the issue of "race-based" self determination. ZOG will only tolerate criticism of white separatism while branding any attempt to question "Jewish supremacy" as anti-Semitic. The fact that many of these and/or very similar cartoons have been reproduced within the ADL's own Web site (*adl.org*) as examples of anti-Semitism may add further credibility to white separatist claims in the eyes of some. Secondly, these cartoons are used to highlight supposed Jewish frustration over media expression beyond their control. This in turn implies the potential vulnerability of ZOG in the face of a growing "free media" exemplified by Web sites such as *stormfront.org*.

As indicated above, attacks on the "controlled media" and enemy Jewish organizations such as the ADL are part and parcel of the same battle from the perspective of white separatists. This fact underlies the unique character of white separatist conspiracy-building, propaganda, and "watchdog" practices on the Web; practices which essentially invert and mirror those of mainstream institutions. To better illustrate this point, it is worth drawing attention to an important precedent set by Harvard Law School reference librarian David Goldman. Concerned with the appearance and spread of racist material online, Goldman created a Web page in 1995 under the title "Guide to Hate Groups on the Internet" (Goldman 2001, 1). What was novel about this Web site, which later went by the name *HateWatch*, was that it provided not only critical commentary concerning racist web sites, but provided links to these sites as well. Goldman defended this practice, which received criticism from many, on the grounds that it was better to expose the nature of hate groups than to practice censorship (Goldman 2001). However, while Goldman has since shut down his Web site, the practice of providing links to "enemy" Web sites has been adopted by numerous other groups concerned with racism as well as by racist organizations themselves. In fact, cooptation of the hate-watch function is now highly visible in the Web sites and Web rings of all three resistance identities covered in this chapter, but takes on a different character in the case of each.

Most white separatist Web sites provide extensive commentary concerning the activities of major Jewish organizations allegedly affiliated with ZOG. Such commentary is used to reinforce key points of identity doctrine in much the same way that media commentary critical of the white separatist movement was shown to have been used within *stormfront.org*. Specifically, attention is directed to the practices of various Jewish/Zionist organizations in their efforts to monitor the activities of numerous social movement organizations, with particular emphasis given to their attempts to ban white separatist Web sites. A typical example may be seen within a Web site entitled *Politics and Terrorism (zog.to)*. This Web site, which is listed within *stormfront.org*'s Links Portal under the sub-heading *Opposition to Zionism and Israeli Terrorism*, advertises attempts by the ADL to have *Politics and Terrorism* taken permanently off-line:

This website is under *threat of a lawsuit* from the $50,000,000.00 a year annual budget of the anti-Defamation League of B'nai B'rith. Their purpose is to get this website shut down. They don't have a case of course, if they did they would long since have brought down the Jew legal hammer. However my ISP appears all too eager to do their bidding. –DL is therefore used to represent "ADL," the trade marked acronym for the anti-Defamation league which I am forbidden from using under threat of a lawsuit. (Politics and Terrorism [a])

In addition to providing commentary concerning the activities of their enemies, many white separatist Web sites make a point of providing links directly to those Web sites which monitor racist and/or anti-Semitic organizations. For example, a subsection of links provided within *stormfront.org*'s portal under the heading *The Other Side*, lists links to well-known "hate watch" Web sites including *Nizkor*, *Simon Wiesenthal Center*, and *Anti-Defamation League*. Each of these links is accompanied by a short explanatory statement. For example, beneath the link to the Simon Wiesenthal Center Web site, appears the following phrase: "The Rabbis at the Wiesenthal Center have been the most active in organizing hate campaigns against ISPs hosting sites they find 'offensive'" (Black [d]).

Significantly, if links to Jewish/Zionist Web sites are in fact followed by those *already holding* white separatist beliefs, viewing their content will likely be understood in terms of "catching ZOG in the act." For such individuals, no discrepancy will be visible between the self-declared goals of "hate watch" organizations and the accusations leveled at these same organizations by white separatists. This point is important since it implies that Web site content which might appear benign to the (more) typical Web user, may contribute to the paranoia of resistance identity members, while simultaneously providing them with additional material with which to reinforce their own Web-based propaganda. For example, the logo of the American Israel Public Affairs Committee (AIPAC), an influential pro-Israel lobby group, has been reproduced within the Web site *Politics and Terrorism* (*zog.to*) in order to visually reinforce the arguments of the latter. A reproduction of the logo, which incorporates the stars and stripes within a Star of David, is accompanied by the following remarks:

This is the AIPAC logo as displayed on their web page. It is attractive and appropriate. The symbolism denotes political entwinement. Is this a warm and fuzzy mutual entanglement, or has the Star of David been stamped over the Stars and Stripes in a sinister way? It leaves no doubt where the loyalty of those to whom it speaks lie. (Politics and Terrorism [b])

White separatists have created Web sites dedicated entirely to the purpose of monitoring the Jewish enemy. The rationale for this practice is summed up in the following advertisement within a Web site hosted by David Duke entitled *whitecivilrights.com*:

Who watches the so-called "Watchdog Groups"?

The Anti-Defamation League of the B'nai B'rith, or ADL for short, presents itself as an organization against ethnic, racial or religious intolerance. In reality, the Anti-Defamation League is an organization that supports Jewish ethnic and religious supremacy, and relentlessly "defames" anyone who dares to point out its own hypocrisy. (European Unity and Rights Organization)

A series of Web pages affiliated with *stormfront.org* may easily be accessed under the heading *Jew Watch* (*jewwatch.com*) with its motto "Keeping a Close Watch on Jewish Communities & Organizations World Wide." Another Web site entitled *ADL WATCH* (*zpub.com*) is dedicated to collecting and providing resources pertaining specifically to the activities of the Anti-Defamation League. These Web pages tend to focus upon the ADL's surveillance activities of dissident groups and its ties to (and alleged coercion of) federal and police authorities. Notably, extensive attention is given not only to the ADL's record of spying on white supremacist groups, but also upon Palestinian, anti-Apartheid, and Black Muslim organizations. These references are used to reinforce the charge of "Jewish hypocrisy" described earlier (ADL Watch).

The "Jew watch" activities of white separatists represent more than what most would consider vulgar propaganda. White separatist fears concerning ZOG, along with their related commitment to the creation of a separate media infrastructure, help to explain why the Jew Watch function has become so widespread within white racist Web sites. The hate watch role adopted within many anti-racist Web sites, especially those hosted by Jewish organizations such as the Simon Wiesenthal Center, are not understood by white separatists as well meaning, anti-racist initiatives, but rather as an extension of Jewish media control and as a disciplinary function of the anti-white and anti-Christian ZOG shadow government. In the minds of white separatists, Web sites such as *ADL WATCH* and *Jew Watch* constitute the "authentic" hate watch Web sites of the legitimate free media. Furthermore, it is the free and patriotic white separatist media which movement leaders clearly hope will someday supplant the corrupt and compromised mainstream mass media. This point will be explored further in chapter 6, where the Web's value as an alternative media infrastructure will be considered with respect to its long term potential for social movement growth and influence.

Kahane.org: Fighting to Eliminate Israel's "Arab Cancer"

While not nearly as numerous as those belonging to white racist organizations, Web sites and Web rings associated with the Jewish far right have become well established on the WWW, and now appear on the lists of some "hate watch" groups. One of the best known of these, *kahane.org*, has gained media attention for some its more sensational content, including threats against individuals associated with the Jewish peace movement and video games in which supposed enemies of the Jewish people, including Palestinian rioters and Israeli "traitors" provide the main targets (Eskenazi 2001, *Jewish Bulletin News* 2003). The ultimate goal of one such game entitled "Escape of the Oslo Criminals" is the assassination of the architects of the Oslo Peace Accords, both Palestinian and Israeli, who are attempting to flee the violence and chaos which they are ostensibly responsible for having created.

Like *stormfront.org*, *kahane.org* makes a wide variety of multimedia identity-based resources freely available to visitors. It also sells various Jewish ultranationalist materials and encourages visitors to become familiar with books and audio files featuring the teachings of the late orthodox rabbi, Meir Kahane. Kahane, after whom this Web site was named, was a well-known and highly controversial figure on the Jewish far right. Unlike the case with most other American Jewish Zionist organizations, Kahane did not encourage his followers to pursue their political goals primarily through conventional, legal channels such as political lobbying. Instead, he advocated the use of violence against anyone daring to harm Jewish interests. In 1968, Kahane founded the militant Jewish Defense League (JDL) with the expressed intent of instilling pride and confidence within the Jewish community by combating anti-Semitism through direct action. An early concern of the organization was responding to crime and expressions of black (African American) anti-Semitism as these impacted working-class Jewish neighborhoods in New York (Lustick 1988; Sprinzak 1991).

In 1971, Kahane moved to Israel to establish the anti-Arab Kach party. The primary goal of Kach was and remains the expulsion of most or all Arabs from Israel and the territories it captured during the Six-Day War of 1967. Kahane believed that what he regularly referred to as Israel's "Arab cancer" represented a long-term demographic and military threat to the Jewish state. In 1985, the Israeli government accused Kahane of inciting racial hatred, and banned his party from running for seats in the Knesset. Since that time, several legal Israeli political parties, including Tehiya and Moledet, have adopted Kach's platform of "transferring" most or all Arabs from "greater Israel" (Sprinzak 1991). Meir Kahane was assassinated in New York in 1990 by an Egyptian-born Islamist who was later implicated in the events of 9/11. After Kahane's death, a Kach splinter group known as Kahane Chai (Kahane lives) was founded in Israel by his son, Binyamin. Binyamin Kahane was killed by Palestinian militants in the West Bank in December, 2000 (Shyovitz 2003, 2).

"Kahanism" is best understood as a militant movement which has emerged within the context of a general growth of Jewish/Zionist fundamentalism after the Arab/Israeli wars of 1967 and 1973 (Lustick 1988; Sprinzak 1991; Kepel 1994). While Kahanists advocate the implementation of religious law in Israel, the bulk of their following has always consisted of secular Jews, and their over-all agenda is better understood as ultranationalist rather than religious funda-mentalist in character. It is important to stress that it was primarily Kahane's vi-olent tactics and disregard for the law, rather than the specific beliefs he advocated, which earned him condemnation from both the Israeli and American governments (Sprinzak 1991). Kahanist organizations have been responsible for numerous violent acts in Israel, the occupied territories, and North America, and the JDL, Kach, and Kahane Chai are all considered terrorist organizations by the U.S. State Department and the FBI. It is those Web sites hosted by Kahanist or-ganizations and/or by Jewish ultranationalist individuals or groups which openly identify with the Kahanist program which are of interest here.

A conspicuous box on the right hand margin of the *kahane.org* home page makes the following statement under the link banner *Kahane.org–Principles and Philosophy*: "The Kahane movement continues to spread the authentic Jewish idea through the Kahane.org website, radio and email transmissions, through our publications and through speeches given by our spokespeople" (Kahane.org). Activating this link takes the reader to "an abridged version of the key principles and philosophy of Kahane.org." Brief summaries of core doctrine are then provided with reference to the following ten guiding principles:

1. Chosen people—Chosen land—Chosen destiny
2. Torah Makes Jews Special
3. Love of Jews—Don't Stand Idly By . . .
4. Persecution of Jews is a Degradation of G-d's name!
5. Faith and Barzel—Strength
6. Israel Belongs To The Jews
7. Exile is A Curse = Immigration To Israel Is A Must
8. No Surrender of Jewish Land to Arabs
9. The Temple Mount is Jewish
10. Religious Ritual and Government in Israel. (Kahane.org)

The idea that a commitment to Kahanist principles represents the most au-thentic expression of Jewish values and the most viable means of defending Jewish interests is also visible in the mission statement on the Jewish Defense League's Web site: "The Jewish Defense League is the most controversial, yet the most effective, of all Jewish organizations. Through its website and chapters, the JDL is firmly committed to its motto, 'Never Again,' by words, deeds and actions"(Jewish Defense League [a]).

Kahanists have long been critical of mainstream Jewish/Zionist organizations which claim to speak for the wider Jewish community, a fact which is readily made apparent within *jdl.org*. The JDL has been particularly critical of its more respected and influential resistance identity rival, the Anti-Defamation League (ADL). For example, a link entitled *The ADL Blows it Again* leads to an article dealing with this organization's legal difficulties after a failed attempt to sue an Evergreen Colorado couple for allegedly making anti-Semitic remarks. Use of an illegally taped telephone conversation resulted in a lawsuit against the organization (Jewish Defense League [b]). The provision of such material within *jdl.org* reflects a general attempt to portray the ADL as being incapable of defending Jewish rights effectively. Such criticism also constitutes a response to the ADL's attempts to discredit Kahanist groups. This may be seen in the quote below, which was taken from a Web page entitled *The ADL Doesn't Help Jews—The ADL Helps Jew-Haters*:

> The Anti-Defamation League spends its time keeping records and publishing reports on the Jewish Defense League. And in 1973, the ADL's Philadelphia office turned over the names of JDL members to the FBI!
>
> The Anti-Defamation League put the JDL's award-winning Web site on their Internet-censoring program so that people cannot find out about the only Jewish organization that goes to the streets to fight for Jewish rights!
>
> *Don't Give Your Money to the ADL!*
>
> *Help JDL Fight Jew-Haters! Support JDL!* (Jewish Defense League [c])

The JDL's attacks on the ADL are consistent with the more general Kahanist claim that both the mainstream Israeli political parties as well as the dominant Jewish/Zionist organizations outside of Israel are generally too ineffectual, misguided, and/or compromised by subservience to the American political establishment to rise to the challenge of defending Israel from its enemies. *Kahane.org* is filled with commentary criticizing the Israeli state's policies towards the Arabs, with even well-known hawks such as Ariel Sharon accused of being too soft or ineffectual in their approach. A related line of rhetoric concerns the "fact" that as a rule, ordinary Jews have been so misled by their supposed leadership that they have become unable to perceive the threat posed to Israel by the Arabs in her midst. This argument, which parallels white separatist assertions concerning brainwashed whites and the threat posed by the growth of minority populations in America, is reinforced within Jewish ultranationalist Web rings in various ways.

One creative method used by Kahanists to discredit project identity rivals entails the use of what may be termed "dummy" or "decoy" Web sites. This technique, which involves the creation of Web sites ostensibly hosted by a rival identity, has also been utilized by other identities online including white separatists. The idea is to trick Web users into accessing propaganda which they would ordinarily avoid. A relevant example concerns a collection of Web pages under the heading *the Church of Rabin and Peace* (CRAP). Notably, this Web site is held within a larger Web ring, "The Jewish Web Webring," which also hosts more mainstream Jewish and Zionist Web sites (Church of Rabin and Peace 1999, 10). The CRAP Web site employs satire and ironic humor to draw attention to the "deluded" activities of Jewish human rights activists, and the "suicidal" policy positions of mainstream Israeli politicians and political parties, while simultaneously eliciting sympathy for Jewish settlers in the occupied territories. Interestingly, decoy Web sites are often created by white separatists as well as Kahanists, but for different purposes. The significance of Web sites of this type for will be given further attention in chapter 6.

Kahanist efforts to establish the authenticity of their movement through use of the Web may usefully be contrasted with the efforts of white separatists. Such comparison is particularly helpful when considering resistance identity responses to dominant media discourse. These responses have shaped the online strategies of both identities, and reflect important similarities and differences concerning the ideological outlook and experiences of actors in each case. First, it should be pointed out that a general parallel exists in terms of perceptions of media bias on the part of each identity. In the case of white separatism, Jewish control over the media is deemed to be responsible for a brainwashed American public; a view which, as will be seen, is echoed within the Islamist web site *radioislam.org*. Conversely, Kahanists and their sympathizers claim that both the dominant mass media and American foreign policy are beholden to "Arab petrodollars." For example, advertisements such as the one reproduced below, have appeared regularly within the anti-Arab *Masada 2000* Web site: "*Frustrated By CNN's Bias against Israel?* The second largest shareholder in AOL/Time-Warner (CNN's parent company) is the Saudi Arabian Prince Allayed bin Talal. Maybe THIS is why CNN consistently and unabashedly puts forth a decidedly pro-Palestinian slant!" (Masada 2000.org [a]).

Similar claims concerning Arab influence over the mass media are regularly expressed within the Web rings of Hindu ultranationalists with whom Kahanist organizations have become allied. Cooperation between these two identities will be considered in chapter 6. For present purposes, it is worth noting that despite a shared belief in "media control," the Kahanist response to perceived media impartiality diverges sharply from that of white separatists. In the case of the latter, hostile media control is understood as near total, and attempts to petition or otherwise influence dominant media institutions are generally understood as futile. As a result, the predominant strategic response of this movement has been to focus upon the development of an alternative communication and information infrastructure for use by white activists. The Kahanist stance towards the dominant media is both more ambivalent and more optimistic, and includes attempts at activism in the form of petitions and lobbying. For example, a variant of the advertisement cited above appears as follows: "*Frustrated by CNN's bias against Israel?* Collect names of companies that advertise on CNN and contact the right people to make a difference. Click HERE to get involved" (Masada 2000.org [b]).

Kahanist attempts at media activism online appear to have been inspired by more prominent Jewish/Zionist project identities in at least two significant respects. First, it should be pointed out that while Kahanist organizations have generally been portrayed negatively in the media, many of their beliefs and goals overlap considerably with those of major Jewish Zionist organizations such as the American Israel Public Affairs Committee (AIPAC), the ADL, the Zionist Organization of America, and others. Many of these organizations have proven highly adept in affecting changes to media discourse concerning the Arab/Israeli conflict, a fact which cannot have gone unnoticed by Jewish ultranationalists. In addition, Kahanists are clearly attempting to send a message to their mainstream competitors; namely, that their movement can represent Jewish interests effectively without the assistance of compromised organizations like the ADL. In this sense, attempts at media activism, such as the examples cited above, may be understood primarily as a form of rhetoric. While media lobbying by Kahanists may hold practical significance when combined with the efforts of more influential Jewish and Christian Zionist organizations, they appear unlikely to have any meaningful impact in isolation from the campaigns of their better-established rivals.

Jewish ultranationalist attitudes towards the dominant media are also reflected in their Web-based responses to mass media commentary. Here, flexibility is required to cope with the presence of both harsh media criticism of Kahanist organizations, and the compatibility which frequently exists between prominent themes in the media and the beliefs of identity members. For example, an article featured on the JDL's home page entitled *It's time to Snap Out of Arab Fantasy Land*, and subtitled "The obvious question is, why are so many so easily deluded by hollow Arab propaganda?," first appeared in Canada's *National Post* (Steyn 2002). This text puts forward arguments repeatedly made by Kahanists themselves; that the Arabs are incapable of responding positively to acts of Israeli goodwill such as the return of Palestinian land, that Jordan already constitutes a Palestinian state, and that Israel should take permanent control over as much of the occupied West Bank as it sees fit. However, while such articles may be employed by Kahanists to back up their arguments with "authoritative" commentary, identity members have also felt compelled to respond to media criticism of their own social movement organizations.

Like *stormfront.org*, *kahane.org* provides an archive of media commentary critical of its own (Kahanist) activities. In the case of *stormfront.org* it was demonstrated that such material was used to help reinforce conspiracy theories concerning the "controlled media." No *direct* rebuttal of media criticism was provided. Instead, the very existence of such articles was used to confirm white separatist beliefs about ZOG. In the perception of Kahanists, however, media bias is clearly not seen as monolithic or beyond repair. Friendly media commentary, such as that cited above, may be used to build the Kahanist case while correctives may be offered when the media "misrepresents" the movement. Hence, media texts critical of the movement are followed by an admonition to "read our response." The responses in question invariably explain media hostility towards Kahanist organizations as an effect of the movement's unwillingness to compromise their program for the sake of appeasing the American establishment and/or left-wing forces in Israel. The tactic of offering such rebuttals makes more sense in a situation where media control is not perceived as absolute, and where the media establishment may behave at different times as both friend and enemy.

As with white separatist Web sites, the practice of providing links to enemy Web sites is also employed by Kahanists. However, due to the fact that Kahanism represents a Jewish fringe movement, and because many or most racist Web sites promote anti-Semitism, Kahanist enemy watch lists often resemble those of mainstream hate watch organizations. As with the latter, Kahanist lists typically include links to the Web sites of white racist groups. However, their approach to these and other enemies differ from those practiced by more widely respected organizations such as the Southern Poverty Law Center, or the ADL in important respects. Most glaringly, Kahanist Web sites frequently contain either implicit or explicit threats of violence against perceived enemies of the Jewish people, or encourage illegal forms of harassment against these same enemies. Recently, for example, the designers of *kahane.org* ran into legal difficulties for making threatening statements against Rabbi Michael Lerner, editor of *Tikkun* magazine (and host of *Tikkun.org*—see chapters 2–3), and a well-known figure dedicated to achieving peace between Israel and the Palestinians based upon an end to Israel's occupation of the Arab territories it captured in 1967 (Eskenazi 2001). Ironically, condemnations of Kahanist threats by mainstream Jewish organizations like the ADL are likely to be incorporated into Kahanist propaganda for reasons which will be clarified shortly.

Calls to harass declared Jewish enemies and/or provision of the means for doing so are common within Web sites openly supportive of Kahanist doctrine.

For example, *massada2000.org*, a Web site which openly professes support for the forced transfer of Arabs from greater Israel, provides a six-page text designed to demonize the Lebanese guerrilla organization, Hezbollah. It then provides a link to the Hezbollah Web site with the admonition "The Hezbollah website for those who are interested, on sending them your regards! (Our Enemies)." It is worth noting that the recommendation of contacting enemy sites through e-mail has also been made within the JDL Web site, where the Islamist site *radioislam.org* (see next section) has been made a target:

> We urge everybody to write to Radio Islam, *radioislam@abbc.com*, and tell Ahmed Rami and the other maniacs what you think about their site. If you flood them with mail, so much the better. Write to *bobh@clever.net* (Vice President) and *abuse@clever.net* and tell them what you feel about their decision to house material defaming the Jewish people on his site. Make him understand that a boycott will be set in motion (that is our intention) if the material of hatred against Jews is not removed from their server. (Jewish Defense League [d])

The call to action cited above was part of a larger campaign by the JDL to have *radioislam.org* taken off-line. In fact, these efforts were partially successful, with its creator Ahmed Rami forced to delete some sections of his Web site. It is also worth noting that the transcripts of exchanges between the JDL and *radioislam.org*'s American ISP are made available not only with the JDL's Web pages, but also within *radioislam.org* itself. Here, they have been used to augment arguments concerning the prevalence of Jewish censorship and propaganda in the Western world (Radio Islam [d]). Rami's use of JDL Web material represents only one example of the highly self-referential nature of the propaganda which characterizes the Web sites and Web rings of all three resistance identities. More will be said about this later.

The Web site of the JDL's close resistance identity rival, the Jewish Defense Organization (JDO), has also consistently advocated the harassment of Jewish enemies. Its "NAZIFIGHTERS HANDBOOK," subtitled "JOIN THE ANTI-NAZI REVOLVE-A-CRANK CALL PLAN," is presented within the organization's Web site, *jdo.org*. The book contains the addresses and telephone numbers of hundreds of white racist organizations and individuals. At one time, this list was accompanied by the following suggestion: "Wanna call a Nazi and express your opinion in a way which is very difficult to trace? Use the internet to make your calls by registering with these companies that offer free calls in return for your having to observe advertising" (Jewish Defense Organization [a], 1).

More recently, no doubt as a result of legal problems, this suggestion has been replaced by the following statement, which allows the JDO to respect the letter if not the spirit of American anti-harassment laws:

PERHAPS THOSE NAZIS ARE OVERDUE FOR A MASSIVE CRANKA-
THON (FROM A PAY PHONE) AND OTHER FORMS OF CREATIVE MON-
KEY WARFARE. AFTER ALL, JEWS, GAYS, PACIFISTS, GYPSIES DID
NOT GET A NICE DAY THANKS TO THE SCUM. THEREFORE YOU
SHOULD MAKE EM SUFFER . . . HOWEVER WE DO NOT URGE YOU TO
DO THIS DUE TO THE ILLEGALITY (Jewish Defense Organization [b], 16)

Much like the online media petitions which periodically circulate within Kahanist Web sites, the illegal or unconventional means of harassing enemies advocated by Jewish militant organizations are best understood as attempts to
"show-up" and outperform allegedly inept and corrupt Jewish organizations
such as the ADL. It should also be kept in mind that an emphasis on direct action has always been central to Kahanist philosophy. Direct confrontation with
"Jewish enemies" is understood by identity members as necessary for the long-
term protection of Jewish lives and culture. The close affiliations existing between more prominent Jewish/Zionist organizations and the American establishment are viewed as dangerous by Kahanists since they tie Jewish loyalties
and resources to a power structure believed likely to become increasingly hostile to both the Jewish people and/or the Israeli state in the future (Sprinzak
1991). The emphasis which Kahanists place upon "Barzel" or "Jewish Iron,"
within their Web sites, allows them to advertise an alternative approach to the
defense of Jewish interests which might prove attractive to some potential recruits to the movement. In this sense, their online harassment practices should
be understood as complementary to rhetoric such as that contained in the aforementioned article, *The ADL Doesn't Help Jews—The ADL helps Jew haters!*

In addition to encouraging the harassment of, and/or threatening violence
against Jewish enemies, Kahanist Web-based "hate watch" activities online
differ from those of their mainstream competitors in an additional, related
way. This concerns their overt attempts to inspire hostility or hatred towards
specific religious/ethnic groups. This point is noteworthy in light of a point
raised earlier; that the uninitiated Web surfer may have trouble distinguishing
"legitimate" hate watch Web sites from those espousing explicitly anti-Arab
and/or anti-Islamic points of view. For example, a Web site entitled *Jewish
Watchdog* (*jwd-jewishwatchdog.ca*) closely resembles better-known hate
watch Web sites in terms of its format. It provides extensive links, complete
with critical commentary, to Web sites deemed anti-Semitic under the heading "ANTI-JEWISH ALERTS." The following rationale is provided: "These
ALERTS contain Internet site links that show a hatred or intolerance against
Jews as individuals or as a people. This includes sub-groups such as neo-nazi,
white supremacist, and anti-Israeli sites" (Jewish Watch Dog, 1).

The lumping together of anti-Semitic Web sites with those critical of Israeli
policies allows this Web site's designer to list *The Universality of Human*

Rights at Risk (*cihrs@soficom.com.eg*)—a Web site hosted by the UN affiliated Cairo Institute for Human Rights—directly beneath a link to *stormfront.org* without appearing inconsistent. At the same time, *Jewish Watch Dog* also provides an extensive list of links under the heading "Friends of Israel." While most of the links provided are to more mainstream Zionist interests, the list also includes links to a number of Jewish ultranationalist Web sites including *masada.org*. The latter, which is virulently anti-Arab and anti-Muslim, calls for the ethnic cleansing of Israel's Arabs, depicts Islam as a religion committed to violence and terror, and regularly presents visual images of Arabs in half human/half animal form. *Masada.org* in turn promotes links to similar Web sites including one hosted by the "anti-Muslim society," wherein attempts are made to prove that Islam condones practices of incest and bestiality (Anti-Muslim Society).

Interestingly, the blurring of boundaries online between "legitimate" hate watch groups and those espousing a Jewish ultranationalist agenda has been exploited in the Web sites of anti-Semitic organizations. For example, *stormfront.org*'s links to *The Other Side* include a link to the Jewish Defense Organization's Web site, *jdo.org*, in addition to those of widely recognized hate watch organizations such as the Simon Wiesenthal Center, *Hatewatch*, the ADL etc. As with other links provided under *stormfront.org*'s *The Other Side*, the JDO link is accompanied by a phrase inserted by *stormfront.org*'s designer, Don Black. In this instance the caption reads, "This one advocates outright terrorism against anyone considered an 'enemy of the Jews'" (Black [e]). In fact, the tactic of depicting all identity movement enemies as part of a fictitious "common front" is easily facilitated by the Web medium and is highly visible within the Web sites of all three resistance identities, the last of which is considered below.

Radioislam.org: Defending Islam and the West from the "Jewish Threat"

In 1987, Ahmed Rami, a former lieutenant in the Moroccan military, began broadcasting *Radio Islam* through a public access Swedish radio station (Anti-Defamation League 2001a, 1). The program was banned after it became clear that Rami was less concerned with providing cultural programming for Sweden's Muslim community than with disseminating anti-Semitic conspiracy theories. Rami first put his Web site, *radioislam.org*, online in 1996. Since that time he was forced to switch Swedish-based Internet Service Providers (ISPs) numerous times before eliciting the services of an American server (ADL 2001a). *Radioislam.org* is a vast Web site which has at least ten home page addresses, offers versions of its content in fifteen languages, and contains thousands of Web pages. Not surprisingly, it has received a great deal of negative attention from a variety of Jewish and/or anti-racist organizations.

A box appearing at the top of the *radioislam.org* home page outlines the purposes for which this expansive and highly elaborate Web site was ostensibly created:

> Radio Islam is working to promote better relations between the West and the Muslim World. Radio Islam is against racism of all forms, against all kinds of discrimination of people based on their colour of skin, faith or ethnical background. Consequently, Radio Islam is against Jewish racism towards non-Jews. World Jewish Zionism today constitutes the last racist ideology still surviving and the Zionist's state of Israel, the last outpost of "Apartheid" in the World. Israel constitutes by its mere existence a complete defiance to all international laws, rules and principles, and the open racism manifested in the Jewish State is a violation of all ethics and morals known to man. (Radio Islam [a])

The explicit attempt to target a Western (non-Muslim) as well as an Islamic audience with identity-based propaganda makes *radioislam.org* an interesting case study. It also distinguishes Rami's site from those utilized by Jihadists who consider themselves to be at war with the West, as well as from the types of Web sites normally considered in conjunction with studies of Islamic diaspora communities (e.g. Bunt 2003; Mandaville 2001). Unlike the latter, Rami's priority is not with establishing a cultural/political resource for use by increasingly mobile Muslim communities, but rather with using his Web site as a vehicle for offering his own unique "Islamist perspective" on world events, while attempting to solicit support for his cause from American Black Muslims, European anti-Semites, or anyone else willing to heed his messages. This orientation raises a further issue of relevance. When considered in terms of its Western target audience, the outlook expressed within *radioislam.org* is clearly the most marginal of the three identities under consideration, carrying with it a double stigma. Not only is anti-Semitism generally viewed as reprehensible in the West, but widespread distrust also surrounds the Arab/Islamist communities for whom Rami claims to speak.

Virtually all of the multi-media materials provided within *radioislam.org* are designed to promote "Ahmed Rami's struggle": "Behind this homepage is a group of freedom fighters from different countries in support of Ahmed Rami's struggle against the Jewish occupation and domination in Palestine and in the rest of the world. You too are welcome as a freedom fighter. Act now! Tomorrow it will be too late!" (Radio Islam [b]).

The quote above appears in conjunction with a call for financial donations to help Rami in his work. Rami insists that his Web site is "politically non-allied" and for all intents and purposes, his "work" may be understood as largely synonymous with the promotion of anti-Semitic propaganda. Likewise, "freedom fighters" may be understood as those who make financial donations to aid in its dissemination. *Radioislam.org*'s purely informational/ propaganda orientation distinguishes it from both *stormfront.org* and *kahane.org*, since in the case of the latter two Web sites, a clearly identifiable resistance identity "community" is being served. Like *stormfront.org* and *kahane.org*, *radioislam.org* is closely associated with both a dominant personality and a distinct ideology. However, unlike the other two Web sites, *radioislam.org*'s messages cannot easily be tied to any specific organization, or even in any clear sense, to a more broadly based social movement.

The ideology expressed within *radioislam.org* may best be understood as representing a relatively new and syncretistic form of anti-Semitism which emerged in the Arab world largely as a response to the ongoing Zionist colonization of Palestine and resulting Arab/Israeli conflict. Researchers who have paid close attention to this issue (e.g. Harkabi 1972; Lewis 1986, 1988; Nusse 1998), point out that while European anti-Semitism first appeared within some segments of the Arab Christian world in the 19th century, its spread was very slow and its impact relatively minor. Anti-Semitism, particularly in an "Islamist" form, did not become a more significant force in the Arab world until the later 1950s and 1960s. It was the repeated and unexpected defeat of Arab forces by Israel which is argued to have created a strong psychological need to account for the Arab inability to stand up to a community (the Jews) traditionally viewed by Arab Muslims as weak and cowardly in battle. According to Doran (2002) and Nusse (1998), this need was satisfied within some segments of Arab/Muslim society through the indigenization or "Islamisation" of European anti-Semitic beliefs.

The ideological framework provided by anti-Semitic tracts such as *The Protocols of the Learned Elders of Zion* has been adapted by some Islamists to reinterpret Koranic passages concerning the historic conflict between the prophet Mohammed and Jewish tribes (Nusse 1998). The Protocols appeared in Russia in the late 1800s, where they were used by professional instigators to promote pogroms against the Jews in that country. These forged documents ostensibly represent Jewish plans for world domination (Cohn 1981). They were translated as *The International Jew* by Henry Ford, in his newspaper the *Dearborn Independent*, from May to October in 1920, and came to have an important influence on the development of Nazi philosophy (Cohn 1981, 158). As Nusse observes, the Protocols, along with other anti-Semitic beliefs of Christian origin, enabled a new image of the Jews as representing a powerful threat: "The image of wretchedness and humiliation associated with the Jews in the traditional Islamic image, which was sustained by the strength and confidence of Islamic civilization until at least the 15th century, is now superceded by that of the powerful Jew, seriously threatening the Muslim community and the whole world" (Nusse 1998, 34).

The new understanding of Israel as the physical center of a powerful world Jewish conspiracy meant that the Arab/Muslim struggle against it no longer needed to be conceptualized in terms of a series of humiliating military defeats. Instead, such defeat is to be expected in the short term, with the long term struggle against Israel understood as a noble and redeeming religious duty (Doran 2002, 36).

Anti-Semitism, in its Arab/Islamist form, should be understood as an ideological current which has come to affect various institutions and sectors of Arab society, rather than the explicit philosophy of any particular Arab, or Islamist, group or movement. While the extent of its influence within the Arab and larger Muslim world is uncertain, anti-Semitic beliefs of European origin have clearly been incorporated into the outlook of some Islamist groups. For example, Article 22 of the original 1988 Charter of the Palestinian militant organization, Hamas, contains references to a global Jewish conspiracy:

> They were behind the French Revolution, the Communist revolution and most of the revolutions we heard and hear about, here and there. With their money they formed secret societies, such as Freemasons, Rotary Clubs, the Lions and others in different parts of the world for the purpose of sabotaging societies and achieving Zionist interests. With their money they were able to exploit their resources and spread corruption there. (Hamas 1988, 12)

Interestingly, the influence of such thinking has apparently faded within Hamas, with distinctions between Zionism and Judaism being made increasingly more explicit within this organization's political statements over time (see Hroub 2000, 49–51). It should also be mentioned that in general, Islamists understand Zionist aggression towards the Arabs as closely tied to the larger project of Western imperialism (Haddad 1991, Hroub 2000). This understanding generally predominates even when anti-Semitic elements are present in the outlook of Islamist organizations. In this sense, *radioislam.org*, with its proclaimed intent of building bridges with the West to confront the common threat posed by the Jews appears novel.

It is important to emphasize that much like the anti-Arab and anti-Muslim hate material which fills Kahanist Web sites, the anti-Semitic arguments put forward within *radioislam.org* are not racist in a narrow, technical sense. Unlike white separatist Web sites, neither Kahanist Web sites nor *radioislam.org* put forward any *explicit* theories or arguments concerning meaningful inherent/genetic differences between racial groups. The intent here is not to justify or downplay the hostility which the latter two identities display towards those they consider to be their enemies. Instead, I wish to point out that the racist

vs. "anti-racist" stance adopted by actors in each case may have important implications with respect to their Web strategies. For example, it will be made
clear in chapter 6 that omissions or assertions in identity-based propaganda
concerning the issue of race may affect a resistance identity's success in
building alliances with other movements. And as discussed below, there may
also be implications in terms of an organization's ability to produce Web-
based propaganda which sounds convincing. This is particularly the case
when the Arab/Israeli conflict is used as a point of reference to reinforce core
identity doctrine.

As previously indicated, the Islamist brand of anti-Semitism which characterizes *radioislam.org*'s content already constitutes an instance of syn-
cretism, or the assimilation of ideological elements originating from one belief system within another. With this in mind, it worth noting that of the
three resistance identities under consideration, the principle of "bricolage"
is relied upon most heavily within *radioislam.org*. Hebdige (1979), and others working from the British cultural studies tradition, have typically employed the term bricolage to refer to instances in which subcultures or other
marginalized actors have appropriated symbols or artifacts associated with
the dominant culture, and then "re-signified" them to reinforce their own
ideological outlook and sense of group identity. The safety pins, army
boots, and earrings adapted to suit the sub-cultural expressions of punk-
rockers provide a classic example. Similarly, Rami has brought together
printed texts, images, and audio recordings of highly diverse origins to reinforce his own world view within *radioislam.org*. Perhaps most notably, he
has attempted to re-signify anti-Semitic arguments traditionally associated
with a racist outlook to promote an agenda ostensibly designed to combat
racism.

To most potential visitors to this Web site, persistent attention to the
Arab/Israeli conflict will likely appear more "natural" within *radioislam.org*
than in the case of white separatist Web sites. Like white separatists, Rami
makes continuous reference to Palestinian suffering and Israeli war crimes in
order to justify his anti-Semitic world view. A key difference is that in the
case of white separatists, their overtly racist doctrine is likely to make their
proclaimed sympathy for the Palestinians difficult for many potential Web
site visitors to take seriously. Conversely, Rami is able to draw freely from
anti-Semitic sources—such as the writings of David Duke or Holocaust de-
nier Ernst Zundel—while simultaneously calling for justice for the Palestinians without necessarily appearing inconsistent or hypocritical. Such charges
may be dodged due to the fact that while *radioislam.org* provides extensive
anti-Semitic resources, including documents such as the *Protocols of the*

Learned Elders of Zion, materials which focus upon "racial difference" are excluded from this Web site. Likewise, while links are provided within *radioislam.org* to Holocaust revisionist Web sites such as that hosted by the *Institute for Historical Review* (*ihr.org*), no links are provided to the Web sites of white separatists.

Attempts to portray the universal threat posed by "Jewish racism" are embellished within *radioislam.org* not only through the selective exploitation of white separatist and holocaust revisionist materials, but also by drawing extensive attention to crimes and racism allegedly perpetrated by Jews against blacks. As with his stated support for the Palestinian cause, *radioislam.org*'s content also parallels white separatist propaganda by exploiting existing tensions between American blacks and Jews. Once again, however, Rami is able to do so without the "racist baggage" which might otherwise weaken his rhetoric. In addition to various Arab/Islamist and (Holocaust) revisionist resources, Rami both borrows from, and provides links to, radical black Web sites such as the *Blacks and Jews Newspage*. This Web site, which is affiliated with the American Black Muslim movement the Nation of Islam (NOI), attributes primary responsibility for the historic black slave trade to "the Jews." In fact, special praise is reserved within *radioislam.org* for the NOI's charismatic leader, Louis Farrakhan, with the latter being credited with "leading the Intifada against the Jewish occupation of the USA" (Radio Islam [c]). The fact that *radioislam.org* appears to be targeting both a white and/or "mainstream" audience as well as a black Muslim audience is a point which will receive further attention in chapter 6.

As suggested above, propaganda within *radioislam.org* derives much, if not most of its rhetorical appeal from the fact that its designer has been able to bring together texts originating from sources which are clearly ideologically incompatible to make a coherent argument. The writings of white supremacist David Duke, the recorded speeches of Black Muslim leader Louis Farrakhan, the U.S. foreign policy critique of Noam Chomsky, the Holocaust denial of Ernst Zundel, the anti-Zionist critique of Holocaust survivor Israel Shahak, the anti-Semitic reflections of Henry Ford, statements by Islamist clerics, quotes from Israeli, Iranian, and American politicians—along with countless other de-contextualized pieces of "information"—are brought together to tell a single story; the universal threat posed by a world Jewish conspiracy. The presentation of these diverse texts also appears designed to place an additional suggestion in the mind of the reader; if all of the groups and individuals in question share a common distrust or hatred of the Jews then perhaps there are good grounds for this universally shared hatred. Perversely,

Rami is able to assemble a "rainbow coalition" of interests within his Web site with which to confront the universal threat allegedly posed by world Jewry. The fact that such reasoning will likely remain either unconvincing or revolting to many or most Web users should not divert attention from the fact that Rami has been able exploit the underdetermined qualities of the WWW to optimal advantage. Within *radioislam.org*, a heavily stigmatized paradigm (anti-Semitism) appears to take on new life via the creative manipulation of hypertext.

Closing Remarks

The case studies above illustrate some of the characteristic ways in which three sets of stigmatized actors have responded to one another's presence within the unique environment of the WWW. Emphasis was placed on the fact that hypertext provides a novel and effective means for resistance identities to engage in propaganda warfare with declared enemies while simultaneously reinforcing their own sense of political mission and social/cultural identity. By exploiting the unusual features of the Web, actors representing each identity are able to take advantage of the proximity of both mainstream and "extremist" enemies; appropriating their texts and symbols to bring greater rhetorical force to their own respective doctrines and arguments. In fact, the more exposure these rival identities have to one another's material online, the more their own convictions and conspiracy theories appear to be reinforced. Further evidence of the self-referential nature of resistance identity Web activities will be presented in chapter 6.

The appeal of the arguments advanced by any given identity will almost certainly be heavily conditioned by the predispositions of anyone visiting their Web sites. Hence, as for the project identities considered in chapters 1 and 2, a tension exists with respect to the Web's usefulness to resistance identities in terms of its narrow-casting versus its broadcasting potential. At the same time, the symbolic and rhetorical uses of the Web considered in this chapter may be closely linked to more practical considerations such as maintaining ideological unity amongst widely dispersed SMOs and individuals belonging to one identity, or attracting new recruits or allies from outside the movement. In the next chapter, the Web's usefulness for addressing these and related concerns will be considered, using the same three resistance identities as points of reference. It will be demonstrated that the impossibility of clearly separating the Web's organizational, resource-sharing, and rhetorical properties constitutes more than simply a methodological challenge for the researcher. There are also significant implications for any social movement hoping to gain greater influence in society.

NOTES

1. *Stormfront.org*'s format was altered considerably following the period during which it was under observation for the purposes of this research, and the iron cross logo no longer dominates the homepage. By comparison, the site now has a less sensational, more mainstream appearance.

2. While Christian Identity doctrine is not the only religious influence within the white separatist movement it has generally been recognized as the most prevalent. For further discussion of Christian Identity and other religious belief systems associated with the far-right in North America see Barrett (1987) and Dobratz (2001).

3. See, for example *Christianity—Religion of the West* and other *stormfront.org* texts authored by Revilo P. Oliver.

4. As a number of social scientists (e.g. Barber 1996; Wallerstein 2003) have pointed out, expressions of ideological racism are incompatible with the needs of global capital, which relies upon the availability of the cheap labor made available by both the offshoring of some types of work on the one hand and continuing immigration of minority groups on the other.

Chapter Six

Hate and Holy War
on the WWW

PART II: THE STRUGGLE FOR INFLUENCE

Forget about Buddha, Allah, Jesus and Jehovah—
Hurry down doomsday the bugs are taking over!

(Elvis Costello, *Hurry Down Doomsday*)

In many respects, internet technology appears ideally suited for resistance identities whose wide geographic dispersal and organizational looseness often appears to mirror the network character of the WWW. Tom Metzger of the White Aryan Resistance (WAR) has described the white separatist movement to which his organization belongs in the following manner: " . . .there is no center. It's like associations or networking. No fancy headquarters, or store fronts, or even book stores. Yet it's all over the place" (Garner 1996, 282–283). And it is certainly not difficult to cite cases where the internet has assisted social movements widely viewed as extremist. It is well known, for example, that Al-Qaeda and its affiliates have used this technology to plan and coordinate acts of terrorism, that neo-Nazi skinheads have used the Net to organize violent demonstrations at European football matches, that the internet makes it easier for the Ku Klux Klan to plan large street marches, and so on. Furthermore, as discussed in the previous chapter, the propaganda produced by these and countless other resistance identities is readily accessible online. Yet, despite the apparent benefits which the internet appears to provide militant fringe groups, it remains unclear just how much this technology may help them to further their political agendas or increase their social influence within information-based societies such as the United States.

In this chapter I will consider the potential significance of the WWW in relation to the long-term viability and success of the three resistance identities examined in chapter 5. The first section will address the Web's importance for social movement integration and growth. Specifically, attention will be directed to the ways in which actors in each network have been able to elaborate upon the identity building and propaganda practices discussed in chapter 5, developing strategies which might allow them to exercise greater social influence and political clout. The primary focus here will be upon the case of white separatism, a social movement which already encompasses a widespread, but shifting and unsteady collection of smaller organizations and networks. Of the three resistance identities, it also represents the movement with the longest history in North America, and the one most concerned with transforming American society as a whole and not just U.S. foreign policy. Evidence suggests that sophisticated Web sites such as *stormfront.org* are well positioned to play a steering or agenda-setting role with respect to maintaining ideological unity across organizational boundaries within the larger white racist movement. More generally, the use of identity-based media infrastructures may allow fringe identities to establish greater credibility as social movements—at least in the eyes of their target audiences—and provide them with additional means for appealing to new recruits.

In the second main section of this chapter, I consider the Web's amenability for coalition building among resistance identities which in most respects appear to have little in common. As was indicated in chapters 1 and 2, the long-standing solidarity between Christian fundamentalists and Jewish Zionists has allowed these identities to wield greater influence with respect to American foreign policy than either one could hope to do independently. The possibility that the Web may aid more marginalized actors such as white separatists, Islamists, or Jewish ultranationalists to achieve solidarity with other social movements could prove significant with respect to their ability to gain greater credibility or social/political influence. As will be demonstrated, however, alliance building among fringe groups on the Web is not a straightforward matter. Rhetorical networks are often difficult to distinguish from organizational ones, a phenomenon which makes the authenticity and/or importance of such activity difficult to assess. It also remains unclear whether allegiances forged entirely through means of the internet will have the same strength or staying power as those developed through interpersonal contact.

In the final section of this chapter, an attempt will be made to reassess some of the contradictory implications of Web use by resistance identities with reference not only to the phenomena discussed in this chapter, but also the rhetorical uses of the Web considered in chapter 5. On the one hand, it will be argued that the WWW provides resistance identities with a unique resource;

one which could potentially contribute to their long-term viability and coherence as social movements. The Web allows resistance identity organizations to experiment with their ideological frameworks and alliance-building strategies with a degree of flexibility and responsiveness to contingency impossible through the use of other media. However, it will also be maintained that despite the apparent boon which internet technology appears to offer militant fringe identities, its ultimate value in furthering the political success of relevant organizations remains in doubt. In important respects, the very qualities of hypertext which so easily lend themselves to inter-organizational networking and the enhancement of identity-based propaganda may also contribute to the increased marginalization of their doctrine, while reinforcing the perceived authority of legitimating voices on the WWW.

Social Movement Integration and Growth

For those social movements which have been stigmatized and relegated to the margins of society, there is a very real chance that the WWW may contribute significantly to their potential consolidation and growth as social movements over the long term. Evidence for this may readily be found within the Web sites and Web rings of the American white separatist movement. Web sites such as *stormfront.org* hold particular importance in this regard due to their double role as both self-contained information resources, and as gateways to vast numbers of other racist Web sites. With respect to both of these functions, it should be recalled that *stormfront.org*'s utility as an effective propaganda and recruitment vehicle for the far right has been enhanced by the fact that attempts are not made within it to discredit racist groups not directly affiliated with Don Black's Knights of the Ku Klux Klan. Instead, *stormfront.org* provides information originating from and/or intended for use by individuals affiliated with a wide range of racist organizations. Similarly, links are provided to Web sites hosted by major organizations on the far right such as the National Alliance, the Sheriff's Posse Commitatus, and Christian Identity Aryan Nations, as well as those of countless less prominent racist groups and individuals.

As the Anti-Defamation League (ADL) has reported, *stormfront.org* "has served as a veritable supermarket of online hate, stocking its shelves with many forms of anti-Semitism and racism" (Anti-Defamation League 2001b: 2). Such is readily apparent when activating *stormfront.org*'s internal *Text Library* link, which takes the reader to Web pages listing collections of articles corresponding to the following topics: *White Nationalist Issues, "Affirmative Action" and anti-White bias, Immigration in America, Racial Differences, Revisionism, National Socialism, Zionism & Judaism.* Each of these links in turn leads to large numbers of texts, many of which have been sub-divided into more specialized categories. Significantly, the main topics dealt with within each grouping of texts correspond in large measure both to the central concerns and to the specific branches of the white supremacy movement. One result is that this internal categorization of resource materials is largely mirrored in the structure of *stormfront.org*'s *Links Portal*. Web links provided within this section of the site are not listed in random order, but are clustered under such headings as *White Nationalism/White Patriotism*, *Ku Klux Klan*, *Christian Identity*, *Legal Defense*, *White Power Music*, *Revisionism*, *International*, etc.

The parallel internal/external structure of *stormfront.org* means that this Web site is able to function as more than simply a racist encyclopedia or supermarket of stocked shelves. Visitors to *stormfront.org* are encouraged not only to approach this Web site as a self-enclosed unit, but also to read any given text(s) held within it as part of larger documents extending beyond the site and dealing with (racist) areas of interest specific to different users. In theory, such multi-linear readings of texts are encouraged within any Web site which provides internal and/or external links. However, the practical dimensions of this aspect of hypertext have been particularly well developed within *stormfront.org*. As was made clear in the previous chapter, Black has acted to ensure that his Web site remains a dominant node within and among various overlapping white racist Web rings. In practical terms, this means that a user with a particular interest in the specific programs or activities of the Ku Klux Klan, European skinheads, or numerous other groups may easily access their Web rings via *stormfront.org*. It also means that those less familiar with racist doctrine, but who have an interest in a particular area of concern to white separatists, such as affirmative action or immigration, may be *drawn* to Black's Web site through a large number of potential hypertext pathways.

Stormfront.org's status a dominant node within larger networks of racist Web sites means that it may serve both as a gravitational center to which Web surfers (primarily identity members) may find themselves drawn, as well as a providing an important point from which ideas and information may flow outward into other networks of Web sites. *Stormfront.org*'s "location" is thus significant from a communicative and organizational standpoint. As Diani (2001, 118) observes, the internet provides social movements—which may encompass a myriad of widely dispersed organizations and memberships—with the potential opportunity to transform their constituents "into a densely aggrieved population, thus solving one key problem of mobilization." And the idea that an alternative white separatist Web-media infrastructure will soon become an essential weapon in the hands of a silent white majority is implicit in much of the commentary within *stormfront.org*. Charismatic leaders of the movement such as Don Black, David Duke, and William Pierce have long hoped that the internet might serve to enable greater white power activism, leading to the eventual creation of a white American state (Goldman 2001, 1).

The ambitious attitude that many white nationalist leaders have adopted toward alternative media may be seen in the following excerpt taken from a text entitled *Program of the National Alliance*. It is worth noting that the ADL (1998, 1) has declared the National Alliance to be the largest and most dangerous racist organization in the United States. The National Alliance Web site, *natall.org*, from which this passage was taken, is regularly endorsed within *stormfront.org*:

> Even our mass media do not attempt to compete with those of the enemy by winning larger audiences. Ours merely aim at reaching the entire White population with our message and making it continually accessible to those who are responsive. We understand that by far the larger part of the White population is and will continue to be more interested in spectator sports or *Star Trek* than in our message, and we will not try to wean them away from their amusements. Only in the very last stages of revolutionary development will we be competing with the Jews for the attention of this mass element, but by then the competition will be on our terms. Our mass media, however, eventually will provide the indispensable tool for communicating with all the elements of the White population during a critical transitional period between the collapse of one way of life and the establishment of another. A successful attainment of governmental power will not be possible without this tool. (National Alliance [a], 2)

While the idea that a massive white power groundswell will soon shake the foundations of the American political establishment might at first sound absurd, it is important to recognize at least two points in relation to white separatist strategizing. First, goals more modest than complete racial separation are regularly advocated in Web sites such as *stormfront.org*. These may include such potentially attainable goals as the outlawing of abortion[1] or the need to roll back affirmative action policies frequently accompanied by online petitions and/or calls for conventional forms of political lobbying. Secondly, leaders on the far right recognize that they face a credibility problem with respect to presenting their long-term goal of a "white state" as realistic. The latter point is made clear in the following excerpt taken from a broadcast by former National Alliance leader Dr. William Pierce[2] (1997), and reproduced in print under the title *America, Israel and Iraq: Exposing the Warmongers*, which appears within *stormfront.org*'s *Text Library*:

> Many people have written to me or spoken to me and have told me that they agree with my analysis of the situation in America and that they share my values and

my concerns. But they also have been much more pessimistic than I am. They tell me, "Oh we have waited too long to take action. It is too late to save this country now. Just look at the numbers. Look at how many Mexicans and Asians already are in our country, and millions more are coming in every year. If we try to straighten things out it will become a bloody mess, and millions of our own people will be killed. Besides, there's no way we can unite our people for such a struggle, because the Jewish grip on the media is too strong." And so they do nothing. (Pierce 1997, 4)

In light of the "problem" identified above, it is worth noting that the white separatist preoccupation with creating alternative media infrastructures, and in particular, Black's attempts to make *stormfront.org* into a vast racist Web portal, complements this Web site's content in a manner which appears to hold rhetorical significance. The Simon Wiesenthal Center has charted well over two thousand racist Web sites (Appleby 2002). Compared to most of these, *stormfront.org* represents a relatively large and elaborate Web site, and one which has remained popular among white racists. Alexa Internet, which offers free tracking services, placed *stormfront.org* as number 28,409 in traffic rankings in 2001. By comparison, the Anti-Defamation League's (ADL) "anti-hate" Web site (*adl.org*) was ranked 59,570 (McKelvey 2001). The point here is that regardless of the actual strength and long-term viability of white separatism as a social movement, *stormfront.org*'s expansive *Links Portal*, which lists and provides ready access to countless racist Web sites, may well leave visitors with the impression that the white separatist agenda is less unrealistic, and the movement far more vital, they had previously imagined.

The potential importance of the integrative function of Web sites such as *stormfront.org* becomes clearer if it is kept in mind that the concerns which have dominated the agendas of various racist organizations in America have not remained static throughout their history. For example, one of the original concerns of the Ku Klux Klan in the United States was with stemming the flow of Catholic immigration. This emphasis was eventually overshadowed by a commitment to keeping blacks legally subservient to whites. Today the main preoccupation of this and other branches of the white separatist movement is with "Jewish power" (Barrett 1987, 20–22, 347–351). Furthermore, differing circumstances presently shape the agendas of various white supremacist organizations based throughout North America and Europe. While white nationalists in contemporary America worry about Hispanic and Asian immigration, racists in Germany and France hope to stem the "Muslim threat" posed by migrants from Turkey and North Africa.

The Web's capacity to facilitate greater ideological unity among widely dispersed white power organizations has not been lost on white separatist leaders. Charismatic leaders such as Don Black, David Duke, and William

Pierce were quick to recognize the potential importance of alternative media such as the internet for unifying the long-term agenda of their movement. Not surprisingly, these individuals host some of the better known and/or most elaborate white separatist Web sites. Furthermore, the influence of these and other key personalities has become highly visible within more extensive racist Web rings. For example, Black, whose credentials as a Web site designer are now well established, has played an active consulting role for other racists attempting to start up their own Web sites. In addition to *stormfront .org*, Black either hosts or co-hosts a series of Web sites including *White Nationalist News Agency*, *White Pride World Wide*, and *Blitzcast* (Anti-Defamation League 2001b: 5). He is also responsible for the *Jew Watch* Web pages discussed in chapter 5; made accessible via an extensive number of URLs and mirror sites.

Significantly, the writings and speeches of Duke, Pierce, and other well-known racist and anti-Semitic commentators such as Yggdrasil[3] and Ernst Zundel, are regularly featured within a broad range of Web sites having no direct affiliation with these personalities. While theories pertaining to both Jewish conspiracies and racial difference have a long history, personalities such as Black, Pierce, and Zundel have worked diligently to readapt racist frameworks to contend with contemporary social and political realities. The potential importance of these and other movement intellectuals in guiding the white nationalist agenda should not be ignored, particularly in light of the off-line activities discussed above. The ease with which "authoritative" texts may be disseminated and reproduced online means that the writings of key personalities may quickly become ubiquitous within resistance identity Web rings, providing inspiration and a common point of focus for disparate organizations within the movement.

The role which the Web has come to play for unifying resistance identity discourse was readily apparent in the aftermath of the 9/11 terrorist attacks. In fact, all three resistance identities considered in this and the previous chapter were quick to exploit these traumatic events to reinforce their respective arguments concerning identity movement enemies. In the case of white separatism, this meant drawing attention to the central role allegedly played by America's Zionist Occupation Government (ZOG) in precipitating the attacks. In this light, it should be noted that while a few racist Web sites—such as that hosted by the Council of Conservative Citizens (*cofcc.org*)—directed most of their ire against Arabs and Muslims, most of the more prominent racist Web sites attributed primary responsibility for the tragedy upon America's "immoral" and/or "foolish" support for the state of Israel. This support was in turn attributed to Jewish control over the American political establishment. Particularly visible online were a series of articles on this topic by

David Duke. Such texts as *Will they dare to ask why?*, *What Price Israel?*, and *The Big Lie*, circulated rapidly on the WWW and remain available for viewing within numerous racist Web sites.[4]

When considered in light of white separatist doctrine, it may not surprise the reader to learn that white separatist leaders exploited the events of 9/11 to reinforce Jewish conspiracy theories. However, it should also be kept in mind that if individuals such as Duke and Pierce expect their interpretations of reality to be accepted by the white separatist rank and file, guiding ideas such as those concerning ZOG must be continuously reinforced. One might reasonably have expected that many, if not most racist individuals would have spontaneously followed the lead of the (mainstream) neo-conservative and/or religious right by directing most of their hostility towards Arabs and Muslims rather than towards Jews in the wake of 9/11. This possibility, and the ideological tensions which it reflects, are visible in the following exchange taken from *stormfront.org*'s discussion forum:

> Post 1) . . . Islam is everything democracy and freedom is against, and Bin Laden would love nothing more than to transform the world into what Afghanistan became when the Taliban took control! That's the major reason he attacked the US! There isn't ONE Islamic country where you have democracy and freedom, and there isn't ONE Islamic country without oil that doesn't have a collapsing economy. These guys are scum! Anyone who's lived with them knows that! They even kill their own constantly (for no reason at all, example: Talking) . . .
>
> Post 2) You're very sick indeed. Or perhaps a Jew. The Islamic countries have what they want. You want to bomb them and kill them because they don't want what you want.
>
> Post 3) (original speaker): All that is Bull****! I say bomb them cause they want everyone to be as oppressed and backwards as they are and will not rest until they get their goal! They would love nothing more! . . . (Stormfront.org 2001, 17–18)

The possibility that "popular" racist understandings of events such as 9/11 may diverge from the white separatist "orthodoxy," along with the perceived need to hold this possibility in check, has clearly been a concern of white separatist leaders. Many of the latter have emphasized the desirability of establishing a world-wide common front against ZOG which would include radicalized Muslims, a topic which will receive further attention in the next section of this chapter. In fact, the exchange cited above was part of a discussion thread preceded by the full text of David Duke's (2001, 1–13) article *The Big Lie: The true reason behind the attack of September 11*. The point being made here is not that racist debate concerning this article ended with everybody agreeing that the Jews pose a more serious threat to Americans than other "racial groups," but rather that white separatist leaders appear to have achieved at least some measure of success as agenda setters within the movement. By exploiting the Web to keep key ideas foremost in the minds of their followers, they have helped set the parameters of racist debate.

It should be noted that the exploitation of moral shocks, such as those surrounding 9/11, may help social movements recruit individuals who previously had little or no personal contact with members of the recruiting organization (Jasper & Poulson 1995). While this would be very difficult to measure with respect to the highly amorphous resistance identity networks considered here, it is clear that all three identities regularly attempt to exploit moral shocks to enhance propaganda within their Web sites. Perhaps the most commonly utilized technique involves the juxtaposition of shocking visual imagery with "wake up calls" directed at the appropriate target audience. For example, Jewish ultranationalist Web sites such as *masada.org* regularly provide gruesome photographs depicting the aftermath of real or alleged Palestinian terrorist attacks. These images are invariably accompanied by sympathetic descriptions of the Israeli victims and calls for Jews to *finally* recognize the need for (greater) Israel to expel its Arab population. Similar tactics are employed within white separatist Web sites where vivid graphics and/or statistics are often used to draw attention to such phenomena as non-white immigration and minority crime. A good illustration is provided within the Web site of the Sheriffs Posse Comitatus [a]. Here, a link is provided to governmental Immigration and Naturalization statistics by activating the following banner: "JOG (Jewish Occupation Government) has notified the American public of the 1999 census that Whites are now a minority in the state of California. Is your state next? When will you wake up sheeple?"[5] (Sheriffs Posse Comitatus [a]).

The potential usefulness of exploitation of moral shocks for recruitment purposes is easier to appreciate if one keeps in mind that each resistance identity is attempting to increase its membership base from within a specific ethnic community or sub-community. For example, the Kahanist tactic of displaying gruesome images involving Arab terrorism is clearly designed to appeal primarily to those "conservative" Jews who may already hold highly negative attitudes towards Arabs. While propaganda within Kahanist Web sites may appear crude or distasteful to many, it is based upon a premise likely to hold strong common sense appeal within certain segments of the Israeli/Jewish community; namely, the impossibility of making a lasting peace with the Arabs. The emotional pressure supplied by such imagery may prove significant for gaining converts from among those individuals already predisposed to Kahanist arguments. Conversely, left-wing Jews are clearly not the main target of Kahanist recruitment efforts. Instead, Jewish "peaceniks" are regularly depicted within Kahanist Web sites as traitors on a moral par (or worse) with the Arab/Muslim enemy.[6]

White separatist recruitment efforts also appear to be aimed at a specific sub-community. While "white Americans" clearly constitute the idealized recruitment pool, evidence suggests that individuals associated with the more mainstream political and religious right appear to be the primary propaganda target. Rhetoric concerning the Arab/Israeli conflict is highly significant in this regard since neo-conservative and Christian fundamentalist organizations in the United States invariably profess strong support for Israel's expansionist policies, frequently attempting to legitimate this support through references to biblical prophecy. As stated earlier, *stormfront.org* and other leading racist Web sites provide extensive materials designed to convince readers that Christianity is inextricably tied to both the previous greatness of Western civilization and the inherent racial superiority of "whites." White separatist references to 9/11, therefore, may help cast doubt upon the political and religious correctness of supporting Israel. Specifically, the supposed role played by the Jews and/or Israel with respect to both America's present state of "moral and cultural decay" and the enhancement of external threats to the nation are emphasized by white separatists. Both of the latter topics also represent major sources of concern within the more mainstream religious and political right.[7]

The strictly propaganda and "information resource" orientation of *radioislam .org* distinguishes it from the white separatist and Kahanist cases. As was mentioned in chapter 5, Ahmed Rami claims not to be affiliated with any specific political organization or interest group. Furthermore, relatively little energy is expended within *radioislam.org* for the purpose of defaming potential Arab or Islamist rivals. While this Web site does contain criticism of pro-Western Arab regimes and the Palestinian Authority, most material focuses upon the alleged machinations of the Jewish enemy. In fact, Rami's struggle appears to consist of making the "truth" known to anyone who cares to listen, rather than promoting particular forms of political action within specific countries. Clearly, Rami would likely have a very difficult time mobilizing any kind of meaningful political activity among Muslims in the United States, the country whose foreign policy is most decisive with respect to the Arab/Israeli conflict. Well-established Arab/Muslim political and cultural organizations in America have generally taken pains to distinguish opposition to Zionism from anti-Semitism; a distinction intentionally blurred within *radioislam.org*.

Nonetheless, some rhetoric within *radioislam.org* may hold resonance within particular Islamist organizations or other social movements in various parts of the world. It was previously indicated, for example, that a great deal of attention is given in this Web site to the African American social movement the Nation of Islam.[8] Rami repeatedly claims solidarity with this resistance identity, offering high praise for its leader Louis Farrakhan as one of his personal heroes. In this light, it is worth noting that the well-known Mid-East expert and neo-conservative, Daniel Pipes—whose *Campus Watch* Web Site was referred to in chapter 2—has suggested that while the Black Muslim movement is becoming more (Sunni) orthodox with respect to their religious beliefs, this community also appears to be becoming more radicalized politically. In addition, Rami is reputed to have direct ties with the Institute for Historical Review, a European anti-Semitic organization dedicated to promoting the claims of Holocaust deniers (ADL 2001). These points call attention to the issues considered in the next section; namely, the possibility that strong ties may be forged amongst identities with roots in radically divergent cultural, political, and/or geographic contexts, and the further difficulty of assessing the depth or even the existence of such ties when they are advertised in the Web sites of relevant organizations or persons.

Building Alliances: Virtual and Real

I will now consider two instances in which the WWW has played a clear role in resistance identity attempts to surmount ideological and/or social network barriers separating them from other social movements. The first example concerns substantial cooperation between Kahanists and Hindu fundamentalists in the form of joint activism both on and offline. The second case involves what appear to be alliance building practices involving white separatists on the one hand, and Islamists and/or project identities belonging to the Arab/Israeli peace camp on the other. Unlike the first example, significant levels of cooperative activity do not appear to be occurring among the latter identities. Instead, the appearance of alliance building among the groups in question is largely the effect of propaganda techniques and unreciprocated overtures engaged in by white separatist organizations. As will be seen, the existence of both real and pseudo-alliances on the WWW, and the difficulty of distinguishing clearly between the two, may have important implications with respect to both the dynamics of propaganda warfare which crosses identity lines, and public perceptions concerning the threat posed by various groups.

It was demonstrated in chapter 5 that the unique experiences and beliefs of resistance identities may condition the manner in which they make use of the WWW. This is visible in the case of Kahanist Web rings, which generally remain isolated from those of the Zionist mainstream. It should also be pointed out that Kahanists actively oppose the politically important alliance between the two most influential expressions of Zionism in the United States; mainstream Jewish ethnic nationalism as embodied by such organizations as AIPAC, the American Jewish Congress, the Zionist Organization of America, etc., and Christian fundamentalism as represented by political lobbies such as the Christian Coalition, the Jerusalem Prayer Team, and countless grassroots Christian fundamentalist organizations across the country. Mainstream Jewish Zionist organizations have generally been willing to overlook anti-Semitic tendencies within the Christian right, choosing to focus instead upon the unqualified support and political lobbying efforts through which Christian Zionists have attempted to facilitate Israeli expansionism (Bruce 1998, 180). By contrast, Kahanists have consistently portrayed the evangelism of Christian fundamentalists as an existential threat to the Jewish people.

Despite the zeal with which the Christian right has worked to support many of the same goals pursued by Kahanists, the latter have persistently portrayed the former as yet another threat to Jewish survival. Specifically, attempts to convert Jews to Christianity, most notably through sponsorship of the Jews for Jesus movement, are viewed by Kahanists (and quite understandably by many other Jews) as attempts to bring an end to the existence of independent Jewish cultural and religious traditions, and hence to Judaism itself. A five-part series in the JDL Web site appearing under the title *The Quiet Holocaust: The Perfidious Plot to Convert Jews*, describes attempts by various Christian organizations to convert Jews as "perhaps the most insidious, dangerous, and hateful" form of anti-Semitism presently in existence (Avraham 2001, 1). However, while Kahanist attitudes concerning this and other issues have contributed to their alienation from the Zionist mainstream, Kahanists have been able to find common cause with another resistance identity which shares their hostility towards proselytizing Christians, leftists, and, most importantly, Muslims.

A militant Hindu Web site entitled "Hindu Unity" (*hinduunity.org*) now functions online in a manner similar to *stormfront.org* and *kahane.org*. Specifically, this Web site has become the predominant gateway to a larger resistance identity Web ring. *Hinduunity.org* represents the ideology of Bajrang Dal, a Hindu ultranationalist movement well established throughout most of India (Hindu Unity [a]). The movement has been involved in many violent clashes with Muslims throughout the country including a campaign which led to the destruction of the ancient Ayodhya Mosque in Northern India in 1992. It has also been involved in attacks on evangelical Christians including one which led to the violent deaths of an Australian missionary and his two young sons in January of 1999 (*Compass News Direct* 2001). *Hinduuinty.org* regularly demonizes internationally known fundamentalist Christians such as Pat Robertson, as well as Catholic missionaries and other expressions of Christianity in India. However, the majority of hostile propaganda within this and similar Web sites is reserved for Muslims. A statement which appeared within *hinduunity.org* following the second anniversary of 9/11 is typical of this Web site's sweeping condemnation of Islam:

> Today, Sept 11th is a sad day for HinduUnity.org as it remembers and prays for our brave men and women who died serving during the WTC disaster. We pray for the families who lost their loved ones in this tragedy. Our wounds shall never heal. Let the Muslims of America and rest of the world know in clear terms that we will not forget nor forgive what Islam and only Islam was responsible for during September 11th, 2001. Let the world know that Islam is not ONLY an American problem but a problem for the rest of the world. Wherever there is a Muslim presence, there will always be terror. The source of this terror is the *Koran* itself. (Hindu Unity [b])

The quote reproduced above appeared beneath a photograph of the (intact) World Trade Center. An Indian flag adorns the left side of the photograph, with an Israeli flag displayed to the right. Significantly, the integration of Israeli symbols within a Hindu fundamentalist Web page display does not represent an anomaly. Praise for Israel and/or the "Jewish people" within Hindu fundamentalist Web sites are now commonplace. For example, *Sword of Truth*, a Web magazine linked to by *Hinduunity.org*, discusses early support for Zionism on the part of Hindu patriots who bravely stood against the "leftist/Muslim/anti-Zionist alliance," which allegedly held a stranglehold on the Indian political establishment before the hard-line Hindu-nationalist BJP party came to power.[9] The Webzine also cites biblical evidence for the existence of ancient bonds and cooperation between Jews and Hindus.[10]

Much of the propaganda within *Hinduunity.org* and other Hindu fundamentalist Web sites directly addresses Jews as well as Hindus. For example, Israeli victims of Palestinian attacks are often listed alongside instances of Indian Muslim violence against Hindus to provide additional illustrations of "Islamic terror." A recent action alert concerning a commemorative stamp issued by the United States Postal Service symbolizing the Muslim holiday of Eid, reads as follows:

> THEY CELEBRATE! WHILE WE MOURN!
> Hindus, Jews and all freedom loving citizens of the U.S.A. are hearby strongly requested NOT TO PURCHASE THIS STAMP of shame, sorrow and pain. If you do, then you have become part of the problem on Sept 11th . . .
> (Hindu Unity [c])

In addition to openly identifying with Jewish ultranationalist concerns, *hinduunity.org* promotes links to several dozen Kahanist Web sites under the heading "Israel Forever." These include links to the better known Kahanist sites, including those hosted by the Jewish Defense League, Kahane.org, and masada 2000, each of which was referred to in chapter 5. Similarly, Kahanist Web sites including *Kahane.org* and *jdl.org* promote links to *Hinduuinty.org*. These links are generally accompanied by expressions of support for organizations associated with the identity being linked to. For example, a link entitled *JDL Supports Hindu Unity* is accompanied by the following phrase: "The Jewish Defense League fully supports the efforts of our Hindu allies in light of the fight against Arab terror; please show your support by visiting *Hinduunity.org*" (Jewish Defense League [f]). This gesture is reciprocated within *hinduunity.org*, where visitors are informed that "HINDUUNITY.ORG SUPPORTS J.D.L TO THE FULLEST!" (Hindu Unity [d]).

Cooperation between militant Hindus and Jews extends beyond the intermingling of their respective Web rings and expressions of solidarity online. Hindu fundamentalists marched alongside Kahanists in the Salute to Israel Parade held annually in New York. And on June 1, 2001, Kahanists joined a protest against the treatment of Hindus in Afghanistan by the Taliban regime outside of the United Nations headquarters (Murphy 2001). Hindus affiliated with *hinduunity.org* have also written to Congress urging that the two major Kahanist organizations, Kach and Kahane Chai, be removed from the State Department's list of foreign terrorist organizations. However, perhaps the most noteworthy form of cooperation between the two resistance identities concerns their joint attempts to ensure the continuation of their propaganda efforts online.

In December 2000, *Kahane.org* was forced to find a new ISP after the Brooklyn-based company Scorpions Communications announced that it would no longer host the Kahanist Web site. Scorpions Communications had been receiving complaints from members of the public, and concerns had also been raised by some of *kahane.org*'s commercial partners (Murphy 2001). Michael Guzofsky, director of the Hatikva Jewish Identity Center, and a leading Kahanist organizer in Brooklyn, had signed a contract with the center six months earlier. After the contract was terminated, Guzofsky was able to convince Gary Wardell—a Christian admirer of Kahane who runs a small business as a Web site designer and Web Service Provider—to host *kahane.org*. In May of 2001, *hinduunity.org* experienced similar problems to *kahane.org* after complaints were made that the Web site advocated violence against Muslims and evangelical Christians (*Compass News Direct* 2001). Immediately after the Web site was shut down, Rohit Vyasmaan, who helps run *hinduunity.org*, contacted Guzofsky, who in turn contacted Wardell. Both Web sites now share the same server, and Guzofsky has stated that if *hinduunity.org* is ever shut down again, *Kahane.org* would provide them with a mirror site (Murphy 2001).

In his consideration of social movements and contentious politics, Ayers (1999, 135) observes that internet technology allows the diffusion of ideas and tactics between individuals and groups to occur very rapidly. He also suggests that the internet may make cultural and interpersonal linkages less relevant to the diffusion of contentious politics. With this in mind, it is worth noting that cooperation between Jewish and Hindu ultranationalists appears to have been based entirely upon recognition of a common Muslim enemy, and was undertaken without any mutual attention to the religious and cultural traditions of the allied identities (Murphy 2001). However, it should also be pointed out that the two communities reside in close proximity in Brooklyn, and it is unclear whether the high levels of mutual trust between the two resistance identities could have been achieved in the absence of regular interpersonal contact. There is at least some empirical evidence that high levels of trust among members of electronically mediated networks are unlikely to develop in the absence of such contact (Fukuyama 1999).

In addition to interpersonal contact, it is important to note that trust between Kahanists and Hindu fundamentalists and their enthusiasm for joint activism has almost certainly been influenced by additional factors, particularly the rapid expansion of economic, intelligence, and military ties between India and Israel since 1992 (Hanley 2003; Janmohamed 2003). Closer ties between the two countries have been encouraged by the Pentagon, and are reflected in the growing cooperation between the recently formed U.S. Indian Political Action Committee (USINPAC) and the American Israel Public Affairs Committee (AIPAC). On July 16, 2003, a joint Capitol Hill forum was held between the United States, USINPAC, the American Jewish Committee, and AIPAC. Congressman David Ackerman stated his enthusiasm for this "great marriage." He also commented that the major problem for India and Israel concerns the fact that "Israel is surrounded by 120 million Muslims [while] India has 120 million Muslims [within its borders]" (Hanley 2003, 33).

The issue of trust is also relevant with respect to the other "alliances" considered in this section. The first concerns repeated attempts by white supremacists to cultivate ties with Islamists. For example, the FBI recently arrested Joshua Caleb Sutter, a member of a Christian Identity group called the Church of the Sons of Yaweh, when he attempted to purchase an illegal firearm. Sutter had previously functioned as the Aryan Nations "Minister for Islamic Liaison" (Roddy 2003). Sutter claims that while in that role he had attempted to form alliances (apparently without success) with anti-American Muslim militants after the events of 9/11 (Roddy 2003). Significantly, attempts by racist organizations to cultivate Arab/Islamist support are highly visible on the WWW. In addition to exploiting the Arab/Israeli conflict to promote anti-Semitism, many white separatist Web sites contain statements expressing some measure of sympathy or solidarity with Arabs and/or Islamic militants. For example, in a radio broadcast transcript made available in *stormfront.org*, William Pierce comments on the depravity and corruption of the American political establishment as follows:

> One can sympathize with those who lash out violently against this situation. One can understand and sympathize with their anger and frustration, even if one does not agree with their tactics. One can even understand the Islamic fundamentalists who denounce America as the "Great Satan" and regard this country as a danger to the whole world. We don't have to accept Islam to agree with them that American society has become dangerously pathological. A self-destructive society which has aircraft carriers and nuclear weapons is a danger to everyone. (Pierce 1997, 4)

The Web site of the National Alliance, the organization formerly led by Pierce, also makes periodic reference to a coming global uprising against ZOG which would at least temporarily unite disparate ethnic identities in the fight against "Jewish supremacy." The comments below were made by National Alliance member Alfred Strom in a radio broadcast entitled *World War IV* (archived within natvan.org), and follow from discussion of alleged Jewish control over U.S. policies in the Middle East:

> I think that what they are doing now, as they did in Germany in the 1920s and in Spain of Ferdinand and Isabella, is more than anything else giving the intelligent and informed people of the world a graduate education in Jewish hubris, Jewish racism, Jewish supremacism, and the Jewish megalomaniac desire to rule the world. And out of that awareness a broad front will arise. It's our job to make sure that there is a substantial White American, White Canadian, White European, White Autralasian, and White South African participation in that inevitable broad front against Jewish supremacism, and that the end result is the self-preservation and assured survival of our race upon this planet. (Strom 2003, 5)

In one rather bizarre example, willingness is even shown to modify racist dogma to demonstrate solidarity with the Palestinians. This may be seen in the Web site of the Sheriff's Posse Commitatus (*posse-commitatus.org*), a racist organization strongly influenced by Christian Identity doctrine. The following remarks appear within a text headed *Responses to the bombing of the World Trade Center*:

> It is said . . . The friend of my enemy is my enemy! Well today we were given the opportunity to learn that our 'friends' in 'Israel' have caused us to be an enemy of a strange lot of people. Bet you didn't know that the Arabs [of Israel] are related to the true Israelites spoken of in the WORD of GOD. True Israelites are

the seedline of Jacob, son of Issac who was the son of Abraham [Abraham fathered Ismael [not Israel] through wife's handmaiden, and thus the arab relatives] . . . (Sheriff's Posse-Comitatus [b])

Perhaps not surprisingly, Web-based "evidence" of an alliance between white supremacists and Islamists has become a source of moral panic within the Web sites of some resistance identities, particularly those hosted by Jewish ultranationalists. For example, under the general heading "ANTI-JEWISH ALERTS," the *Jewish Watchdog* Web site warns readers about a white racist Web site entitled *Jews in Technology*: "This is a dangerous site. An affiliation between the Aryans and the 'Palestinians' is not something I would want to have to deal with. Then again maybe they would wipe each other out!" (Jewish Watch Dog, 2).

A text appearing within the right-wing Israeli Web site *Arutz 7* discusses the ties allegedly being consolidated between white separatists and "the Muslim world" under the heading *Jew Hatred in America*. Notably, *radioislam.org* receives special attention (ben Hyka 2002, 1). Similarly, the Web site of the Jewish Defense Organization (*jdo.org*) features an article under the heading *Islamic Terrorists and Nazi Scum are one in the same*. The piece in question, which first appeared in *FORWARD* magazine under a different title, is admittedly far more cautious and subdued in tone than the adjoining JDO commentary. However, it is worth taking into account the fact that much of the evidence presented within this text concerning potential racist/Islamist cooperation is based upon the appearance of articles by Duke and Pierce within some Islamist Web sites after the attacks of 9/11 (Donadio 2001).

The existence of an alliance between Islamists and white supremacists has even been referred to within Hindu fundamentalist Web sites. In the example below, *radioislam.org* is again cited as evidence: "A new nexus of Islamists and Nazis is forming, not content with what Hitler had committed. Ahmed Rami's site of Radio Islam has long been the centre of anti-Semitic propaganda, linked to sites of white Nazis who would if true to their ideology expel or even gas this Arab 'wog'" (Singh 1999, 5).

Even relatively cautious human rights organizations such as the Southern Poverty Law Center have warned about a potential alliance of Islamists and racists. In an article in this organization's Web site entitled *The Swastika & the Crescent*, Martin E. Lee discusses the existence of contacts between neo-Nazis and Islamists in Europe. He then states that since the terrorist attacks of Sept. 11, "there are a number of signs including a spate of articles by American neo-Nazis that have appeared in Islamic publications and Web sites that an operational alliance may take shape in America as well" (Lee 2002, 12–13). The point being made here is not that such cooperation could never, or has never occurred between Islamists and white supremacists, but rather that Web-based *evidence* of resistance identity alliances may give a highly misleading impression concerning the magnitude of any potential threat in this regard. Certainly, it is worth noting that the hosts of at least some of the Muslim Web sites which featured articles by Pierce and Duke were initially unaware of the racist background of these individuals, and removed the offending texts shortly after receiving complaints from their readership (Donadio 2001).

Importantly, substantial cooperation between resistance identities may remain largely invisible. Such appears to have been the case with respect to practical cooperation between militant Jewish groups and neo-Nazis in France, before this cooperation was revealed in a 170-page report on the subject by MRAP, a leading French anti-racist group. According to the report, 26 Web sites traced to neo-Nazi and Jewish militant groups in France operated from the same server in the United States between 1999 and March 2003 (Diderich 2003). Between 2001 and 2003, the groups are reported to have sent 1000 messages per day. These messages contained incitement to attack mosques in order to provoke a civil war between Arabs and other French people, and calls for the assassination of president Chirac. The two groups involved apparently shared technical know-how, including advice on how to send messages without leaving electronic trails (Diderich 2003).[11] Interestingly, the *Reuters* article that reported these events became the object of discussion within *stormfront.org* (2003). A debate ensued in which the "threat" posed to the West by Arabs and Muslims was weighed against that presented by world Jewry.

One problem faced by white separatists online in their attempts to court Islamists concerns the absence of any significant reciprocity in the form of Muslim-hosted Web sites openly supportive of the white separatist program. The absence of such support is perhaps unsurprising when one considers the multi-ethnic and multi-racial composition of many Islamist organizations and movements. It should be noted that even the most militant and ideologically narrow Sunni and Shiite Islamist organizations are inherently anti-racist with respect to who may belong to the community of believers (Castells 2004, 15, 111–115).[12] With respect to the specific case of *radioislam.org*, it is worth observing that while some white separatist Web sites, such as those of the *Posse Commitatus* and *Aryan Nations*, do provide Web links directly to this Web site, Rami's open support for the American Black Muslim movement makes such demonstrations of solidarity appear rather awkward. However, hypertext has provided *stormfront.org*'s designers with an interesting means for resolving this issue.

Under the heading *Opposition to Zionism and Israeli Terrorism*, *stormfront.org* provides a link to a Web site entitled *Politics and Terrorism* (*zog.to*).

While no link is provided from *stormfront.org* to Rami's Web site, it is interesting to note that *zog.to* bears a suspicious resemblance to *radioislam.org*. As with the latter, discourse within *Politics and Terrorism* is devoted almost entirely to considerations surrounding the Arab/Israeli conflict, with the exploitation of Palestinian suffering serving as the primary tool used to promote anti-Semitism. In addition, links are provided to many of the same Islamist web sites linked to by *radioislam.org*, and even the design and color scheme of *Politics and Terrorism* matches that of Rami's site. The main differences concern the continual use of the ZOG acronym within the former, along with the addition of "racist theory" in the form of commentary concerning the *genetic* constitution of Jews, and an absence of any support for the cause of Black Muslims in the United States. Additional searching provides clues that *zog.to* may not represent an Islamist Web site, including the host's self-description as a "righteous gentile" and the use of the "Christian" symbol of knight in armor swinging a sword.

In addition to Islamists, white separatists have attempted to conflate their messages with those of other identities on the Web, including those associated with the Arab/Israeli peace camp. For example, a number of prominent white separatist Web sites, including *duke.org* and the Web site of the Institute for Historical Review (*ihr.org*), now promote a link to a site entitled *No War For Israel* (*nowarforisrael.com*). While clearly created by white separatists, this Web site bears a superficial resemblance to popular left-wing, anti-war sites such as *antiwar.com*. *Nowarforisrael.com* draws attention to "Israeli Apartheid," quotes Israeli leftists, lists Israeli human rights violations in the occupied territories, and provides links to Web sites hosted by "Jewish Groups No War For Israel Supports." Most importantly, an overt attempt is made to identify directly with activists belonging to the International Solidarity Movement (ISM). The Web's site's name, "no war for Israel," allegedly corresponds to the last words of American ISM activist Rachel Corrie before she was crushed to death by an Israeli bulldozer (see chapter 3). An image of Corrie appears on the Web Site's home page with the adjoining phrase "Martyr for Peace." Clicking on this image leads to numerous photographs relating to the tragedy of her death.

Closer inspection of *No War for Israel* reveals that the intended propaganda function of this Web site is to win converts to a line of reasoning put forward by David Duke (2002) and other white separatists concerning U.S. motives for the war(s) on Iraq. Specifically, it is intended to convince readers that an interest in Middle East oil has nothing to do with U.S. intervention in the region. Instead, the war on Iraq is to be understood as having been entirely orchestrated by "Jewish supremacists" whose only goal is to empower Israel and consolidate Jewish global control. More so than with respect to *Politics and Terrorism*, the *No War for Israel* Web site, with its frequent references to "Jewish supremacism," appears unlikely to confuse visitors as to its hosting identity for very long. Rather, the intent appears to be to hold the attention of readers just long enough to convince them that common ground exists between white separatists and activists on the left, and/or to create a greater semblance of respectability for white separatist Jewish conspiracy theories.

The existence of Web sites such as *nowarforisrael.com* will almost certainly add to the difficulties experienced by organizations on the political left attempting to fight for Palestinian human rights. *Free Palestine Now!*, the Web site of a Virginia Commonwealth University-based student activist organization, makes the following comments concerning the street tactics of the National Alliance: " . . . The National Alliance has been unsuccessfully attempting to hijack the Palestinian movement to spread anti-Semitism. They have held anti-Israel demonstrations numerous times in Washington DC. Usually Palestinians and Israelis protest this idiotic and hateful group arm in arm . . ." (Free Palestine Now!, 1).

On the same Web page, complaints are made concerning the frequent attempts of mainstream Zionist organizations to equate criticism of Israel with anti-Semitism, and the role played by ZOG supporters in exacerbating this problem:

> The ADL was once a legitimate organization that fought anti-Semitism in the US. They now seek to de-legitimize any cause of justice whether it be global economic justice or freedom for the Palestinian people by opportunistically labeling them anti-Jewish. They attempt to prove that the Palestinian solidarity movement is Anti-Semitic by pointing to the small group of fascist right-wing ZOG supporters who opportunistically use mass demonstrations to promote their anti-Semitic views. (Free Palestine Now!, 1)

It is worth noting that the ADL's Web pages, which keep tabs on organizations belonging to the racist fringe, also provide lists and information concerning "anti-Israel protest groups." Most of these correspond to project identity organizations such as those considered in chapter 3 (Anti-Defamation League 2001c, 1–5). The designers of *nowarforisrael.com* clearly hope to capitalize on the frustrations experienced by student activists and other project identity actors in their attempts to avoid defamation by mainstream Zionist interests. This may be seen in a headline on this Web site's home page which states "THE NEW THOUGHT POLICE: The Campaign to criminalize criticism of Israel (No War for Israel)." Interestingly, the Web's amenability to the conflation of disparate streams of discourse appears to benefit resistance identities—both powerful and marginal—at the expense of project identities belonging to the Arab/Israeli peace camp. Certainly, this is apparent with respect to fringe groups who have nothing to lose by exploiting Palestinian suffering to bolster their anti-Semitic conspiracy theories. And as implied above, such rhetoric may in turn provide fuel for the propaganda campaigns of powerful resistance identities such as those belonging to the Zionist mainstream.

While the overtures of the far right have consistently been rebuffed by organizations associated with the Arab/Israeli peace camp, the tactics of organizations such as the National Alliance have provided useful fodder for the propaganda campaigns of the mainstream political and/or Zionist right. A good illustration is provided within the publication *Foreign Policy* (Nov./Dec. 2003). In an article entitled *Antiglobalism's Jewish Problem*, Senior Editor Mark Strauss (2003, 58) suggests that anti-Semitic conspiracy theorizing is drawing the "Brownshirt and Birkenstock crowds" together. Strauss (2003, 63) also includes Islamists in the new anti-Semitic alliance, arguing that "Islamists and secular nationalists alike portray globalization as the latest in a series of U.S-Zionist plots to subjugate the Arab world under Western economic control." More importantly, this argument is conjoined with the observation that "the very same antiglobalization movement that prides itself on staging counter-protests against neo-Nazis and links arms with protestors who wave the swastika in the name of Palestinian rights" (Strauss 2003, 63–65).

Interestingly, the main propaganda technique utilized in the article cited above closely mimics the rhetorical networking strategies pursued by white separatists on the WWW when *attempting* to win left-wing and Islamist support. It takes little mental effort to realize that when left-wing protestors wave the swastika (appropriately or not) in their attempts to draw attention to the "racist," "Nazi-like" behavior of the Israeli government, that their use of this symbol implicitly represents a condemnation, and not an endorsement of Nazi philosophy. In other words, the practice in question is ideologically consistent with the action of staging anti-neo-Nazi counter-protests. However, the rhetorical technique utilized by Strauss, one which is regularly employed in advertising, does not depend upon the use of argumentative logic, but rather upon the principle of associative logic. The reader is encouraged to make connections of a categorical nature among otherwise unrelated phenomena (i.e. the philosophies of neo-Nazis and leftists) due to their repeated juxtaposition. The amenability of the WWW to precisely this form of propaganda construction and its potential significance for weak and powerful actors making use of the Web is a topic which will be revisited in the next section.

Discussion

Evidence presented in chapters 5 and 6 suggests a paradox. The very qualities of the WWW which seem most likely to benefit resistance identities in their efforts to achieve greater viability and cohesion as social movements

and/or build coalitions with other identity networks may also serve to under-
mine the credibility of their messages in the eyes of the public, potentially
alienating them even further from the political mainstream. The dynamics
which underlie this paradox are best appreciated by focusing upon the Web's
two-fold capacity as a representational medium. On the one hand, hypertext
may readily be employed for the purpose of creating and disseminating
highly sophisticated propaganda among the constituent elements (individuals
and organizations) associated with a given resistance identity. Such intra-
identity representation may be used to complement other Web-based resource
functions such as the provision of practical information, action alerts, and discussion forums in ways which may help to unify and empower the community in question. However, these efforts must be contrasted with resistance
identity attempts to utilize the Web as a mass medium, where the intent is to
present identity doctrine to the public in a manner which will convince outsiders as to the virtues of its program.

The two aspects of Web-based representation referred to above clearly
overlap, and are often indistinguishable with respect to the content of resistance identity Web sites. For example, organizations such as the National Alliance likely hope that much of their Web-based ideological expression will
serve both to inspire greater enthusiasm and confidence among their rank and
file, while simultaneously providing "education" to the uninitiated. Nonetheless, there are important reasons for making methodological distinctions between internally versus externally directed propaganda and identity-building
practices among relevant groups. It was suggested in chapter 3 that the proliferation of countless resistance identity and project identity Web sites may
contribute to public doubts concerning the authority and authenticity of information obtained online. It seems likely that the Web-based networking
practices engaged in by fringe groups such as those considered in this chapter will contribute further to such doubts. In fact, public suspicion may be
aroused not only with respect to resistance identity Web sites such as those
considered here, but also in the case of other less well-known groups—such
as the peace camp Web sites considered in chapters 2 and 3—to whom resistance identities provide links for rhetorical effect. One result is that the appeal
of trusted brands and/or household names, such as CNN or MSNBC, as reliable sources of information about the world may increase.

The internal (within identity Web sites and Web rings) and external (across
identity Web rings) use of bricolage has allowed each of the three resistance
identities considered in this chapter to *expand* their arguments, counter the
propaganda of their enemies, and network with potential allies in a highly
elaborate, if solipsistic, manner. Relevant rhetorical techniques include drawing attention to the statements of enemies to reinforce identity-based propa-

ganda claims, "gathering" legitimate arguments and factual information to back up spurious conspiracy theories, the employment of "decoy" Web sites to mislead Web users, actively imitating the "hate watch" activities of project identities, and numerous other practices which depend for their effectiveness upon the transgression of identity-based networks and/or the incorporation of hypertexts simultaneously being used by rival organizations. In an important sense, each of the fringe identities considered in this chapter have demonstrated their ability to exploit the Web's interconnected and underdetermined properties in a manner which allows them to "coexist" online with other social identities in a symbiotic manner. The problem facing each identity from a *mass media* perspective is that for those unfamiliar with their doctrines, there is no obvious "authoritative center" or standpoint from which to appreciate the subtleties of resistance identity propaganda.

Within the de-centered environment of the WWW, the strength of resistance identity claims and arguments hinge upon the reader's willingness to follow particular hypertext pathways. This willingness in turn depends upon the reader's predisposition to accept or reject the underlying premises which inform the world view of the identity in question. For this reason the Web-based rhetoric of the groups considered in this chapter will likely appear very powerful to members of a given identity and/or to "borderline" individuals, but suspicious, repulsive, or completely nonsensical to outsiders. By contrast, the "common sense" premises which underlie dominant interpretations of reality conveyed by the mainstream mass media—such as those considered in chapter 4—are generally accepted by the public without any conscious intent. Generally speaking, individuals do not *decide* to "adopt the agenda" of the corporate-owned media, but nonetheless come to depend upon it as a primary source of information about the world. This is not to say that most individuals are completely uncritical of the news media. The important point here is that the propaganda dimension of corporate media framing practices is far more likely to go unnoticed by most members of the public than it will in the case of groups widely perceived as extremist.

While resistance identity propaganda warfare and efforts to utilize the internet as a mass medium may further erode their credibility with the general public, evidence also suggests that the Web's capacity to allow resistance identities to *represent themselves to themselves* may benefit these social movements in important ways. In the section, *social movement integration and growth*, it was argued that ideological self-representation within resistance identity Web sites and Web rings may work synergistically with other strategies in ways which may contribute to the long-term viability of a given social movement. For example, it was suggested that the ability to conjoin the Web structures produced by disparate and widely dispersed racist actors may aid the efforts of white separatist leaders in their attempts to unite the agendas of these diverse elements within a more coherent ideological framework. The speed with which messages and texts may circulate online combined with the capacity to experiment with various ideas in discussion forums provides an important means through which movement "intellectuals" may help set the parameters of identity discourse and debate.

When viewed in terms of the agenda-setting capacities discussed above, white separatist attempts to cultivate ties with Islamists should be understood as more than simply attempts to bring about alliances on the ground. Such efforts may also be appreciated in terms of their potential importance for guiding social movement ideology and maintaining the movement's dominant paradigm, belief in ZOG, in light of contemporary political realities such as America's support for Israel. At the same time, the presence of contradictory themes within this movement's ideology, and their continued circulation online, may aid white separatism as a social movement in abeyance. For example, the implicit admiration for Jewish "race-consciousness" expressed in some Web sites and/or recognition of Arab "darkness" may allow for greater flexibility in terms of attenuating identity doctrine within the movement during periods of rapid social or political change. These points hold particular importance in light of relevant national and global political and economic trends. It appears highly unlikely that racist movements will make significant political headway in the foreseeable future, an issue which will be revisited in chapter 7.

It was suggested earlier that regular face-to-face contact may be needed to maintain long-term cooperation between identities coming from very different cultural or political backgrounds. Nonetheless, even temporary coalitions may prove significant with respect to achieving more narrow or short-term goals such as mobilizing street rallies or petitioning the media. Furthermore, even relatively independent actors like Ahmed Rami may employ the Web to supply other actors with overlapping goals with useful information resources. However, it should also be pointed out that the marginal status of all three identities will almost certainly limit their influence in American society as *independent* social movement actors. For example, it was indicated that the Jewish/Hindu militant alliance considered in this chapter echoes, and perhaps marginally reinforces, the more politically significant cooperation taking place between India and Israel and their respective lobbies in Congress. Yet, the political impact of Kahanists as a unique force in the United States will almost certainly remain marginal precisely to the extent that they reject mainstream Zionist political methods and alliances with other groups. Similarly, the Web may allow white separatists to more effectively rally their forces in support of the anti-abortion campaigns or anti-immigration efforts pursued by more mainstream political forces. However, such efforts will do little if anything to promote white separatism as an independent voice in society.

All things considered, there appear to be few grounds for believing that the Web's value for the three resistance identities with respect to identity building, resource pooling, and disseminating propaganda will translate into either political power or greater ideological influence within the general public in the foreseeable future. As Margolis & Resnick (2000, 19) have observed, the internet technology is no magic bullet, and for the most part marginal movements will remain marginal. To better appreciate why this is the case, it is necessary to look beyond cyberspace to broader local and global realities. In particular, the efforts of all the actors considered in this book need to be examined in light of ongoing changes to the character of civil society and forms of political engagement which have arisen in tandem with the spread of the global economy. These and related concerns will be addressed in light of several overlapping areas of theory in the remaining chapter of this book.

NOTES

1. Legalized abortion is typically portrayed by white separatists as part of a ZOG-inspired plot to reduce the birth rate of whites.

2. Dr. William Pierce, a former professor of physics, was the author of the underground novel, *The Turner Diaries* (1978). This fictional account of the white revolution and race war long-awaited by white separatists has been referred to by the FBI as "the Bible of the racist right." Pierce's book allegedly had a profound influence upon Timothy McVeigh, who bombed the Federal Building in Oklahoma City in April 1995 (Kinsella 1995: 114–115). Pierce died in July 2002, and the National Alliance is now chaired by Erich Gliebe (National Alliance [b]).

3. The pen name of a racist whose tracts may be found within many racist Web sites, including *stormfront.org*.

4. The rapid circulation of such articles has been noted by Donadio (2001) and Lee (2002), both of whom draw specific attention to the appearance of texts produced by Pierce and Duke within some Muslim Web sites and community periodicals. See related discussion in the next section of this chapter.

5. White Americans who remain uninvolved in the white separatist movement are often referred to as sheep in this and other racist Web sites due to their meekness and general refusal to recognize the alleged peril facing white civilization.

6. In addition to condemning Jewish peace groups, the Web site of the Jewish Defense League also provides links to their Web sites under the heading *Unmasking Frauds: Uncovering Anti-Israel "Jewish" Sites* (Jewish Defense League [e]).

7. After the events of 9/11, televangelists Jerry Falwell and Pat Robertson, two of the most prominent figures on the American Christian right, attributed partial responsibility for the attacks to liberal civil liberties groups, feminists, and homosexuals.

The latter were accused of turning God's anger on America (Harris 2001). Significantly, these same enemies are frequently identified by organizations and individuals belonging to the racist right with the notable addition of "the Jews" and/or ZOG.

8. Most notably, Pipes (2003, 126–132, 233–244), makes the controversial claim that the Black Muslim movement has become increasingly anti-American and anti-Semitic largely as a consequence of contact with Islamist movements of foreign origin. The veracity of such claims is very difficult to assess. The Black Muslim movement has a long history in the United States, has frequently changed course with respect to its core doctrine, and has given rise to numerous splinter movements.

9. As is typically the case with respect to both anti-Semitic and Zionist propaganda, Hindu ultranationalists do not make distinctions between religious and cultural expressions of Judaism on the one hand and Zionism as a modern ethnic-nationalist movement and philosophy on the other.

10. See the article *Jews and Hindus are Brothers* by Ranbir Singh (1999).

11. For an interesting discussion of the "pro-Zionist" versus "pro-Palestinian" split within the French far right, see Billig (1991, 107–121).

12. The American Black Muslim movement is perhaps the one notable exception. However, the importance of race to African American converts to Islam appears to have diminished in tandem with an increasing identification with orthodox Sunni Islam (Castells 2003, 56–63; Curtis IV, 2002).

Chapter Seven

Hegemony Reconsidered:
The Internet, Civil Society,
and Social Fragmentation

Many recent approaches to civil society contrast the decline of class and labor as bases of social solidarity with the growing plurality of identity-based social movements, religious communities, sub-cultures, and ethnic associations which have increasingly come to characterize Western liberal democracies. These "new" social groupings may in turn be understood as constituting a series of overlapping and competing public spheres, oriented in varying degrees to both a larger, common "national sphere" and/or to identity networks which transcend state borders. It is against this backdrop that the previous case studies should be (re)considered. In the past six chapters, it was demonstrated that competing identity networks based primarily in the United States use the Web extensively, and for a variety of purposes, in their attempts to influence government policies and public opinion. It was also suggested that some types of social actor benefitted, and will likely continue to benefit disproportionately from their use of internet technology. In this chapter, I will defend this claim in light of relevant theory. More specifically, I will argue that when considered collectively, the Web-based activities of resistance, project, and legitimating identities appear likely to reproduce, and possibly even deepen existing inter-identity rivalries, while simultaneously reinforcing discourses favorable to state and corporate power.

I will begin by briefly reviewing several lines of argument, each of which deals with the interrelationships between technologically mediated communication, pluralist societies, and public attitudes and behavior. The first of these concern observations about the evolving character of civil society and related arguments about changes to popular forms of political engagement encouraged by the widespread use of the internet. A second area concerns the culturally vital and integrative role played by journalism and news production within democratic societies. After highlighting the most relevant points of each, I will attempt to reconcile these strands of thought, which might at first appear incompatible, through reference to Ellul's (1965) observations about the workings of propaganda within modern state societies and related ideas from hegemony theory. This will allow for a more coherent integration of arguments pertaining to the case studies raised in chapters 2 through 6, and hence for a better appreciation of the ways in which the WWW may be contributing both to processes of social fragmentation and ideological hegemony, simultaneously.

Without doubt, the alleged fragmentation of the public into diverse identity-based enclaves has been attributed to more than simply the appearance of internet technology. Perhaps most importantly, an increasing mobility of labor has clearly led to ever more ethnically diverse societies around the world, and particularly in the global north. At the same time, the decline of the welfare state in the wake of global capitalism has dealt a serious blow to older ideals of shared citizenship and political deliberation (Habermas, 1998). As governments have become less active in promoting the common good through public works and social programs, traditional bases for a shared collective identity have steadily eroded. Cultural communities, both old and new, have in turn demanded a greater say in running their own affairs, particularly in such areas as education and religious expression. And, in many cases allegiances to cultural networks which cross state borders remain as strong, if not stronger than those accruing to the state. Furthermore, citizen-based groups and identity networks of all persuasions are increasingly able to rely upon their own communication and information media, ostensibly decreasing their dependence on state and corporate gatekeepers.

These and related changes have led some researchers to conclude that both the state and/or the mass media are no longer able to play their traditional legitimating functions in terms of forging a common cultural and political identity. For example, Castells (2004) maintains that this reality is reflected in the decline of American party politics and in the subsequent growth of political lobbying among citizen-based groups espousing narrow, ethnically, and religiously based agendas. This development—encouraged by the proliferation of digital technology—is argued to fit with the larger trajectory of the global network society. Locally based, but often internationally affiliated, grassroots actors now approach the state in much the same manner as trans-national corporations. That is to say, they attempt to gain control over the mechanisms of the state to better assert their will and serve their own interests regardless of any domestic consensus (Castells 2004, 358). These changes are argued by Castells to be occurring not only within a context where "native" and/or diaspora communities may preserve their own identities via the internet, but also one in which privatized media do not play a legitimating role vis-à-vis state power.

In a similar vein, Bimber (1998; 2003) argues that the Net is contributing to what he terms "accelerated pluralism" in American political life. On the one hand, he maintains that there is unlikely to be any significant relationship between greater public access to the internet and higher levels of participation among the citizenry with respect to traditional forms of party politics. At the same time he argues that the Net will almost certainly lower the obstacles to grassroots mobilization and organization faced by political entrepreneurs, activists, and other "issue-publics," thus speeding the flow of politics (Bimber 1998, 156). In particular, the lower costs of organizing made possible by the Net will encourage greater mobilization among those outside the boundaries of traditional private and public institutions, business and professional establishments, and the constituencies of existing government agencies and programs. While the limitations of this line of reasoning were examined in chapters 2, Bimber (2003) is likely correct about general changes to the means and pathways through which grassroots actors engage in politics. And unlike the case with Castells, Bimber's analysis allows for the possibility that the mass media will remain a significant integrative force in state societies. This point will be revisited shortly.

An isolated focus on the trends and arguments touched upon above make it easy either to overlook, or to dismiss as marginal, the continued role of the mass media as a primary basis for a common national and/or Western culture. As Bimber (1998) has emphasized, the so-called mass audience often invoked in considerations of public opinion is better understood as "many issue publics" rather than as a single engaged and informed polity. Nonetheless, evidence suggests that the social and cultural importance of the mass media remains as strong as ever. Certainly, popular forms of entertainment continue to be overwhelmingly mass-produced. As noted by Hesmondalgh (2002, 245), magazines are arguably the most niche-oriented of all the culture industries, with over 18,000 consumer and business titles published in the United States alone in 1997. And yet, of the $25.8 billion brought in by the top 300 titles, over 26 percent of revenue was captured by the 10 largest consumer magazines (Hesmondalgh 2002). In the case of other media the situation is even more revealing. The film industry hinges upon the production of mass market blockbusters, the recording industry still relies upon the hits of superstars, and mass appeal network television continues to be the mainstay of American viewers.

Even more importantly for present considerations, Americans, much like the general publics of other Western democracies, continue to rely upon their own major national media above all else for information about the world (Sparks 2005). And traditional American news outlets such as *CNN.com*,

MSNBC.com, and *USA Today* represent the most subscribed sites on the Web (Bimber 2003, 248). To better appreciate why this situation should persist in an era of identity network proliferation and do-it-yourself digital media, it is worth considering a hypothetical scenario created by Michael Schudson (1995) in the introduction to his book *The Power of News*. Here, the reader is invited to imagine a world in which the practice of professional journalism has been "momentarily abolished"; in which governments, lobbyists, candidates, churches, and social movements deliver information directly to citizens. Simply by utilizing their home terminals, citizens may . . .

> . . . tap into any information source they want on computer networks. They also send their own information and their own commentary; they are as easily disseminators as recipients of news. The Audubon Society and the Klu Klux Klan, criminals in prison, children at summer camp, elderly people in rest homes, the urban homeless and the rural recluse send and receive messages. Each of us our own journalist. (Schudson 1995, 1)

Having created the vision of a society in which every citizen acts as his or her own journalist, Schudson proceeds to argue that were such a situation actually imposed, large-scale practices of mass communication and traditional forms of journalism would quickly reestablish themselves. Furthermore, they would do so primarily in response to popular need and demand. According to Schudson (1995), this is primarily because people would want ways to make sense of the endless and confusing torrent of information made available to them. He notes, for example, that while it might seem appealing to be able to call up documents such as the latest Supreme Court decisions, few people would feel competent enough to identify key paragraphs and place them in appropriate context (Schudson 1995, 2). Following a line of reasoning first expressed by Walter Lippman in *Public Opinion* (1922), Schudson maintains that media workers and other knowledge specialists play a vital role in democratic societies, since most members of the public have neither the resources, nor the time and inclination to play the role of journalists.

By emphasizing the *cultural* role of news—its importance not only for information delivery, but also for "interpreting and explaining"—Schudson (1995) implicitly acknowledges the role of the news media as a legitimating identity, one which serves to uphold collectively shared myths and dominant ideologies.[1] Significantly, these ideologies and myths transcend the more narrow interests and perspectives of the specific social groupings and organizations which, when taken together, constitute the public as a whole. Hence, for most people, information provided by recognizably partisan interests—the Audubon Society, KKK, criminals in prison, children at camp, etc.—would not be deemed as credible or reliable as information provided by professional journalists via mainstream news outlets. A similar line of reasoning was drawn upon in the previous case studies. Specifically, it was argued that when social movement organizations (SMOs) present Web-based information about the Arab/Israeli conflict from perspectives which appear incommensurate with dominant media frames, they are likely to be viewed with suspicion by people unaffiliated with the identity in question.

When reflecting upon the ideas above, it is worth recalling Bimber's (2003) argument that widespread use of the Net will be unlikely to lead to higher levels of political participation among the citizenry. In fact, Bimber suggests that this will be the case for *any* new communication/information technology. This is because greater access to such technologies will not alter the fact that for most people, most of the time, engaging in politics is not a priority (Bimber 1998, 155). Furthermore, people are highly selective in their attention to political issues and their assimilation of information. They tend to care relatively intensely about a few issues while remaining disinterested and uniformed about most. Furthermore, Bimber (2003) maintains that the cognitive structure of human beings necessarily limits the individual's will and capacity to assimilate information systematically. Drawing upon recent research findings in the areas of political psychology, mass media, political information, and issue publics, he argues that there is now overwhelming evidence suggesting that political engagement is limited by the fact that people are not psychologically equipped to do more than express interest and focus attention on more than a limited number of issues to the near exclusion of others (Bimber 1998, 141–142).

Interestingly, both Bimber (1998; 2003) and Schudson (1995) build upon Lippmann's ideas concerning human cognitive limitations in the face of information overload to support their own disparate lines of argument. Significantly, Lippmann was preoccupied with the role of the mass media in maintaining democracy. Holding that the workings of modern democratic societies are too complex to be properly apprehended by any given member of the public, he also believed that it was unrealistic to expect the media to keep citizens *fully* informed, and hence politically engaged, with respect to most of the major social, political, and economic issues affecting their lives. Hence, for Lippmann (1920; 1963) democracy as popularly understood is largely an illusion, but also a necessary one. He argued that in addition to keeping the public *relatively* well informed with respect to a limited number of key issues, media professionals and other knowledge elites played an important role in society by upholding the ideology and mythology of democracy. In particular, citizens need to be encouraged to maintain their faith in democratic state institutions, which, while imperfect, represent the best political system available.

A similar understanding of the integrative role played by the media in modern state societies informed the work of Jacques Ellul (1965). However, while Lippmann stressed the media's importance for maintaining democracy, Ellul preferred to approach the issue of mass media influence through reference to the concept of propaganda. Importantly for present purposes, Ellul saw a complementary relationship between the "integration propaganda" which serves to legitimate state and/or corporate power, and the "propagandas" produced by a wide range of competing social/political organizations and institutions within the nation/state. His reasoning on this matter rests upon several interrelated lines of argument. These concern the modern individual's "need" for propaganda, important differences between traditional forms of community and the social groupings which exist within modern nation/states, and the observation that propaganda often works according to the principle of divide and rule. It is worth briefly outlining these arguments before considering their relevance with respect to the Net-based activism, and competing agendas of legitimating, project, and resistance identities on the WWW.

All of the theoretical positions adopted by Ellul (1965) in *Propaganda: the Formation of Men's Attitudes* rest upon the widely accepted premise that people require coherent world-views in order to function as social beings. Importantly, however, when outlining the necessary conditions for the existence of propaganda, Ellul (1965, 90–116) also insists that the belief systems within traditional societies differ markedly in character from those adopted by individuals and groups within modern states. These differences have less to do with belief system content per se, than with the manner in which world views come to be shared by the members of a given community. In pre-modern societies, belief systems and codes of behavior emerged spontaneously and consensually from *within* the community. Individuals within traditional societies had regular face-to-face contact, shared the same interests and goals, and their ideals and social hierarchies were a direct by-product of their common experiences and needs. Furthermore, they had little or no exposure to competing ideological systems. When such exposure did occur, the strong communal bonds and closed world-views of these communities generally shielded their members from outside influences.

In much the same manner that Durkheim contrasted organic with mechanical forms of social solidarity, Ellul (1965, 97) maintains that the new form(s) of social cohesion demanded by the modern "technological society" are inherently incompatible with traditional forms of community. It is only in the creation of an individualist society *and* a mass society, he argues, that both the "material means and dictatorial will of the state take shape." The modern state must be a mass society to allow for the implementation of modern economic and governmental systems, but also individualist, since people must be cut loose from earlier communal ties and loyalties. As a result, the isolated individual, no longer protected by traditional communal bonds, is left vulnerable to the influence of propaganda. Furthermore, he or she *needs* propaganda. When traditional forms of solidarity are disrupted or destroyed through the processes of industrialization and state-building, the individual is forced to look elsewhere for new sources of self-identity and a sense of personal worth. According to Ellul (1965, 96), propaganda responds psychologically to this situation by addressing the individual's craving for a coherent ethos and sense of purpose. Propaganda provides the individual with the means for "recognizing" their own necessity and importance within an otherwise alienating mass society.

Before proceeding further, it should be pointed out that Ellul (1965) does not always distinguish clearly between the various types of propaganda he identifies, and other processes of socialization within modern states. Furthermore, "propaganda" is a loaded term, and one which many would be reluctant to apply to media content in democratic countries. However, to apply Ellul's ideas concerning propaganda for present purposes, one need only accept two readily defensible premises. The first is that all societies partake of collective ideologies and myths which ultimately serve to legitimate their underlying economic and/or political systems. Secondly, these legitimating myths and discourses could never remain either coherent or influential across the vast "imagined communities" of modern nation-states if they were not actively sustained through institutionalized practices of mass communication (Anderson 1991; Gellner 1983). These two ideas may readily be brought together with respect to the specific case of news production. The repeated selection of "newsworthy" events and framing of social and political issues in a manner which ultimately serves to legitimate the dominant political/economic system and/or reinforce national ideologies may be understood as roughly corresponding to what Ellul terms integration propaganda.[2]

Significantly, Ellul (1965) argues that the new social groupings which emerged within modern societies cannot protect their members from the effects of propaganda. This is because the very formation of the new groups takes place in tandem with the development of the legitimating institutions of the larger society. They develop within the state and are integrated into its systems. As such they represent nodal points or "loci of propaganda" in the sense of being subsumed within the dominant system(s) and dependent upon its techniques. According to Ellul (1965, 97–98), the new primary groups, including political parties and unions, serve as relay stations in the flow of propaganda. The very rationale for the existence of such groups hinges upon their implicit acceptance of the prevailing economic/political order, since it is within this order that they must attempt to advance the interests of their constituencies. In addition, Ellul

(1965) makes numerous references to ethnic, religious, and other identity-based groupings within the state, but stresses that these new groups only superficially resemble their traditional counterparts. Much like labor unions and political parties, these communal identities necessarily accept the legitimacy of the dominant political and economic order, adopting its organizational and communicative techniques, even as they pursue partisan goals within it.

Ellul's (1965) arguments about propaganda are largely consistent with the tenets of hegemony theory. As Hall (1984) has observed, most individuals and cultural or political groupings in society accept the hegemonic or dominant definitions of the larger social and political contexts within which they operate. This generally remains the case even when self-identified groups are actively engaged in fighting for their collective rights and/or pursuing their own narrow political agendas. In most instances, challenges to the status quo consist of attempts to negotiate more favorable treatment within the prevailing social/political order. Activism and protest in such cases essentially amount to attempts to "cut a better deal" on behalf of the group in question, rather than to alter the underlying conditions which ultimately enable some groups to dominate others. Importantly, however, even if some social actors do consciously adopt what Hall refers to as "oppositional codes," or doctrines which directly challenge the legitimacy of the larger political and economic system, Ellul's (1965, 213) analysis suggests that in a "partitioned society" legitimating forms of propaganda will likely remain effective.

According to Ellul (1965, 97), the partitioning of modern societies takes place on numerous levels, via such actors as unions, religious organizations, classes, political parties, and beyond that a partitioning of nations. The result is that while groups and individuals can resist "one particular propaganda," they remain vulnerable to "the general phenomenon of propaganda":

> In the first place, it maintains its effectiveness towards the mass of undecided who do not yet belong to a group. Then too, it is possible to affect those who belong to a group of a different sort: for example, Communist propaganda that will not affect militant Socialists might affect Protestants; American propaganda that will not affect a Frenchman in his capacity as a Frenchman might influence him with regard to capitalism or the liberal system.
>
> Because one knows that the doctor will not read a magazine on city-planning, and because one knows that the public at large will not read any of the specialized journals, and because one knows that the Ukrainians will not read Georgian newspapers, one can, according to necessity, make contradictory assertions in any and all of them. (Ellul 1965, 214–215)

A related argument line of argument—one supported by a growing body of research—suggests that the more information people have access to, the more likely it is that this information will be assimilated in a manner whereby pre-existing political dispositions and related beliefs about the social world are reinforced. Furthermore, people tend to seek out information which reinforces the views they already hold (see Bimber 2003, 207–209). There can be little doubt that the internet encourages such tendencies, which are directly connected to what Wilhelm (2000) has termed "the balkanization of cyberspace." Disparate social movements, religious groups, activists, lobbies, etc. are clearly exposed to the world views and endless amounts of information provided by others on the Web. However, evidence presented throughout this book suggests that such exposure is more likely to encourage sectarian tendencies and more elaborate forms of propaganda construction, than it is to break down communication barriers between groups. While this was most apparent in the case of the conspiracy-minded far right and other militant fringe groups, evidence presented by other researchers, including Bimber (2003), Wilhelm (2000), and Robins & Webster (1999), suggests that this phenomenon is in fact pervasive on the Web.

Rather than being mitigated, the dynamics identified by Ellul (1965) as integral to the modern technological state appear to have taken on new life within the context of the "postmodern" global network society. Its defining technology, the internet, readily facilitates greater partitioning among communities at both the global and local levels, even as it reinforces the authority and spread of discourses serving to legitimate American global dominance and an accompanying expansion of "free markets." One result is that some types of social movement network appear to be benefiting disproportionately from the existence of the Net. Conversely, evidence suggests that many of the apparent benefits which the World Wide Web (WWW) ostensibly offers to marginalized grassroots actors may have little, if any, real value in terms of affording them the opportunity to gain greater political influence, or more widespread popular support.

The rise of identity politics on a global scale has been attributed, at least in part, to localized expressions of resistance in the face of an invasive and homogenizing Western consumer culture. This argument is perhaps most strongly developed by Barber (1996) who maintains that the growing prevalence of "Jihad"—the term he uses when referring to exclusivist, militant expressions of religion and nationalism—is in large measure a negative, but community-affirming response to the threat posed by global capitalism to traditional cultures and value systems. In turn, the forces aligned with global markets, or "McWorld," gain greater legitimacy by counter-posing their "civilizing" and unifying project against the unsavory reality of ethnic strife and ideological extremism. Crucially, Jihad and McWorld are understood by Barber (1996) as representing opposing poles locked into an ongoing dialectic through which the programs of each side are continually reinforced. It is important to note, however, that McWorld may at times be embraced rather than opposed by the forces of Jihad; a point which has important implications when attempting to assess which identity networks are most likely to benefit most from the spread of internet technology.

As discussed in chapters 2 and 3, the agendas of both Christian fundamentalist and Jewish Zionist organizations square well with the overall trajectory of U.S. foreign policy. And this is not only the case with respect to the Middle East. As Lienesch (1993, 136) has indicated, there is near unanimous agreement within the American Christian right that conversion provides the only real solution to poverty, whether at home or in the Third World. This belief is invariably tied to opposition to public welfare programs, an alternative emphasis on Christian charity, and, increasingly, to the related notion that free markets are divinely sanctioned (Kintz 1997; Leinesch 1993). Furthermore, in addition to championing the spread of free market capitalism and a more aggressive U.S. foreign policy towards Islamists and other perceived enemies of the state, Christian and Jewish Zionist goals also mesh with the new legitimating discourses of the national security state. Likewise, peace activists and members of the American Muslim and Arab communities have ranked highest on the receiving end of the new computerized surveillance capacities and other special powers of the state which expanded substantially after the events of 9/11.

While the institutions and mode(s) of political integration formerly associated with the welfare state are clearly in decline, this should not be taken to mean that legitimating institutions are either absent or impotent in the "information age." Inattention to, or outright denial of this important fact is perhaps the most glaring weakness in Castells's otherwise impressive analysis of the global network society.[3] That the corporate media remain a crucial legitimating institution in relation to U.S. foreign policy was made clear in chapter 4, where it was further argued that the Web environment allows relevant narratives to be reinforced in new and effective ways. Commenting on the imperialist mindset which continues to inform popular conceptions of America's role in the world, Said (1994, 324) observes that the commonest sequence "is the old one that America, a force for good in the world, regularly comes up against obstacles posed by foreign conspiracies, ontologically mischievous and 'against' America" (Said 1994, 324). In recent years, mainstream news organizations such as CNN and ABC—under fire from the political right for their alleged "liberalism"—have come under pressure to strike an even more "patriotic" tone (McChesney & Foster 2003).

The points raised above hold considerable relevance when attempting to assess the Web's capacity to function as an effective public sphere. This is readily apparent when considering the conundrum faced by peace activists attempting to present their case to the public. On the one hand, the interconnected, hypertext environment of the WWW has provided legitimating identifies such as *CNN.com* with a new means for subverting project identity legitimacy based on universal principles of social justice. Through the use of hypertext, these same values may readily be co-opted and attributed to the American state. Project identity narratives have also been attacked from "below" by stigmatized racist groups hoping to bolster their own perceived legitimacy through the exploitation of Palestinian suffering. This reality, in combination with a relative lack of access to traditional media channels, has left peace camp activists vulnerable to the charges of "guilt by association" regularly leveled at them by influential Zionist and neo-conservative organizations. The ironic result is that networks genuinely committed to upholding widely shared principles of social justice may come to be viewed with increasing public suspicion, even as powerful resistance identities espousing exclusivist ideologies remain better positioned to consolidate their perceived status as forces of political moderation.

Online networks have several distinct advantages over "real communities," the most important of which include the internet's ability to facilitate social bonding among individuals without the requirement of close proximity, "either spatially or temporally" (Etzioni 1997, 295). And there can be little doubt that for virtually all social movement actors, the Net provides tremendous advantages in terms of enhanced potentials for communication and identity building. Certainly, this has proven to be the case for "hate groups" and other stigmatized identities. Among other benefits, hypertext provides relevant actors with the means to exploit the co-presence of enemies online, allowing them to construct novel forms of propaganda and build more cohesive identities in the process.

As Castells (2004) has commented with respect to the American militia movement:

> Such a diverse, almost chaotic, movement cannot have a stable organization, or even a coordinating authority. Yet, the homogeneity of its core vision and, particularly, its identification of a common enemy are remarkable. This is because linkages between groups and individuals do exist, but they are carried out through the media (radio mainly), through books, pamphlets, speaking tours, and alternative press, by fax, and, mainly, through the Internet. (Castells 2004, 94)

Similarly, in chapters 5 and 6 it was suggested that the creation of identity-based Web portals, and a related ability to circulate key texts rapidly within a widely dispersed identity network, may hold considerable importance in terms of allowing for greater ideological cohesion amongst racist groups which might otherwise lack a common political focus. The Web portal provided within *stormfront.org*, and the series of articles distributed online by David Duke and his supporters in the wake of 9/11 were discussed as cases in point. Nonetheless, the long-term success of political fringe movements must be judged in light of more than simply how well they are able to exploit new technologies. The goals of white separatists are clearly incommensurable with a global order in which the mobility of cheap labor—and hence the persistence and growth of ethnic diversity in technologically advanced societies—remains a prerequisite for the effective functioning of McWorld. The persistence of this reality, rather than a demonstrated ability to "master the logic of networks," will almost certainly remain the most critical determinant of the white separatists' long-term success.

As Said (1994, 324) observes, "centrality is identity, what is powerful, important and *ours*." And centrality "gives rise to semi-official narratives that authorize and provoke certain sequences of cause and effect, while at the same time preventing counter-narratives from emerging." These insights hold as much relevance when considering the Net's amenability to new forms of political mobilization, as they do when attempting to come to grips with the unusual characteristics of the WWW as an interconnected, hypertext medium. The internet changes the rules by which actors compete—providing novel means for disseminating information, locating allies, constructing propaganda, and challenging authority—even as it allows for the enhancement of older activist strategies and techniques. Nonetheless, the weight of evidence suggests that it is ultimately those forces closely aligned with established institutions of power which will continue to benefit disproportionately from its use. As Ellul made clear in 1965, both the disparate propagandas of competing groups and interests, *and* the integration propaganda of dominant institutions are endemic to the modern technological society. Perhaps this is why the twin phenomena of social fragmentation and ideological hegemony, so readily facilitated by internet technology, also appear so familiar.

NOTES

1. Schudson (1995) readily concedes that the messages carried by the corporate news media are strongly influenced by the state and/or corporate interests to which they are closely tied. The existence of both grassroots and political economy influences upon news content are acknowledged by Schudson and are not seen as mutually exclusive phenomena. Such an understanding is essential if the corporate news media are to be understood as a legitimizing identity whose authority is widely recognized among the citizenry.

2. The term could also be applied to many or most products of the culture industries, where popularized media products such as books and films arguably serve to reproduce hegemonic interpretations of reality.

3. While Castells emphasizes the importance of the corporate media as the "space of politics in the information age" he also maintains that the profit orientation of the media enterprise serves to guarantee the media's political neutrality. Media messages are understood by Castells to reflect prevailing cultural/political norms, but their role in shaping popular conceptions of reality in a manner which serves the interests of dominant elites is never acknowledged. See *The Power of Identity* (2004, 367–414).

Works Cited

ADL Watch. There are many places online to get background about the Anti-Defamation League of B'Nai B'rith. *zpub.com*, http://www.zpub.com/notes/adl2.html. (accessed Nov. 3, 2003).

AIPAC. (a). How to Get Involved. http://aipac.org/documents/involved.html. (accessed July 20, 2004).

———. (b). AIPAC: The American Israel Public Affairs Committee. http://ww.aipac .org/. (accessed July 20, 2004).

Ackerman, Seth. 2001. The Illusion of Balance: NPR's coverage of Mideast deaths doesn't match reality. *FAIR*, Nov.–Dec. http://www.fair.org/extra/0111/npr-mideast .html. (accessed Feb. 17, 2004).

Ahmad, Eqbal. 1999. Settler Colonialism: Peace of the Weak to Wye's Rebirth of Apartheid. *The Washington Report on Middle East Affairs*, March, 11–12.

Akenson, Donald H. 1991. *God's Peoples: Covenant and Land in South Africa, Israel, and Ulster*. Montreal & Kingston: McGill-Queen's University Press.

Al-Awda. (a) Media Accomplishments 2003. *Al-Awda.org*, http://www.al-awda.org/ mediaaccomplishments2003. (accessed June 7, 2003).

———. (b) Who We Are. *Al-Awda.org*, http://www.al-awda.org/whoweare/. (accessed June 7, 2003).

———. (c) What You Can Do. *Al-Awda.org*, http://www.al-awda.org/whatyoucando/. (accessed June 7, 2003).

———. (d) What is PRRC/Al-Awda position on Racism and Anti-Semitism? *Al-Awda.org*, http://www.al-awda.org/faqsonalawda/. (accessed July 3, 2004).

al-Haddad, Laila. Activists say Israel hides human rights abuses. *The Daily Star*, http:// www.palsolidarity.org/inthenews/lebstardec03.php. (accessed Nov. 20, 2003).

Alterman, Eric. 2007. The Politics of Pundit Prestige. . . *The Nation*, April 23. http://www.thenation.com/docprint.mhtml?=20070423&s=alterman.

Anderson, Benedict. 1991. *Imagined Communities: Reflections on the Origin and Spread of Nationalism*. Rev. ed. London: Verso.

Anti-Defamation League. 1998. Anti-Semitism-USA. *ADL.org*, Sept. 24, 1998. http://www.adl.org/presrele/asus_12/3240_12.asp. (accessed Sept. 23, 2003).

———. 2001a. Holocaust Denial: Ahmad Rami. *ADL.org*, http://www.adl.org/poisoning_web/rami.asp. (accessed July 8, 2003).

———. 2001b. Don Black: White Pride World Wide. *ADL.org*, http://www.adl.org/poisoning_web/black .asp. (accessed July 8, 2003).

———. 2001c. Anti-Israel Protest Groups. *ADL.org*, http://www.adl.org/Israel_protest_calendar_groups.asp. (accessed Dec. 2003).

Anti-Muslim Society. Islam = short for "Insanity of sex, Looting And Murder." http://www.geocities.com/am_society/. (accessed July 24, 2003).

Appadurai, Arjun. 1996. *Modernity at Large: Cultural Dimensions of Globalization.* Minnesota: University of Minnesota Press.

Appleby, Timothy. 2002. Net Growing as tool to spread hate: study. *Globe & Mail*, Nov. 23, sec. A.

Associated Press. 2001. Mideast tensions spill over into Internet photo contest. March 2. http://groups.yahoo.com/group/arabhumanrights/message/223. (accessed March 2, 2001).

Avraham, Meira Bat. The Quiet Holocaust: The Perfidious Plot to Convert Jews. *JDL.org,* http://www.jdl.org/enemies/quiet_holocaust. (accessed Jan. 2, 2001).

Ayers, Jeffrey M. 1999. From the Streets to the Internet: The Cyber-Diffusion of Contention. *The Annals of the American Academy of Political and Social Science* 556: 132–143.

Barber, Benjamin R. 1996. *Jihad vs. McWorld: How Globalism and Tribalism are Reshaping the World.* New York: Ballantine Books.

Barrett, Stanley R. 1987. *The Rebirth of Anthropological Theory.* Toronto: University of Toronto Press.

ben Hyka, Yaakov Reuven. 2002. Jew-Hatred in America. Aug. 8, ttp://www.israelnn.com/print.php3?what=article&id=1241. (accessed Jan. 24, 2003).

Bennett, Lance W. 2004. Communicating global activism: strengths and vulnerabilities of networked politics. In *Cyberprotest: New Media, citizens and social movements*, ed. Wim van de Donk, Brian D. Loader, Paul G. Nixon, and Dieter Rucht, 123–146. London: Routledge.

Billig, Michael. 1991. *Ideology and Opinions: Studies in Rhetorical Psychology.* London: Sage Publications.

Bimber, Bruce. 2003. *Information and American Democracy: Technology in the Evolution of Political Power.* Cambridge: Cambridge University Press.

———. 1998. The Internet and Political Transformation: Populism, Community, and Accelerated Pluralism. *Polity* 31: 133–160.

Bird, Eugene. 2000. Camp David Negotiations Fail to Resolve "Core Issue" of Jerusalem. *Washington Report on Middle East Affairs*, Aug.–Sept., 6+.

Black, Don. (a) Mission Statement. *Stormfront.org*, http://www.stormfront.org/.(accessed July 14, 2003).

———. (b) What the controlled media has to say about Stormfront. *Stormfront.org*, http://www.stormfront.org/dblack/press.htm. (accessed July 14, 2003).

———. (c) untitled. *Stormfront.org*, http://www.stormfront.org/dblack/press051195.htm. (accessed July 14, 2003).

———. (d) Simon Wiesanthal Center. *Stormfront.org*, http://www.stormfront.org/links/against.htm. (accessed Feb. 9, 2002).

———. (e) Jewish Defense Organization. *Stormfront.org*, http://www.stormfront.org/links/against.htm. (accessed Feb. 9, 2002).

Boggs, Carl. *Gramsci's Marxism*. 1976. Southampton: Pluto Press.

Brownfeld, Allen C. 2003. Can "Road Map" for Mideast Peace Withstand Assault of Israel's U.S. "Friends"? *Washington Report on Middle East Affairs*, June, 57–58.

———. 2003. Will Election Year Domestic Politics Derail "Road Map" to Mideast Peace? *Washington Report on Middle East Affairs*, Sept., 58–59.

Bruce, Steve. 1998. *Conservative Protestant Politics*. Oxford: Oxford University Press.

Bunt, Gary R. 2003. *Islam in the Digital Age: E-Jihad, Online Fatwas and Cyber Islamic Environments*. London: Pluto Press.

Butterfield, Jeanne. 1991. U.S. Aid to Israel: Funding Occupation in the Aftermath of the Gulf War. In *Beyond the Storm: A Gulf Crisis Reader*, ed. Phyllis Bennis and Michael Moushabeck, 103–111. New York: Olive Branch Press.

Campus Watch. Campus Watch: Monitoring Middle East Studies on Campus. *campuswatch.org* (accessed July 9 2003).

Carter, Jimmy. 2006. *Palestine: peace no apartheid*. New York: Simon & Schuster.

Castells, Manuel. 2004. *The Information Age: Economy, Society and Culture: The Power of Identity*. 2nd ed. Oxford: Blackwell Publishers Ltd.

———. 2000. The Rise of the Network Society. 2nd ed. Oxford: Blackwell Publishers Ltd.

———. 1997. *The Information Age: Economy, Society and Culture: The Power of Identity*. Oxford: Blackwell Publishers Ltd.

Chester, Jeff, and Gary O. Larson. "Sharing the Wealth an Online Commons for the Nonprofit Sector." Pp. 185–205 in *The Future of Media: Resistance and Reform in the 21st Century*, edited by Robert McChesney, Russell Newman, and Ben Scott. New York: Seven Stories Press, 2005.

Chin-Chuan Lee, Joseph M. Chan, Zhongdang Pan, and Clement Y. K. So. National Prisms of a Global "Media Event." In *Mass Media and Society*, ed. James Curran and Michael Gurevitch, 295–309. 3rd ed. London: Arnold.

Chomsky, Noam. 1999. *Fateful Triangle: The United States, Israel & the Palestinians*. Rev. ed. Montreal: Black Rose Books.

Christensen, John. 1999. U.S. and Israel: such good friends: "Quite an extraordinary relationship." http://www.cnn.com/SPECIALS/1999/israeli.elections/stories/israel.us/ (accessed Dec. 12, 2002).

Christian Coalition. 2003. For America and Israel: The Interfaith Zionist Leadership Summit. http://www.cc.org/events/interfaithzionist.htm. (accessed May 23, 2003).

Church of Rabin and Peace. 1999. The World Wide Web's #2 Rabin Memorial Web Site! http://church-of-rabin.tripod.com/ (accessed July 8, 2003).

CNN.com. 1998. At-A-Glance: Facts and figures on the state of Israel. http://www.cnn.com/SPECIALS/1998/israel/at.a.glance/ (accessed Dec. 10, 2002).

———. 2001a. The Balfour Declaration. http://www.cnn.com/SPECIALS/2001 mideast/stories/timeline/balfour.html (accessed Dec. 10, 2002).

———. 2001b. Palestinian borders and Jewish Settlements. http://edition.cnn.com/ SPECIALS/2001/mideast/stories/issues.borders/indexhtml (accessed Dec. 10, 2002).

———. 2001c. Status of Jerusalem. http://edition.cnn.com/SPECIALS/2001/mideast/ stories/issues.jerusalem/index.html (accessed Dec. 10, 2002).

———. 2001d. Palestinian refugees and the right of return. http://edition.cnn.com/ SPECIALS/2001/mideast/stories/issues.refugees/index.html (accessed Dec. 10, 2002).

———. 2001e. Special Report: Mideast Land of Conflict. http://www.cnn.com/ SPECIALS/2001/mideast/ (accessed Dec. 10, 2002).

———. 2001f. Related Sites. http://www.cnn.com/SPECIALS/2001/mideast/stories/ related.sites/index.html (accessed Dec. 10, 2002).

———. 2002a. In-Depth Special: Victims of Terror.http://www.cnn.com/SPECIALS/ 2002/terror.victims/page1.html (accessed July 16, 2002).

———. 2002b. CNN.com presents new online look. http://www.cnn.com/2002/US /09/19/redesign.letter/index.html (accessed Dec. 10, 2002).

Cockburn, Andrew and Leslie Cockburn. 1991. *Dangerous Liaison: The Inside Story of the U.S.-Israeli Covert Relationship.* Toronto: Stoddart Publishing Co. Ltd.

Cohen, Avner. 1998. *Israel and the Bomb.* New York: Columbia University Press.

Cohn, Norman. 1981. *Warrant for Genocide: The myth of the Jewish world-conspiracy and the Protocols of the Elders of Zion.* USA: Scholars Press.

Couldry, Nick. 2003. Beyond the Hall of Mirrors? In *Contesting Media Power: Alternative Media in a Networked World,* ed. Nick Couldry and James Curran, 39–56. Lanham: Rowman & Littlefield Publishers, Inc.

Curran, James. 2000. Rethinking Media and Democracy. In *Mass Media and Society,* ed. James Curran and Michael Gurevitch, 3rd ed. 120–154. London: Arnold.

Curtis IV, Edward E. 2002. *Islam in Black America.* Albany: State University of New York Press.

Dalistan Journal. 2001. "Hit List" Of Christian Evangelicals On Hindu Extremist Website. Dec. 26. http://www.dalistan.org/journal/hindutva/htv001/htva0006.html (accessed July 8, 2003).

Diani, Mario. 2001. Social movement networks: virtual and real. *Culture and Politics in the Information Age: A New Politics?,* ed. Frank Webster, 117–128. London: Routledge.

———. 2003. Networks and Social Movements: A Research Paradigm. *Social Movements and Networks: Relational Approaches to Collective Action,* eds. Mario Diani, and Doug McAdam, 299–319. Oxford: Oxford University Press.

Diderich, Joelle. 2003. Neo-Nazis, Extremist Jews Unite. *Reuters,* Sept. 28, http://www .wired.com/news/culture/0,1284,59662,00.html (accessed July 17, 2003).

Dobratz, Betty A. 2001. The Role of Religion in the Collective Identity of the White Racialist Movement. *Journal for the Scientific Study of Religion* 40: 287–302.

Donadio, Rachel. 2001. Radical Islam, Neo-Nazis Are Seen Sharing Hate Rhetoric. *Forward,* Nov. 23. http://lists.village.edu/cgi-in/spoons/archive_msg.pl?file=anar...

Doran, Michael S. 2002. Somebody Else's Civil War. *Foreign Affairs* 81(1): 22–42.

Dordoy, Alan, and Mellor, Mary. 2001. Grassroots environmental movements: mobilization in an Information Age. In *Culture and Politics in the Information Age: A New Politics?*, ed. Frank Webster. London: Routledge.

Draper, Theodor. 1991. American Hubris. In *The Gulf War Reader: History, Documents, Opinions*, eds. Micah L. Sifry and Christopher Serf, 40–56. New York: Random House.

Duke, David. 2001. The Big Lie: The true reason behind the attack of September 11. Oct. 3, http://www.stormfront.org/forum/showthread.php?s=&thread=3064 (accessed June 18, 2003).

———. 2002. The Iraqi War: Its not about the oil, stupid! *David Duke Online Radio Report*, Nov. 2, http://www.davidduke.com/radio (accessed Aug. 26, 2003).

Ellul, Jacques. 1965. *Propaganda: The Formation of Men's Attitudes*. New York: Vintage Books.

Eskenazi, Joe. 2001. JCRC condemns site that published Lerner's address. *Jewish Bulletin News*, June 1, http://jewishsf.com/bk010601/sfp9a.shtml (accessed July 8, 2003).

Etzioni, Amitai and Oren Etzioni. 1997. Communities: Virtual vs. Real, *Science*. 277 (295). http://www.cs.washington.edu/homes/etzioni/editorial.html.

European-American Unity and Rights Organization. Who watches the so-called "Watchdog Groups"? *whitecivilrights*.com, http://whitecivilrights.com/ (accessed July 4, 2003).

Fallows, James. 2003. Who Shot Mohammed Al-Dura? *Atlantic Monthly*, June http://www.theatlantic.com/issues/2003/06/fallows.htm. (accessed Oct. 14, 2003).

Fiske, John. 1993. *Power Plays, Power Works*. London: Verso.

Free Palestine Now! Rogues Gallery: Fascism, Anti-Semitism, Anti-Muslim, and Zionism Watch. *Free Palestine Now!* http://www.studentorg.vcu.edu/fpn/rogues.html (accessed July 7, 2003).

Fukuyama, Francis. 1999. *The Great Disruption: Human Nature and the Reconstitution of Social Order*. New York: The Free Press.

Gabor, Ivor, and Willson, Alice Wynne. Dying for Diamonds: the mainstream media and NGOs—a case study of ActionAid. In *Global Activism, Global Media*, ed. Wilma de Jong, Martin Shaw and Neil Stammers, 95–109. London: Pluto Press.

Garner, Roberta. 1996. *Contemporary Movements and Ideologies*. USA: McGraw-Hill Inc.

Giddens, Anthony. 1990. *The Consequences of Modernity*. Stanford: Stanford University Press.

Goldberg, Michelle. 2003. Osama University? *Salon.com*, Nov. 6. http://www.geocities.com/ivorytowersorg/OsamaUniversity.htm.

———. 2004. Outlawing Dissent. *Salon.com*, Feb.11.http://www.ccmep.org/2004_articles/civil%20liberties/021104_outlawing_dissent.htm.

Golding, Peter, and Graham Murdock. "Culture, Communications and Political Economy." Pp. 70–92 in *Mass Media and Society*, 3rd ed., edited by James Curran and Michael Gurevitch. London: Arnold, 2000.

Goldman, David. 2001. Cyberhate Revisited. Interview by *Southern Poverty Law Center: Intelligence Report*, Spring. http://www.solcenter.org/cgi-bin/intelligence-project/ (accessed July 8, 2003).

Greenwald, Glenn. 2007. Neocons' rejection of the Rule of law extends to the personal level. *Salon.com*, May 8. http://www.salon.com/opinion/greenwald/2007/05/08neocons/index.html.

Gross, Max. 2003. Evangelicals Adopt Settlers. *Forward*, June 13. http://www.forward.com/issues/2003/03.06.13/news7.html.

Gruneau, Richard. 1988. Introduction. In *Popular Cultures and Political Practices*, ed. Richard Gruneau, 11–32. Toronto: Garamond Press.

Habermas, Jurgen. 1998. The European Nation-State: On the Past and Future of Sovereignty and Citizenship. Trans. Ciaran Cronin. *Public Culture*, 10, 397–416.

Hadawi, Sami. 1967. *Bitter Harvest: Palestine between 1914–1967*. New York: New World Press.

Haddad, Yvonne Yazbeck. 1991. Operation Desert Shield/Desert Storm: The Islamist Perspective. In *Beyond the Storm: A Gulf Crisis Reader*, ed. Phyllis Bennis and Michael Moushabeck, 248–262. New York: Olive Branch Press.

Hall, Stuart. 1984. Encoding/Decoding. *Culture, Media, Language*. ed. Stuart Hall, Dorothy Hobson, Andrew Lowe, and Paul Willis, 128–139. London: Hutchinson.

Hallin, Daniel C. 1986. *'The Uncensored War': The Media and Viet Nam*. New York: Oxford.

Hamas. 1988. *The Covenant of the Islamic Resistance Movement (Hamas)*. Aug. 18. http://mideastweb.org/hamas.htm (accessed June 22, 2003).

Hanley, Delinda C. 2003. A Friendship Forged in Steel and Weaponry. *Washington Report on Middle East Affairs*, Oct., 33.

Harkabi Y. 1972. *Arab Attitudes to Israel*. Jerusalem: Keter Publishing House.

Harris, John F. 2001. God Gave U.S. "What We Deserve," Falwell Says. *Washington Post*, Sept. 14, sec. C3.

Hart, Alan. 1984 *Arafat: Terrorist or Peacemaker?* London: Sidgwick and Jackson Ltd.

Hebdige, Dick. 1979. *Subculture: The Meaning of Style*. London: Methuen.

Herman, Edward S., and Noam Chomsky. 1988. *Manufacturing Consent: The Political Economy of the Mass Media*. New York: Pantheon Books.

Hersh, Seymour M. 1991. *The Samsom Option: Israel's Nuclear Arsenal and American Foreign Policy*. New York: Random House.

Hesmondhalgh, David. 2002. *The Culture Industries*. London: Sage Publications.

Hindu Unity. (a) Promoting & Supporting the Ideals of the Bajrang Dal. http://hinduunity.org/ (accessed Aug. 17, 2003).

———. (b) NEVER FORGET! NEVER FORGIVE! http://hinduunity.org/ (accessed Aug. 17, 2003).

———. (c) They Celebrate! While We Mourn! wysiwg://24/http://www.hinduunity.org/ (accessed Feb. 9, 2002).

———. (d) HINDUUNITY.ORG SUPPORTS J.D.L. TO THE FULLEST! wysiwyg://10/http://www.hinduunity.org/jdl.html (accessed Dec. 31, 2000).

Hroub, Kaled. 2000. *Hamas: Political Thought and Practice*. Washington DC: Institute for Palestine Studies.

Huntington, Samuel P. 1997. *The Clash of Civilizations and the Remaking of World Order*. New York: Touchstone.

If Americans Knew. Accuracy in Israel/Palestine Reporting: New London Day (March–June 2003). http://ifamericansknew.org/media/nl/report.html (accessed Feb. 17, 2004).

Inhofe, James. 2002. Seven Reasons Why Israel is Entitled to the Land. *CBN News*, March, 4. http://cbn.org/CBNnews/news/020308c.asp? (accessed May 26, 2003).

International Solidarity Movement. 2001. Mission Statement. Dec. http://www.pal solidarity.org/about/mission.php (accessed Feb. 10, 2004).

——. You're just anti-Semitic aren't you? palsolidarity.org/about/antisemite/php (accessed July 3, 2004).

Israeli Committee Against House Demolitions. Frequently Asked Questions. *icahd.org*, http://www.icahd.org/eng/faq.asp?menu=9&submenu=1 (accessed May 20, 2004).

Jackson, Michele H. 1997. Assessing the Structure of Communication on the World Wide Web. *Journal of Computer Mediated Communication*, 3.1 http://jcmc.huji.ac.il/vol3/issue1/Jackson.html.

Jackson, Thomas. What is Racism? *American Renaissance*, http://stormfront.org/whitenat/racism.htm (accessed July 7, 2003).

Jacobs, Ronald N. 2000. *Race, Media and the Crisis of Civil Society: From Watts to Rodney King*. Cambridge: Cambridge University Press.

Janmohamed, Zahir. 2003. Burgeoning Alliance Reinforces Intolerance. *Washington Report on Middle East Affairs*, Oct., 32.

Jasper, J. M., and J. D. Poulson. "Recruiting strangers and friends: moral shocks and social networks in animal rights and anti-nuclear protests." *Social Problems* 42, no. 2 (1995): 493–512.

Jerusalem Prayer Team. 2004 President Bush, Let Israel Have a Fence! *jpteam.org*, http://tool.donationnet/unavailable/petition_rt.cfm?dn=1032&sour... (accessed Feb. 6, 2004).

Jewish Defense League. (a) opening statement (untitled). http://www.jdl.org/ (July 5, 2002).

——. (b) ADL Blows It Again. http://jdl.org/news/index.shtml#Anchor-ADL-8500 (accessed July 5, 2002).

——. (c) The ADL Doesn't Help Jews—The ADL Helps Jew Haters. http://www .jdl.org/action/jdl_and_adl.html (accessed Feb. 2, 2001).

——. (d) Armchair Activist: Silence "Radio Islam." http://www.jdl.org/action/armchair/radio_islam.shtml (accessed Sept. 2, 2003).

——. (e) Armchair Activist: Unmasking Frauds: Uncovering Anti-Israel "Jewish" Sites. http://wwwjdl.org/action/armchair/frauds.shtml (accessed Feb. 21 2003).

——. (f) JDL supports Hindu Unity. http://wwwjdl.org/ (accessed Dec. 31, 2000).

Jewish Defense Organization. (a) ADDRESSES, PHONE NUMBERS AND LINKS. http://www.jdo.org/nazi.htm (accessed July 15, 2001).

——. (b) NAZIFIGHTER'S TACTICAL MANUEL: JOIN THE ANTI-NAZI REVOLVE-A-CRANK CALL PLAN. http://www.jdo.org/nazi.htm (accessed May 16, 2003).

Jewish Watch Dog. ANTI-JEWISH ALERTS. http://www.jwd-jewishwatchdog.ca/alerts/jwd_02-anti-jewish.html (accessed May 23, 2003).

Jimmy Carter Library & Museum. Links to Related Sites. http://www.jimmycarter library.gov/links/ (accessed Aug. 10, 2004).

Johnson, Chalmers. 2001. *Blowback: The Costs and Consequences of American Empire*. New York: Henry Holt and Company.

Kahane.org. Kahane.org: Principles and Philosophy. http://kahane.org/home.htm, and http://kahane.org/philosophy.htm (accessed Aug. 3, 2003).

Kaplan, Esther. 2004. The Jewish Divide on Israel. *The Nation*, July, 20–24.

Kepel, Gilles. 1994. *The Revenge of God: The Resurgence of Islam, Christianity and Judaism in the Modern World*. Cambridge: Polity Press.

Khalidi, Rashid I. 1980. *British Policy towards Syria & Palestine 1906–1914: a study of the antecedents of the Hussein-McMahon correspondence, the Sykes-Picot Agreement, and the Balfour Declaration*. London: Ithaca Press.

Khouri, Fred J. 1985. *The Arab-Israeli Dilemma*. 3rd ed. Syracuse: Syracuse University Press.

Kimmerling, Baruch. 2003. *Politicide: Ariel Sharon's War Against the Palestinians*. London: Verso.

Kinsella, Warren. 1995. *Web of Hate: Inside Canada's Far Right Network*. Toronto: HarperCollins.

Kintz, Linda. 1997. *Between Jesus and the Market: The Emotions That Matter in Right-Wing America*. London: Duke University Press.

Klein, Naomi. 2003. On Rescuing Private Lynch and Forgetting Rachel Corrie. *Guardian Unlimited*, May 22, http://www.guardian.co.uk/israel/comment/0,10551, 961025,00.html.

Knightly, Philip. 1991. Imperial Legacy. *The Gulf War Reader: History, Documents, Opinions*, ed. Micah L. Sifry and Christopher Serf, 3–15. New York: Random House.

Landow, George P. 1992. *Hypertext: The Convergence of Contemporary Critical Theory and Terminology*. Baltimore: John Hopkins University Press.

Lash, Scott, and Urry, John. 1994. *Economies of Signs & Space*. London: Sage Publications Ltd.

Lee, Martin. 2002. The Swastika & the Crescent. *Southern Poverty Law Center: Intelligence Report*, Spring, http://www.geocities.com/johnathanrgalt/ Swastika_Crescent .html (accessed Aug. 28, 2003).

Leinesch, Michael. 1993. *Redeeming America: Piety and Politics in the New Christian Right*. Chapel Hill: The University of North Carolina Press.

Lerner, Michael. 2001. Peace for Israel and Palestine. *Tikkun.org*, Dec. 4, http://www .tikkun.org/community/index.cfm/action/community/article... (accessed May 27, 2003).

Lewis, Bernard. 1986. *Semites and Anti-Semites: An Inquiry into Conflict and Prejudice*. New York: W. W. Norton & Company.

———. 1988. Anti-Semitism in the Arab and Islamic World. In Present-Day Anti-Semitism. ed. Yehuda Bauer. Jerusalem: The Hebrew University of Jerusalem.

Lippman, Walter. 1922. *Public Opinion*. New York: The Macmillan Company.

———. 1963. The Limits of Public Opinion. In *The Essential Lippmann: A Political Philosophy for Liberal Democracy*, ed. Clinton Rossiter and James Lare. New York: Random House.

Lockman, Zachary. 1999. Railway Workers and Relational History: Arabs and Jews in British-ruled Palestine. *The Israel/Palestine Question*, ed. Ilan Pappe. London: Routledge.

Lorek, L.A. 1995. Since Oklahoma City Bombing, some Internet sites featuring hate materials shut down, others flourish. *Fort Lauderdale Sun-Sentinel*, May 11, http://www.stormfront.org/dblack/press051195.htm (accessed July 14, 2003).

Lustick, Ian S. 1988. *For the Land and the Lord: Jewish Fundamentalism in Israel.* New York: Council on Foreign Relations.

Lustick, Ian S. 2006. *Trapped in the war on terror.* Philadelphia: University of Pennsylvania Press.

MacMillan, Margaret. 2001. *Paris 1919: Six Months That Changed the World.* New York:Random House.

Mandaville, Peter. 2001. *Transnational Muslim Politics: Reimagining the Umma.* London: Routledge.

Margolis, Michael and David Resnick. 2000. *Politics as Usual: The Cyberspace Revolution.* Thousand Oaks: Sage Publications.

Marsden, George M. 1980. *Fundamentalism and American Culture: The Shaping of the Twentieth-Century Evangelism; 1870–1925.* Oxford: Oxford University Press.

Marshall, Rachel. 1995. A Jewish State Brings Back the Pale. *Washington Report on Middle East Affairs* June, 7+.

Martin, William. 1996. *With God On Our Side: The Rise of the Religious Right in America.* New York: Broadway Books.

Masada 2000.org. Frustrated by CNN's Bias Against Israel? Retrieved: 5 July 2001 http://www.masada2000.org/ (accessed July 15, 2001).

Mason, Bruce, and Bella Dicks. 1999. The Digital Ethnographer. *Cybersociology* 6, http://www.socio.demon.co.uk/magazine/6/dickmason.html.

Massing, Michael. 2006. The Storm over the Israel Lobby. *The New York Review of Books*, June 8. 53(10).

McAdam, Doug. 1996. Conceptual origins, current problems, future directions. In *Comparative Perspectives on Social Movements: Political opportunities, mobilizing structures, and cultural framings*, ed. Doug McAdam, John D. McCarthy, and Mayer N. Zald, 23–39. Cambridge: Cambridge University Press.

McArthur, Shirl. 2003. A Conservative Tally of Total Direct U.S. Aid to Israel: $97.5 Billion and Counting. *Washington Report on Middle East Affairs*, May, 32+.

McChesney, Robert W. and John Bellamy Foster. 2003. The "Left-Wing" Media? *Monthly Review.* 55.2 http://www.monthlyreview.org/0603editr.htm.

McChesney, Robert W. 1998. Media Convergence and Globalization. In *Electronic Empires: Global Media and Local Resistance*, ed. Daya K. Thussu, 63–82. London: Arnold.

McChesney, Robert W. 2004. *The Problem of the Media: U.S. Communication Politics in the 21st Century.* New York: Monthly Review Press.

McKelvey, Tara. 2001. Father and son team on hate site. *USATODAY.com*, July 16, http://www.usatoday.com/life/2001-07-16-kid-hate-sites.htm.

McMurtry, John. 1998. *Unequal Freedoms: The Global Market as an Ethical System.* West Hartford: Kumarian Press, Inc.

Mearsheimer, John and Walt, Stephen. 2006. The Israel Lobby. *London Review of Books*, March 23, 28(6).

Merkley, Paul C. 1998. *The Politics of Christian Zionism 1891–1948.* London: Frank Cass Publishers.

Meyer, William H. 2004. *Security, Economics, and Morality in American Foreign Policy*. Upper Saddle River: University of Delaware.

Moeller, S. 2004. Media Coverage of Weapons of Mass Destruction. March 9, 2004. Center for International and Strategic Studies at Maryland.

Moughrabi, Fouad. 2001. Battle of the Books in Palestine. *The Nation*. Oct. 1. http://www.thenation.com/docprint.mhtml?i=20011001&s=moughrabi.

Mouly, Ruth W. 1985. *The Religious Right and Israel: The Politics of Armageddon*. Midwest Research Monograph Ser. 2. Cambridge MA: Political Research Associates.

MSNBC.com. 2000. The Year in Pictures 2000. http://www.msnbc.com/modules/ps/yip_2000/launch.asp?b=hi (accessed July 4, 2003).

Murdock, Graham. 2000. Reconstructing the Ruined Tower: Contemporary Communications and Questions of Class. In *Mass Media and Society*, ed. James Curran and Michael Gurevitch. 3rd ed. 7–26. London: Arnold.

Murphy, Dean. 2001. Two Unlikely Allies Come Together in Fight Against Muslims. *New York Times*, June 2, metro. late ed.: sec. B1.

National Alliance. (a) Program of the National Alliance. http://www.natall.com/what-is-na/na3.html (accessed July 31, 2003).

——. (b) Dr. William Pierce 9-11-33 to 7-23-02. http://www.natall.com/ (accessed July 15, 2004).

National Vanguard Magazine. Who Rules America? http://stormfront.org/jewish/whorules.html (accessed July 14, 2003).

No War for Israel. Rachel Corrie: Martyr for Peace. http://www.nowarforisrael.com/ (accessed May 4, 2003).

Nusse, Andrea. 1998. *Muslim Palestine: The Ideology of Hamas*. Amsterdam: Harwood Academic Publishers.

Oliver, Revilo P. Christianity—Religion of the West. http://stormfront.org/whitnat/religion.html (accessed July 14, 2003).

Our Enemies. Hezbollah. http://www.ourenemies.org/Hezbollah.htm (accessed July 24, 2003).

Pappe, Ilan. 1988. *Britain and the Arab-Israeli Conflict, 1848–51*. Oxford: Macmillan Press.

Perelman, Marc. 2001. Judge Slams ADL for Hurting Couple Tarred As "Anti-Semites." *Forward*, April 13. http://fpp.co.uk/docs/ADL/Denver/Forward130401.html (accessed July 22, 2004).

Philo, Greg and Berry, Mike. 2004. *Bad News From Israel*. London: Pluto Press.

Philo, G. 2002. Television News and Audience Understanding of War, Conflict and Disaster, *Journalism Studies* 3(2): 173–186.

Pickerill, Jenny. 2001. Weaving a Green Web: environmental protest and computer-mediated communication in Britain. In *Culture and Politics in the Information Age: A New Politics?*, ed. Frank Webster, 142–166. London: Routledge.

Pierce, William. 1997 America, Israel and Iraq: Exposing the Warmongers. *American Dissident Voices*, Nov. 22. http://stormfront.org/jewish/iraq_adv.htm (accessed 16 July 2003).

Pipes, Daniel. 2003. *Militant Islam Reaches America*. New York: W. W. Norton & Company.

Politics and Terrorism. (a) ZOG,-DL JOG. http://zog.to/indexhtml (accessed May 23, 2003).

———. (b) AIPAC Index. http://zog.to/3/aipac/ap-ind.htm (accessed May 23, 2003).

Poster, Mark. 2001. *What's the Matter with the Internet?* Minneapolis: University of Minnesota Press.

President. UNC/LIA. http://www.ibiblio.org/lia/president/president-info.html (accessed Aug. 10, 2004).

Presidential Libraries. Presidential Libraries of the National Archives and Records Administration. *NARA: Presidential Libraries* http://archives.gov/presidential_libraries/about/about.html (accessed Aug. 10, 2004).

Quigley, John. 2005. *The Case for Palestine: An International Law Perspective*. Durham & London: Duke University Press.

Radio Islam. (a) opening statement (untitled). http://www.abbc.com/islam/english/english.m (accessed July 14, 2003).

———. (b) (untitled). http:/www.radioislam.net/islam/index-.htm (accessed July 14, 2003).

———. (c) Louis Farrakhan: Leading the Intifada against the Jewish Occupation of the USA. http://radioislam.org/islam/fotos/amfarak.htm (accessed Aug. 2, 2003).

———. (d) A combat with unequal weapons. http://abbc.com/islam/english/radiois/plot.htm (accessed Aug. 2, 2003).

Robins, Kevin and Frank Webster. 1999. *Times of the Technoculture: From the Information Society to the Virtual Life*. New York: Routledge.

Roddy, Dennis B. 2003. Federal investigators infiltrate extremist groups. *Pittsburgh Post-Gazette*, Feb. 23. http://www.rickross.com/reference/hate_groups/hategroups.351.html (accessed Aug. 25, 2003).

Rose, Adam. 2003. The Truth of Muhammed al-Dura: A Response to James Fallows. *Support Sanity*, http://www.supportsanity.org/Articles/The%20Truth%20of%20Moh . . . . (accessed Feb. 17, 2004).

Rosenblatt, Dana. 1999. Expatriate finds Israelis very much involved in politics. *CNN.com*, http://www.cnn.com/SPECIALS/1999/israeli.elections/stories/expatraite/diary (accessed Dec. 10, 2002).

Roy, Sarah. 2005. Strategizing Control of the Academy. *The NEA Higher Education Journal,* Fall.

Ryan, Sheila. 1991. Countdown for a Decade: The U.S. Build-Up for War in the Gulf. In *Beyond the Storm: A Gulf Crisis Reader*, ed. Phyllis Bennis and Michael Moushabeck, 91–102. New York: Olive Branch Press.

Sabawi, S. 2006. Editorial Delusions at the Globe and Mail. *Counterpunch*, Feb. 23. http://www.counterpunch.org/sabawi.org/sabawi02232006.html.

Said, Edward. 1994. *Culture and Imperialism*. New York: Vintage Books.

———. 1996. *Peace and its Discontents: Essays on Palestine in the Middle East Peace Process*. New York: Vintage Books.

——. 1997. *Covering Islam: How the Media and the Experts Determine how we see the rest of the World*. Rev. ed. New York: Random House.

Schiller, Herbert I. 1998. Striving for communication dominance: a half-century review. In *Electronic Empires: Global Media and Local Resistance*, ed. Daya Kishan Thussu, 17–26. London: Arnold.

Schudson, Michael. 1995. *The Power of News*. Cambridge MA: Harvard University Press.

——. 2000. The Sociology of News Production Revisited (Again). In *Mass Media and Society*, ed. James Curran, and Michael Gurevitch. 3rd ed. 175–200. London: Arnold.

Schudson, M. 2003. *The Sociology of News*. New York: W.W. Norton & Company.

Schwartz, Edward. 1996. *Net Activism: How Citizens use the Internet*. Sebastopol, CA: Songline Studios.

Scott, Joan W. 2006. Middle East Studies Under Seige. January–March. *The Link*, 39(1). http://www.ameu.org/printer.asp?iid=265&aid=575.

Shahak, Israel. 1997. *Jewish History, Jewish Religion: The Weight of Three Thousand Years*. London: Pluto Press.

Sheriff's Posse Comitatus. 2000. (a) Immigration and Naturalization. http//www.posse-comitatus.org (accessed July 22, 2003).

——. (b) Responses to the bombing of the World Trade Center... wysiwyg:// main.174/http://posse-comitatus.org/ (accessed Aug. 13, 2003).

Shields, Rob. 2000. Hypertext Links: The Ethic of the Index and Its Space-Time Effects. In *The World Wide Web and Contemporary Cultural Theory*. ed. Andrew Herman and Thomas Swiss, 145–160. New York/London: Routledge.

Shyovitz, David. 2003 Rabbi Meyer Kahane (1932–1990). *Jewish Virtual Library*, http://www.us-israel.org/jsource/biography/kahane.html (accessed July 8, 2003).

Simon, Roger. 1991. *Gramsci's Political Thought: An Introduction*. London: Lawrence & Wishart.

Singh, Ranbir. 1999. Hehudi-Hinu Bhai Bhai (Jews and Hindus are Brothers). *Sword of Truth Magazine*, Dec. http://www.swordoftruth.com/cgi-bin/printfriendly.pl (accessed July 8, 2003.

Solomon, Norman. 2001. Bias and Fear Tilting Coverage of Israel. *Media Beat*, April 19. http://www.fair.org/media-beat/010419.html (accessed July 8, 2004).

Southern Poverty Law Center. 2001. Cyberhate Revisited. *Intelligence Report*, No. 101. http://www.splcenter.org/gi-bin/printassist.pl?=/intelligenceceprojec...

——. 2005. Media and the Global Public Sphere: An Evaluative Approach. In *Global Activism, Global Media*, ed. Wilma de Jong, Martin Shaw, and Neil Stammers, 34–49. London: Pluto Press.

Sprinzak, Ehud. 1991. *The Ascendance of Israel's Radical Right*. New York: Oxford University Press.

Stein, Kenneth. 1998. On Israel's 50th, the glass is half full. *CNN.com*, http://www.cnn.com/SPECIALS/1998/israel/stein.essay/ (accessed Dec. 10, 2002).

Steinberg, Gerald M. 2000. Palestinian Child Sacrifice. *Israel Foreign Ministry*. Oct. 25, http://www.isrinfo.demon.co.uk/articl35htm (accessed Nov. 7, 2003).

Stevens, Richard P. 1970. *American Zionism and U.S. Foreign Policy: 1942–1947*. New York: Pageant Press, Inc.

Steyn, Mark. 2002. It's Time to Snap Out of Arab Fantasy Land. *National Post*, April 18, nat. ed. sec. A16. http://www.jdl.org/israel/fantasy.shtml (accessed Aug. 11, 2003).

Stork, Joe, and Martha Wenger. 1991. From Rapid Deployment to Massive Deployment. In *The Gulf War Reader: History, Documents, Opinions*, ed. Micah L. Sifry and Christopher Cerf, 34–39. New York: Times Books.

Stormfront. 2001. Stormfront White Nationalist Community: The Big Lie. (discussion thread) Oct. 3. http://www.stormfront.org/forum/showthread.php?s=&thread=3064 (accessed June 18, 2003).

——. 2003 Stormfront White Nationalist Community: Jews and Right Wing Extremists unite? http://www.stormfront.org/archive/t-78917 (accessed July 18, 2004).

Strauss, Mark. 2003. Antiglobalism's Jewish Problem. *Foreign Policy*, Nov.–Dec., 58–67.

Strickert, Fred. 2001. War on the Web. *The Christian Century*, May, 20–23.

Strom, Alfred. 2003. World War IV. *American Dissident Voices*, April 12, http://www.natvan.com/pub/2003/041203 (accessed July 29, 2003).

Sullivan, Terry (a). Introduction: Camp David Accords Framework for Peace. *PRESIDENT* and the *Jimmy Carter Library*. http://wwwibiblio.org/sullivan/CampDavid-Accords-Intro.html (accessed Dec. 10, 2002).

——. (b) The Tour. *PRESIDENT* and the *Jimmy Carter Library*. http://www.ibiblio.org/sullivan/CampDavid-Accords-Tour.html (accessed Dec. 10, 2002).

——. (c) Arab-Israeli Conflict. *PRESIDENT* and the *Jimmy Carter Library*. http://www.ibiblio.org/sullivan/CDPrelude-conflict.html (accessed Dec. 10, 2002).

——. (d) American Diplomatic Efforts. *PRESIDENT* and the *Jimmy Carter Library*. http://www.ibiblio.org/sullivan/CDPrelude-efforts.html (accessed Dec. 10, 2002).

Suzman, Mark. 1999. *Ethnic Nationalism and State Power: The Rise of Irish Nationalism, Afrikaner Nationalism and Zionism*. Wiltshire: MacMillan Press Ltd.

Swedenburg, Ted. 1999. Palestinian Peasantry in the Great Revolt (1936–9). In *The Israel/Palestine Question*. ed. Ilan Pappe. London: Routledge.

Taylor, Philip M. 2000. The World Wide Web goes to War, Kosovo 1999. In *Web Studies: Rewiring media studies for the digital age*, ed. David Gauntlett. USA: Oxford University Press.

Tikkun. 2001. Core Vision and Founding Principles. http://www.tikkun.org/community/index.cfm/action/core_vision.html (accessed May 27, 2003).

——. 2003a. Rapid Response Media. July 4, http://www.tikkun.org/community/index.cfm/action/community/article . . . (accessed Aug. 10, 2003).

——. 2003b. Media Distortions. May 27, http://tikkun.org/community/index.cfm/mode/category/id/23/acti... (accessed Aug. 10, 2003).

Tillman, Seth P. 1982. *The United States and the Middle East: Interests and Obstacles*. Bloomington: Indiana University Press. 1982.

United Nations (a). Jerusalem. *Question of Palestine*, http://www.un.org/Depts/dpa/qpalnew/glossarycollapsible.htm (accessed April 27, 2003).

——. (b). 1994. The United Nations and the Question of Palestine. *UNISPAL*, http://domino.un.org/UNISPAL/9a798adbf322aff38525617b006d . . . (accessed April 27, 2003).

Urry, John. 2000. *Sociology Beyond Societies: Mobilities for the twenty-first century.* London: Routledge.

van de Donk, Wim., Loader, Brian, Nixon, Paul G. and Rucht, Dieter. 2004. Introduction: Social movements and ICTs. In Cyber protest: New media, citizens and social movements, eds. van de Donk, et al. London: Routledge.

Weir, Sarah. 2003. Reversing Reality: Newspaper Coverage of Israel and Palestine. *Washington Report on Middle East Affairs*, Sept., 22–23.

Wilhelm, Anthony G. 2000. *Democracy in the Digital Age.* New York: Routledge.

Williams, Ian. 2000. Camp David Talks Addressed Letter, But Not Spirit, Of U.N. Resolutions. *Washington Report on Middle East Affairs*, Aug.–Sept. 12+.

Winseck, Dwayne. 2003. Netscapes of Power: Convergence, Network Design, Walled Gardens and Other Strategies of Control in the Information Age. In *Surveillance as Social Sorting: Privacy, Risk and Digital Discrimination*, ed. David Lyon. London: Routledge.

Yggdrasil. White Nationalism FAQ. http://stormfront.org/whitenat_nationalism_faq .htm (accessed July 14, 2003).

Zerbisias, Antonia. 2004. The truth is out there, somewhere. *TheStar.com* Jan. 8 http:// www.thestar.com/NASApp/cs/ContentServer?pagename=thestar . . .

Index

AIPAC. *See* American Israel Public Affairs Committee

Al-Awda, 29–32, 36n3, 40–41, 52

Al-Dura, Mohammed, 45, 49–52

Al-Qaeda, 66, 115. *See also* terrorism

America Online (AOL), 56, 79, 86n9, 111

Althusser, Louis, 9

American Enterprise Institute (AEI), 32

American Israel Public Affairs Committee (AIPAC), 30–31, 33, 41, 53, 65, 96, 102, 121, 126, 129

ADL. *See* Anti-Defamation League

ADL watch. *See* Jew Watch

American Palestine Committee (APC), 24

American Zionist Emergency Council (AZEC), 24

Anti-Defamation League (ADL), 94–97, 100, 102–103, 105–6, 117, 119–20, 125, 134

anti-Semitism, and Islam, 107–12, 124; and white separatism, 94, 103, 117, 129, 133–34. *See also* Christian Identity movement; and mainstream Zionist propaganda, 33, 134–35

AOL. *See* America Online

APC. *See* American Palestine Committee

Arab/Israeli wars, 27, 31–32, 62–63, 67–69, 71–72, 77, 98–99, 103

Arafat, Yasser, 73

architecture, of the Web, 56, 80

Atlantic Monthly, 52

AZEC. *See* American Zionist Emergency Council

Bajrang Dal. *See* Hindu ultranationalism

balkanization of the Web, 17, 43, 149

Balfour Declaration, 25–26, 61–62

Barber, Benjamin, 113n4, 149

Begin, Menachem, 31, 86n6

Bimber, Bruce, 17, 20, 22–23, 143–45, 149

Black, Don, 90, 93–94, 96–97, 106, 116, 118–121

Black Muslim Movement, 44, 97, 107, 111, 125, 132–33, 140n8,12

Bricolage, 110, 136

British Mandate, in Palestine, 62–63

Cable News Network (CNN), 5, 14–16, 41, 53, 55–86, 91–92, 101–2, 136, 143, 150–51

Zionist Occupation Government (ZOG), 91–92, 94–97, 121–22, 130, 133–34, 138–39, 140n7
Zionist Organization of America (ZOA), 32, 102, 126

ZOA. *See* Zionist Organization of America
ZOG. *See* Zionist Occupation Government
Zundel, Ernst, 110–11, 121